FUTURE
SOLUTION

RICHARD WAYNE HATLEY

DEDICATION

THIS BOOK IS DEDICATED TO THE L TEAM. THE BEST WIFE, DAUGHTER, MOTHER AND MOTHER-IN-LAW ANY MAN SHOULD EVER BE FORTNUNATE TO HAVE TELL HIM WHAT TO DO NEXT. THEY HAVE ALL HEARD IT BEFORE.

Future Solution

v

ACKNOWLEDGMENTS

Acknowledgements are sometimes just like the speeches that we made when we were in Kindergarten. Or the tapes of our graduation ceremonies if we had to take courses over in Summer School. When we look back at them with old eyes and ears they don't quite sound or look the same as we believed that they were. Sometimes they come across similar to the speech that the high school. Basketball player in Hoosiers gave when he was telling the class what he was thankful for in the High School Civics class that the Coach was trying to teach. I will try not to repeat that scene. I need to remember the people that encouraged me to keep trying. Especially JD who talked with me and tried to teach me Racket Ball and how to use a PC.

I sure am glad that I didn't join you at that CPA firm in Houston that is no longer with us. Whoa, We sure dodged that one. And thank you Rusty. I would have never thought about using the term Muligrubbers if you hadn't told JD about how everybody was complaining about their status of life in Baton Rouge.

Thank you Pat and Mike.
Thank you Charles.
Thank you Rush and Shawn.
Than you Coach Bob
Thank you Ron
Thank you Mr. Bill
Thank you John and Bobby
Thank you Rick
Thank you Bubba and Carl

And especially some of the hard working people in Lexington that told me to make a living with my mind, because if I tried to make a living with my hands, I would starve.

Introduction

So, you bought the book? If I were sitting there with you right now, what would you want to ask me? "Why did you write this book and what's in it for me?" Good questions. Well, I'll start with what's in it for you. It's in your Own Self-Interest to have a Future. Yes, a Future that can look a lot different from the problems that we are wrestling with at this time. You know all of those problems: The Deficit, Healthcare, Unemployment (or lack of Jobs) and hanging on to your own little piece of America.

Well, this book is about all of those problems and some solutions that we could use to solve those difficult problems. What's so different about this book than what you have heard on your favorite Television and Radio talk show? A lot. This book is about what is important **to** you. Yes, this book is about making sure that everybody's Self-Interest is considered.

This book doesn't try to blame the Liberals or the Conservatives. The solutions that we will arrive at to solve our problems ask an important question. What will work and what are the Self-Interests that are involved in solving those problems?

We will spend a lot of time talking about those problems and how it all started in the first place. We will even go back and look at a little bit of history and economics. The whole time you will feel as if we are all talking about these problems together. You will be right. This book was written with the purpose of stimulating thought and discussion of these major problems: Discussion and thought that will translate into action. A Plan of Action.

As Samuel Taylor Coleridge said, "Works of imagination should be written in very plain language; the more purely imaginative they are the more necessary it is to be plain." Yes, this book is about trying to have a future rather than putting off difficult decisions. This book looks at some of our major problems and solutions that we can adopt to have our Future, all in language that all of us can understand. This

1

book is for everybody that has been disappointed by what our leaders promise us and then what they actually do when they get elected. This book is for all of the people who feel that this country has let them down. This book is for all of the people who know deep down in their hearts that there has to be a better way.

Well, this book is for you. There are other solutions to our problems. Solutions that all of our leaders have never tried to show us. Solutions that have been there all the time. This book looks at our problems for what they are. Problems that can be solved if only we have The Will to try.

Now back to your first question. Why did I write this book? I have been thinking about the material in this book for several years. People who have known me for some time will see some things that we have talked about in our conversations together. They may even recognize some of the conversations that take place in this book.

I started to seriously think about this book after the last election. You remember the famous election of 1992? Yeah, the one when we all felt as if we didn't really have a choice. Well, I spend the whole summer of 1992 talking about how President Bush had let all of us good Republicans down. I also started to get interested in what candidate Bill Clinton was saying about being a new Democrat.

Yes, I thought candidate Clinton might be my kind of guy and I was telling all of my family about how we should give him a chance. They all looked at me as if I had lost my mind or worse fallen in love with Jane Fonda. No, the summer of 1992 was kind of hard around my house.

When the election finally rolled around my wife gave me a choice. I could either vote with her for good old George or I could go live with Billie. And according to her that would mean moving to Arkansas on my part. You can imagine how I felt when I finally went into that election booth to pull the lever. Would it be for good old George and my wife or would I be moving over to Arkansas?

Well, blame it on my genes because my arm would not let me pull any lever but the good old Republican lever. That night I thought about what I had just done. I had voted for somebody that I did not believe could do the job. I also kept asking myself, what were the alternatives? What were the other options? There were no other options. Not then. But that got me to thinking about conversations that I had had in the past.

Most of those conversations ended with somebody asking me a key question. "You may have a good point, but what are you going to do about it? You know it's always easier to criticize than to come up with what you think will work? What are you going to do to make it better?"

This book is my attempt to make it better for you and me. You see, for too long a lot of us have kind of stayed on the sidelines. You have heard it before. "What's the use of trying? Things have been like that for years. It would take years to fix all of those problems? It just would be too hard. People would never change. We are all going to the Dogs."

Well, this little Southern Boy wants to try and make a difference. He wants to try to have a better Future. What about you? Do you really want to see that Future? Here's a good suggestion on how to read this book.

Make sure that you have a special place to read this book where you can be alone and where you can think. When I was writing this book, I thought about all of times that I had solved difficult problems in my past. Most of those problems were solved when I had the time to think them through in a quiet place.

It's also very important for you to ask yourself a major question when you read this book. Ask yourself, "How does this apply to my problem and what's in it for me?" You won't have to read for too long in this book before you realize that it is important for all of us to feel as if we have a self interest in solving all of these important problems.

It will also help you when you read this book if you can imagine in your mind some difficult struggle or problem that you have seen others overcome. In my case, I have a favorite movie that I've watched over and over to give me additional inspiration. That movie was **Hoosiers.**

If you have seen that movie, it will help you to see that movie over and over in your mind as you read about our struggle with the Deficit, Healthcare, Jobs and the other problems. That gets at the heart of why I wrote this book. You see, we think that our problems are so great that we can't solve them. Just like in the movie, "If we put all our effort into doing the best we can, then we won't be losers. We will be winners."

So go ahead and get yourself something cold to drink. Go up the stairs to that special room of yours. Get comfortable and enjoy this book. As you read this book you may even think that you know somebody that has felt like me.

Who knows, enough people may even agree enough to really start the process of Change. Yes, this book is about real change. Change that will and can work. Are you ready?

What are you going to do?

1 THE WAY THINGS ARE TODAY
THE GOVERNMENT

You know what our problem is today? The government just won't listen to the people. The President said one thing and look at what he's doing. Doesn't he know that we didn't elect him and them to do that? Anything but That! You know what we ought to do. We ought to have another Boston Tea Party. No not that Tea Party the one that they had way back in the day. Show them what we think of their taxes.

Their taxes and spending sounds like we have a King or maybe even a Queen and we are just a bunch of surfs working the master's land for our room and board. Well, whose country is this and how did all of this tax and spend problem start? Looks like we need to go back and look at our history books. You know the books that all of the other kids carried to study hall. You know, the kids that weren't going to college. The ones that didn't have to take Spanish or Latin.

The ones that took **DE** and **History** instead.

Well, if we have to look back in our history, let's start at the beginning. What does the **Constitution** say? What are my rights? "I know I have rights, they're written down somewhere in the Constitution. You know the thing that the Supreme Court protects for all of us so we don't have to go back to working the land and bowing down to Kings and Queens."

But wait, is that the beginning or is there something else that all of the old people did before they gave all of the Wise Men & Women in **Black** on the Supreme Court a life time job? Seems to me that I remember having to memorize something that started out with----

The Declaration of Independence

When, in the Course of human events, it becomes necessary for one people to dissolve the political bands which have connected

them with another, and to assume, among the Powers of the earth, the separate and equal station to which the Laws of Nature and of Nature's God entitle them, a decent respect to the opinions of mankind requires that they should declare the causes which impel them to the separation.

We hold these truths to be self-evident, that all men are created equal, that they are endowed by their Creator with certain unalienable Rights That among these, are Life, Liberty, and the pursuit of Happiness. That, to secure these rights, Governments are instituted among Men, deriving their just Powers from the consent of the governed.

That, whenever any form of Government becomes destructive of these ends, it is the Right of the People to alter or to abolish it, and to institute new Government, laying its foundations on such Principles, and organizing its Powers in such form, as to them shall seem most likely to effect their Safety and Happiness.

Wow, if that's the beginning of our Country, I wonder what that thing that those people in **Black** keep reading really says.

The Constitution of the United States of America

We the people of the United States, In Order to form a more perfect Union, establish Justice, insure domestic Tranquility, provide for the common defense, promote the general Welfare, and secure the Blessings of Liberty to ourselves and our Posterity, do ordain and establish this Constitution for the United States of America.

Gee, it sounds as if we started this country not by the labels we know as the **Liberals** and the **Conservatives**. I bet that back in the good old days they didn't have our problems and they had a real government back then. You know the kind of government that listened to the **Real** people, not the **Rich** people that control everything. Yeah, back then the government was **By and For the People**.

Everybody knows that good old George never told a lie and he was the father of our country. Yeah, back then there were no tax and spend problems. Wait a minute, seems as if I remember something about some type of energy tax or was it the Whiskey Tax? Let me see what does my good old history book say? No, not mine but the one that Jamie Lee left in my car the night of the prom.

Excise taxes, especially on alcoholic beverages, were unpopular in the eighteenth century. A cider tax nearly caused rebellion in England in 1763, and so did a rum tax in Massachusetts in 1754. By 1794 the federal excise tax on liquor did cause rebellion or what looked like it, in Pennsylvania, Farmers in the western part of the state generally turned their surplus grain into whiskey.

This could be transported over the mountains more easily than wheat or corn, and it brought a better price in the Eastern markets. But the profit was small, and there was much evasion of the tax. In July 1794, the United States marshal, summoning offenders to court, met with mass resistance.

The governor of the state, Thomas Mifflin, thought that the courts could handle the situation. But Washington, urged on by Hamilton, decided that the challenge to national authority called for military action, and in October he marched fifteen thousand militiamen to Philadelphia, leaving Hamilton to complete the arrest of the ringleaders. (The National Experience Second edition, A History of The United States, 1968 by Harcourt, Brace & World, Inc.)

Gee, it looks as if they had problems back then too. How did it get so expensive? Did the **Rich** pay their **Fair** share back then? I bet that back then the government made sure that everybody paid their **Fair** share and that fellow Richard Nixon or was it Ronald Reagan changed the tax system so that their **Rich** friends didn't have to pay their **Fair** share.

What did you say? Come on don't tell me that in 1913 we had to change the Constitution in order for the Federal Government to collect income taxes. Yep, there it is in that good old book of mine. Amendment XVI states, "*The Congress shall have power to lay and collect taxes on incomes, from whatever source derived, without apportionment among the several States, and without regard to any census of enumeration."*

For over 100 years we didn't even have an income tax. I wonder what changed. What went wrong? Why do we have to worry about paying our **Fair** share? Well, Virginia, what went wrong is the rest of the story. We went wrong. We wanted it all: Not just the freedom and the chance to try and fail, but it **All**.

Prior to World War II, our government and its Tax and Spend policies closely resembled our Declaration of Independence and The Constitution. There was even something like a French Thing that summed it all up. What was that phrase? Oh yeah, it was called *Laissez Faire*. That was probably dreamed up by George Bush. You know the guy who liked to travel abroad.

What? Thomas Jefferson used that phrase. Come on now, not **The** Thomas Jefferson that the new Democrats say they want to be like.

Yes, that Thomas Jefferson who thought "that a wise and frugal government should not control all of the actions of men and their commerce." Yes, that means some of those people who don't always pay their **Fair** share. What does *Laissez Faire* really mean? It means that governments should not control the actions of men and their business.

You know, don't act like Russia. Don't try to make business sell 100 sausages for $1.00 a piece when there are 1,000 surfs that want sausages. Let the Market Place set the price.

"Why would you want the government to not care and forget about the little guy? Don't you know that people have to eat? The government should make sure that sausages only cost $1 and not let the people who don't pay their **Fair** share set the price. If we left them alone why sausages could cost $100. That not **Fair!**"

Wait a minute what does the dictionary say that **Fair** means? **Fair** unprejudiced, impartial, equitable, evenhanded, treating all sides alike, just, unbiased, affording no undue advantage, dispassionate, objective, legitimate, disinterested, honest, reasonable, square, upright, honorable, aboveboard, according to the rules, proper and justified. And these are only some of the positive meanings of the word. I wonder what some of the less kind meanings are: average, moderate, pretty good, middling, mediocre, passable, reasonable, satisfactory, decent, tolerable, respectable, medium, ordinary, indifferent and run of the mill. (Webster's New World Dictionary, Second edition, 1984, Simon & Schuster, Inc.)

Gee, **Fair** can mean almost anything you want. Sounds as if **Fair** can mean whatever the user wants it to mean? **Fair** means help me not them, make them pay and don't make me pay.

Now we are getting somewhere. We started out with a country that had a really big riot in some of the big cites to protest the Government's taxing and spending programs and created a government that believed that everyone was created equal and that governments should not take away from anyone's ability to enjoy the fruits of their labors. We have now added that **Fair** word. The word that can mean almost anything. That's kind of like the original George.

No, not the George that liked to travel abroad or the George who always told the truth, the George that stayed at Home in England and supported all of his wife's social programs. What is our government? It's not an empire or a kingdom. Somewhere I remember reading that we have a Republic and we have representative government.

Yeah, the government represents me so I don't have to take time from working and looking at what everybody else has on Television and thinking that they didn't pay their **Fair** share. Yes, **The President and Congress** represent me.

That's the problem and when the next election comes around I'll fix that problem. I'll get somebody else in there that will represent **Me** and make everybody **else** pay their **Fair** share. Wait a minute, seems as if I remember reading that down South, no not Arkansas or Mississippi, I mean really down **South** like in South America that they have Revolutions that throw the bums out and fix the problem. Yeah, every other year they have these revolutions and throw out the bums.

I wonder why they keep having revolutions. Don't they know how to pick the good guys? You know the ones that will do what the people want and make everyone pay their **Fair Share**.

What did you say? Are you saying that they have been using the **Fair Thing** for years and they are going to something called a Market Approach? That can't be right. You know the big Wigs and Capitalists always take advantage of the little guy. You mean to say they used that line for over a hundred years in Mexico and everybody finally figured out that didn't work.

Seems as if all those governments in Mexico just took the money from everybody and the little guy still didn't have any money and couldn't even drink the water. This can't be what's happening in the Good old USSR is it?

Yeah, you know the country that used the writings of Karl Marx. You know, another **French thing**, that they called **Communism.** Old Karl had it all figured out way back then when he wrote his **Communist Manifesto** or something like that.

Karl was the first really smart guy to figure out what the **Rich Cats** were really doing. How was it that my old Economics professor used to describe Karl?

Yeah, what Karl Marx said was that **Rich Capitalists** were always trying to exploit the working class. If a hard working guy worked in a factory and made $20 bucks a day (this was a long time ago) and he married a hard working gal who also made $20 bucks a day, then the Capitalist would pay both of them together $30 bucks for the same working day.

Karl had a way to fix that problem. He was going to turn all of the land and power over to the **People**. Workers would all get their **Fair** share for their labor. There's that double meaning word again. But what did happen to all of those hard working guys and gals? Seems as if just like down in Mexico all that happened was that a bunch of **Government People** got all of the good stuff and the hard working guys and gals still weren't any better off. Maybe throwing out the bums is not the solution to the problem? Maybe as my old buddy Clem used to say, "I is the problem."

Now we are getting somewhere. Maybe it's like that commercial that I saw on Television the other day. You remember that commercial with an old Viking watching all of his troops get slaughtered. They were trying to fight a battle with swords when their opponent was using guns and explosives. He was trying to fight today's battle with yesterday's technology. Do you remember the look of pain and frustration on his face as he saw his plans for victory going up in smoke?

But what does all of that mean? Let's regroup, I want the government to listen to me and deal with my problems and I want them to get someone else to pay **Their Fair** share. Maybe that's why politicians are always using words that can mean anything, because somewhere somebody has to pay.

What was that lesson that my math teacher tried to get me to understand when I was trying to out **Word** holler Otis? Oh yeah, it was something about paying my Credit card bill. Let me see how did it go. I owe $1,000 for the stereo and VCR that I bought on credit and they charge me 1.5 % interest each month and I can only afford to pay $10 each month.

Seems like even though, I'm reducing my debt, I'll never pay this thing off, and why can't I charge anymore until I have reduced my balance. That's has to be against the law or at the least it's not **Fair**.

Surely this doesn't apply to **The Deficit**!

Yes, Virginia, it does and so does Representative government and trying to give everyone what they think that they told you they wanted. It applies to all of this and more, much more: giving people what they think are their rights and making someone else pay their **Fair** share. That's the problem, we want more and we want someone else to pay for what we think is our rights.

There is only one little problem. There is not enough money in the whole world to satisfy those needs and rights when somebody else is paying for those rights? There also is a major truth that we all have been avoiding for too long.

Truth Number 1: **The Government does not have any money of its own. All of the money that the Government has comes from somebody who has to earn that money first.** We are getting ahead of ourselves. Let's go back to the Government. You know the one that keeps not listening to us. Do we need a **Revolution** to get them to change? Wasn't there something called a **Reagan Revolution the New Covenant and Hope and Change** (Oh, I forgot that was one of the early changes.

Seems as if a lot of people really did know what that word was supposed to have meant.)

No, Virginia, we don't need a **Revolution**. We had one. Remember the **Declaration of Independence and the Constitution**? This government was created for us and receives its power from us. No more bowing down and working the land as Serfs. But what has happened and what do we need to do now? Why do I keep hearing about Hope and Change and then things never seem to change? The answer is that we **have** had changes and we didn't even see them coming.

Virginia, don't you remember the story I told you about the **2nd Wave**. You remember the little boy who was in a really bad storm and how a wave of water came crushing down on his house and made a real mess of his house.

Yes, remember how after the **Wave** had engulfed his house he went running out of his house to see what had happened. Then the **2nd Wave** came crashing down on him. Yes, the first wave was only a warning of the really big wave that was coming.

He thought that **1st Wave** was the danger when the real danger was in the **2nd Wave**. The wave that he didn't even see. We have had our warning that there is a second wave coming. The wave that will force us to make some major changes in our country and what we expect of

Government to do for us. We have tried to make some adjustments that we thought were real changes. We haven't really understood what was the 1st wave that was changing all of us. We changed from a land of opportunity to a land of **Rights** and **Fair Share** and our Government changed with us.

They are us and we are they. We ask them to right ever wrong and to make someone else pay.

Yes, they are the ones that made out last time. The ones who grabbed the bull by the horn and left us only to watch. But how did we hange? Aren't we just like our fathers and mothers? You know the ones that fought and struggled just so we could have a better life and to go on to college and make something of ourselves and to have it better than they did.

Now, Virginia, now we are getting somewhere. When have you ever heard anybody talk about sacrificing for our children? What have we heard? Let me see what are the key issues of today?

How about the abortion issue? Wrong! That's not about sacrificing for your children or tomorrow. You know, women have the right to decide how their bodies are treated. That's not being selfish? That's being for the underdog and people that can't help them? Wrong, Virginia, that's a present problem that eliminated the **Future**. The **Future** of a little baby who never will get to dream.

Well, enough about this abortion thing! You know that I'm sensitive about this and I thought we were going to talk about **Economics**. What's this got to do with economics? Everything, Virginia but let's get back on the subject of government. Let's take the budget problem and what that says about now versus the **Future** of the little ones who want to dream. Remember the lesson that my math teacher tried to teach me about **Finance**? Now think about the **Deficit**.

We have this big problem where we are spending a lot more money each year than we have coming in. So our government leaders will come up with a program that they will call a Deficit Reduction Program and the **Deficit** will go up less each year than if they had not done anything. Will this reduce the **Deficit** in total? No. "Why would we want to do that? Then we couldn't do all of the things that we were elected to do. Have you lost your mind?

We'll tax people their **Fair** share, that's what we'll do." Okay, let me get this straight. We are going to keep spending more than we have and to make it less of problem, but we'll tax people their **Fair** share. But tell me when does the **Deficit** go away? You know somewhere I read that right now the government is spending over **15%** or more of its money just in interest on the national debt. Isn't that a problem?

Yes, Virginia, it is a problem and it's at the heart of how we have changed. The children did not grow up and become like their parents. Maybe all of us just followed the advice of Dr. Spock and became our own little persons. Maybe we need to **Really Change**. Maybe we need to look to the **Future**. But first let's look at how our parents were.

You know, back then according to my mother, when she was young, everybody had 4 choices.

1. Be born Rich and grow up learning how to spend money.
2. Be born Poor and grow up with smarts, go to college and learn how to become a #1.
3. Be born Poor, grow up hard and work for a living.
4. Be born Poor, grow up lazy and avoid working for living.

Mother grew up as a #3 and tried her hardest to get me to become a #2. Being a #3 meant that she worked hard at a low paying job that never provided her with enough money to spend for all of the things that her kids saw on Television, which in our situation was a small black and white RCA 19 inch Television (if you don't count the times that we went over to a #2 neighbor and watched **The Life of Riley and The Ed Sullivan Show**)

Mother also sold Avon and I sold Christmas greeting cards, delivered the Memphis Press Scimitar in the afternoon after school, worked for good old Elmo at the local Dairy Bar and helped out at Mr. Davies' local Drug Store. The most that I ever made was **50 cents** an hour. Yes, I said cents, not dollars.

You know them little copper things that turn your hands green and the waitress puts in the bowl for sales taxes at the local bar. But hey, that's the way that **a # 3** did it in those days. Whenever, we were over at a #1 or a #2's watching the color Television and something such as a new Corvette would be advertised on Television, mother would just remind us that those kinds of things were for #1's who were soon to have children that would become #4's.

Basketball shoes? There weren't any basketball shoes. Your choices were either some cheap Japanese white slip on and off tennis shoes or black or white Keds. I never saw my hero Mickey Mantle or Stan the Man say what kind of shoes he wore.

No, everything was not **Ozzie and Harriet**. In fact it probably for me was really just my mother and grandmother. You see my father didn't work. He had come from a #1 family and turned into a #4 person and spent the rest of his life talking about how things just weren't **Fair**. Sounds a lot like today. It just wasn't **Fair** that the money ran out and he never went to college and learned how to provide for himself or his family.

I remember my father talking about the **Big Job** down at the local hospital that he didn't get. The one that they had open for a Hospital Administrator. Seems as if they didn't even talk to him. It just wasn't **Fair**. Why didn't he qualify with his 18 years of experience as a Chief Petty Officer Hospital Corpsman? It was only after I got to college that I found out that what he was missing was a college education.

But he didn't think that it was Fair. They should have given him a chance. Translation: They should have given him the job.

So life was still hard even then, when we didn't have that Budget Problem. But what did we have? We had what they gave us in the beginning. We had our Freedom. We had an Opportunity. My father wasted his and we are trying to waste ours. Where did we make the wrong turn? Could it be our own fault?

Probably a good place to start is with jobs. Right now, according to my mother everything starts with work. What kind of people were we back in the Fifties? No, I don't mean were we a bunch of #1's or #3's?

What kind of workers were we? I know from my good old history book that until the turn of the century we were primarily farmers, craftsmen and unskilled labors. I bet that by the fifties we had changed to more college educated and professional workers. You know that by the Sixties and Seventies that all of the Television soap operas showed how the Doctors and Lawyers never worked real hard but got to spend all kinds of money and get into all kinds of trouble.

Maybe we were not all working in factories, manual labor or other low paying jobs. Could it be that we had educated our people up in class and out of those low paying jobs? You know, we had created a larger middle class. Yeah, I remember in my history class hearing that there wasn't really any middle class until the fifties when more kids of lower class families went to college and became Doctors and Lawyers.

A whole lot of people really believed that this was the land of opportunity and made something of themselves. Yeah, those are the ones that don't pay their **Fair Share.** So a lot of people left low paying jobs and moved up to higher paying jobs.

Where did those low paying jobs go? Somebody had to have taken those jobs away from us. I know, every time I go into a "**Seven Eleven**" all you see is some kind of foreigner who has taken a job away from an **American.**

Yeah, that is the problem! We are losing all of our jobs to foreigners. Send them back to their own country. America for Americans. What do you mean the job only pays minimum wages? I can't live on that! Are you crazy? Who would work for that? A person has got to live? That's not **Fair!** Maybe that explains why we can't just tax and spend our way out of this **Budget** Thing.

Slow down Virginia, I know I've jumped a whole lot to get here, but something just hit me right between the eyes. You know that **Jobs Bill** that I keep hearing about. What kind of jobs were they talking about anyway? Sounds like unskilled labor to me. You know like working down at "Wendy's" or "McDonald's".

You know the jobs that some of the people said no to when Los Angeles had their little Party. Maybe we are like that old Viking that's using yesterday's weapons to fight today's battles. Maybe we have changed too much. Too much for that.

If, according to my mother, everything starts with work maybe that won't do anything except cost more money. Now, let's think about that for a minute. I wonder if that has anything to do with us losing all of those factory jobs. Could it be that we have become just too good for those kinds of jobs. I remember reading somewhere about some type of pyramid of needs.

Yeah, as people were able to meet their basic needs their **Future** needs became more and more difficult to meet. At the first level or bottom of those needs was the need to provide basic food and shelter and at the top were the much more complicated needs like **Self-Fulfillment.**

Could it be that most of our people are looking to meet those higher needs with minimum wage skills? Does that remind you of that old Viking trying to fight the big battle with swords when his opponent was using guns and explosives? Not a pretty sight.

"Hold on Richard, you know our biggest problem is the government, why are you talking about such things as circles or pyramids of needs? They are the ones who have screwed everything up for all of us. Why it's the government's fault. I was doing all right until they came in. It's their fault."

Well, we will have plenty of time to talk about them and how that can be solved, but right now it is very important to think about us. It is kind of like fighting a war. Before you start to fight a war you need to ask and answer four questions.

1. What are your reasons for fighting in the first place?
2. What is your plan for the battle?
3. What is your level of commitment to that plan?
4. How long are you committed to that plan and how will you get your troops in and out of that battle?

You see Virginia; we really do have Representative Government. Our Government is trying to give us what they think that we want. Did you hear what the former Representative from Illinois said the other day? I think his name is Dan Rostenkowski or something that I never could spell and he was the chairman of the House Ways and Means Committee. Well, good old Dan said that Congress is just like you and me.

They are having a real hard time trying to give us all of the things that we all want and at the same time still not raise everybody's taxes. He was right. The problem is very complicated and there is not a big source of money that all of government can just use without asking us to pay more in taxes.

Oh, I know it would be real neat if we could just blame one person or group. Yeah, then we could fix the problem in time for everybody to go to supper just as they do on the Network News.

But that's not the real world. In our world, the solutions will come from that **Good Old All of The Above**. The starting point for our solutions has to involve all of us. We have to look at ourselves first. We are all part of the problems and all of us must be part of the solutions. Any other way will just be trying to run away from the problems and hope that it will go away on its own.

"Wait a minute, Richard, you can't be trying to tell me that good old me Bubba, caused the Government to run up a Four Trillion dollar Deficit are you? Heck, if it had been me spending that kind of money, I sure would have spent it a lot differently. Why I would have bought me a Corvette or two and some real nice threads. I wouldn't have just wasted it on people who don't even want to work for a living."

Unfortunately Bubba, you did. When they were spending all of that money that they didn't have what were you doing? Did you ever try to stop them? Did you try to get other people to join together and stop them? No, you stayed on the sidelines and just watched. You did complain and agree with the other complainers but you didn't try to stop them. You know why you didn't try to stop them? Because you thought that there was something in it for you.

Yes, Bubba, the Government didn't just run up a big deficit for any one thing. No, they make sure that there were a lot of programs that would benefit different people. People who would reelect them back in office. That's how the system works. We are voting for people who get in office based on what they can do for everybody. Why would they cut our benefits or raise our taxes? That sure wouldn't get them reelected.

Remember Truth Number 1: The government doesn't have any money of its own. All of the government's money comes from somebody that has to earn that money first.

So, for whatever the reason that the government wants to spend money it should look at spending that money just as you and I do.

"What do you mean Richard? Don't tell me that you want the Government to spend their money the same way that I do? You really don't mean that? Do you?"

Well, Bubba, I don't mean that the government should spend money like the way you look for deals. You know, don't worry about: ' does the deal make sense'. Just make the deal work because you really want the deal and you don't care about how much it costs.

Why it is somebody else's money anyway. No, what I am talking about is the way that you buy suits. You remember how you wear those real inexpensive suits. How did you phrase it? Oh, yeah, you wouldn't want to spend three or four hundred dollars of **your** money on suits. Why, you couldn't sleep at night knowing that you had four hundred dollars hanging on a rack in your closet. It would give you the heepe geepes. Wouldn't it?

Why have we allowed the government to operate differently than how we all have to deal with things in our everyday life? Do we think that the government is some kind of God and can operate from a different level than the rest of us? What's our answer? The answers have to start with each of us.

That's why we have to look at ourselves first and ask ourselves what we are willing to do to solve our problems. I know that's kind of backwards from the way that we normally look at a problem. You know, what's in it for me? But to truly solve these difficult problems, we have to be willing to be part of the solution. As long as we are just looking for somebody else to blame and an easy way out then the government will keep giving us what they thought that we asked for in the first place. What are you willing to do about it? Just what are you prepared to do?

Is this is a real problem that we need to deal with or is it just something that we can all just keep complaining about and hope that it will go away when we all wake up?

Think about that for a minute Bubba and then we can start looking at how we can improve our Government.

2 THE WAY THINGS ARE TODAY
THE BUDGET

Gee, I sure do remember it being a lot simpler way back then. You know when we didn't have to worry about the Budget Thing. What do you mean? Don't I remember worrying about the **Red Thing**? You mean watching all of those films about radiation and how to get under your desk at school. How all of the #1's were building all of those underground shelters and buying up all of the dried beef and Pet milk, just in case the Red Thing really got out of hand.

Yes, I remember that, but what's that got to do with the Budget Thing? A lot Clem, a lot. Now we have to look at a little bit of **Economics** and a little bit of history and remember that just like in school, **E** always comes before **H**.

The **Economics** of Government can be really simple if you don't fall into the trap of the numbers. You know, climbing a tall building or a mountain isn't hard as long as you don't look down. Well, we kind of over did it with that concept. Remember that Senator from Illinois who coined the phrase. "A million here and a million there. Sooner or later you're talking about spending **Real Money**."

No, Mikey, I'm not picking on the Liberal Left. I think that senator was the Republican Minority Leader, Everret Dirkson and he said that back in the sixties. Whoa boy, I'm starting to get into history and you know that I haven't even started talking about the

E Thing

The Economics of this thing is really very simple. We're spending more than we have to spend. Forget everything else and think about that for a minute. What would you do if you had a son or daughter that had $2,000 in monthly income but was spending $2,500 a month? And let's say that you first tried to give her an extra $600 a month to help her pay some of her bills.

21

What do you think would happen next? You have got that right! Now she is spending $4,000 a month. Would you continue to give her more or would you set her down and have a simple math discussion? Right, you'd have that talk.

That talk would go something like this. "Now Virginia, don't you know that you can't spend more money than you have coming in?"

"Well, Dad you know that there are a lot of needy people out there and I'm helping Tammy Sue pay for that abortion that she needed and I'm also helping Billy Ray pay for the car that he needs to drive all of us down to the shelter."

"But, Virginia, how can you afford to keep doing that on your monthly salary? Don't you known how to budget and prioritize your spending? You can't keep spending your money like that! Don't you know that sooner or later you'll get in trouble and they'll take away all of your assets and put you in jail?"

"But Dad, that's what you're for, to bail me out. Don't you know, I'm depending on you to help me out? Didn't you always tell me that we should be good people and help out other people who can't help themselves?"

Yes, Virginia, I did say that, but I also said that you had to live within a budget. Don't you remember the talks we used to have about pies and how we cut up the pie so everybody gets a slice of the pie? Maybe not all that they want, but a good slice for all and to also help Mom out so she didn't have to work in the kitchen and keep having to bake more pies."

"Yes, Dad, but that budget thing is not a lot of fun. It's more fun to pass out the extra pie. Besides, it just isn't **Fair**."

That, in a nut shell, is the heart of the problem. Passing out the extra pie is fun.

Spending only what you have is no fun and that is not only a problem for our government, it's a problem for all of us. You see there is just one little problem with the government passing out the extra pie.

Who does the government turn to when it runs out of the stuff to make the pies? Who does the government turn to help them out? Does the government have a big daddy that can bail them out? Don't you remember? **Truth Number 1: The government does not have any money of its own. The Government only has the money that it takes from somebody that has to make that money first.**

"Now, dad really. You are just too much! You are starting to bore me with all of this talk about the government not having any money. Don't you care about all of the good things that the government does? Don't you know that if the government didn't help out all of those needy people then there would not be anybody to help them out?"

Think about what you just said, Virginia. If the government didn't spend somebody's money for some things, then nobody would spend their money of their own free will.

Where will the money come from if it doesn't come from people who want to help people with their own money? What makes people want to help other people in the first place? Isn't there some kind of rule or something that tells people how to handle this?

I remember sitting in an economics class when I was going to College and hearing a very interesting lecture about the evolution of economic thought and how Supply and Demand economics really worked. The lecture was so enjoyable that I complimented the instructor and told him that if only we would teach this subject in high school that it would really improve all of our viewpoints on jobs and government.

Do you know what his comment was? You would have thought that he would have appreciated my compliments and expanded on the issue of how important economics was in all of our lives.

That would have made sense since that was supposed to have been what the lecture was about. What he felt was more important to be taught in high school was birth control.

Guess why he was more interested in birth control than economics? You guessed it. He had a daughter and right now birth control was very important to him and her. Does that prove an important point about us and our problem?

Yes, all of us. You see, all of us have a concept of the world that includes only us. All of us approach the world from our own point of view. Think I'm wrong?

Next time you're talking to anybody just keep talking about you and see how long the conversation lasts. No, people want to talk about things that relate to them. Sure they are interested in you and what you are doing. But they also are real interested in how you relate to them. Even your mother has a whole lot of things that she wants to tell you when you finally call her.

She even wants to tell you about some people and things that you moved away from so that you didn't have to hear people reminding you about them.

Rule Number 1:. Everybody acts in their own best Self-Interest.

Yes, everybody. Even Mother Theresa acted in her own best self-interest. She did a whole lot of good for people. People that you and I would never even stop on the street to talk with or lend a dime of our money. It was in her own self-interest to help people. For her that was more important to her than having a fine house, car, jewelry or clothes. When she helped people she got a tremendous sense of self satisfaction.

"Now calm down Virginia, you don't have to cry." This doesn't mean that we are all a bunch of mindless people just thinking about ourselves.

Self-Interest means looking at the things in this world from the standpoint of how it affects us.

When you take your first look at the morning sun, whose eyes do you look through? Yes, your eyes. When someone asks you to a question on anything, how do you respond? Yes, you answer their question from your understanding of the question.

We all have to live in this world from our own viewpoint. We all react in this world based on our concept of how everything relates to us. Now, some people are so centered on themselves that they do not place any value on how their actions benefit others. These types of people have always been called **Selfish people**. They give no consideration for anyone other than themselves. This is one end of the **self-interest** gauge.

There are other people that place a lot of value on how their actions affect others. These are the people we see doing what we consider high moral actions for others. They have a self-value system that gives them a tremendous sense of self-value when their actions benefit others. We view these people as not being **selfish**.

This is the other end of the **self-interest** gauge. Most people are in the middle. All people have a self-value system; a system of looking at the world and the actions of others and themselves that places values and benefits on these actions.

Take the example of two married people who find themselves on a sinking ship. There is only enough room in the last remaining lifeboat for one more person. When the Husband makes the decision to let his Wife go on the life boat, he has made a decision for her to live and him to die.

To him, his wife being able to live when he will die satisfies his **self-interest**. He may love her very much and love does affect his value of his **self-interest**, but he still has made this decision based on how this will affect him. He may not have been able to live knowing that, she gave up her life for him. His **self-interest** placed a higher value to Him on her living than for him to live.

So how does rule number #1 fit in with economics? Simple, we have delegated to our government the role of being our daddy. The daddy who can bail us out when we run out of money to help people because we do want those other things. The government's **self-interest** is in appearing to be all things to all people. Their self-interest is also in getting reelected.

You also have to remember: **Truth Number 2: The government has to keep acting as if it can solve our problems.**

The Government can't get us to pay for those things that we think that the government should do for us. The government over in Russia has a really big problem right now. They have changed their government to a Democratic government where the people elect the leaders. They are also having some of our same kind of problems. What kind of problems? Problems dealing with change and avoiding the second wave.

You see the second wave is like being in a real bad storm. You know those kinds of storms that the other people that live in Florida close to the Gulf of Mexico have every year. Yes, I 'm talking about Hurricanes.

Well, in Hurricanes, you have to make sure that you don't come out too early when the first storm comes over your house. Sure, if you go outside you will see some improved weather and it may even look real sunny and peaceful. The reason that it is so peaceful is that you are in the center of the storm and the second wave of the storm is fixing to hit.

This is the second wave and is more deadly than the first wave. When there are major changes in any system, institution or organization that effects people lives there will be more than one wave of change.

The first wave is always the easiest and slowest. The second wave is the one that really hurts because it is about real change. The Russian leaders thought that they had the answer in the Communist Party's belief that the state should own all of the wealth in the country and make sure that all of the working people got their **Fair Share**. It didn't work did it?

No, it didn't work and right now Russia is getting hit with the 2nd wave. Yes, Russia is now a Democracy and the people get to vote. Sure, they wanted change. They just didn't think that it would be that hard. Maybe they are just like the Hebrews that finally got out of Egypt and started to complain about how hard it was to walk to the promise land. Didn't they want to go back to Egypt where at least there was food even if it meant going back into slavery?

No, that second wave can be a really dozy can't it? Unfortunately for all of us math still works. 2 + 2 still = 4 and we can't make 2 +2 = 5. Life is hard and you have to have it before you spend it. Is there anything else to it than that? What about the **History** thing? How does all of this fit together? Well, the **History** of this thing is very important. Do you remember George? No, not the one that liked to travel and talked about all of those points of light.

You mean the one that took all of our money to spend on all of his wife's social causes. Yeah, Good old King George that was across the pond in England.

Well, he lost this country because he couldn't figure out how to say no to her. Instead he kept trying to come up with new and inventive ways to get our money to give to her. Let's see what were some of Good Old George's Taxes?

1. **Sugar tax.**
2. **Stamp tax.**
3. **Lead tax.**
4. **Paint tax.**
5. **Paper tax.**
6. **Glass tax.**
7. **Tea tax.**

Now, why would the King of England pick those items to tax? The answer is simple: Any one item didn't hurt but together they raised a lot of money that the King needed. Why did the King need all of those taxes? His national debt had more than doubled in the last ten years and the huge interest cost on the debt was starting to hurt.

I bet you never heard that before. Also the King and his Minister of Finance never questioned the current cost for what they were spending. To them it was more important to get more money. If you lived back then you heard a lot of talk in England about the colonies paying **their fair share**.

You didn't hear the King asking the English people to pay **their fair share**. No, if he had said that, then a King in England would have been the first to have an appointment with the **French Thing** and not the King of France.

You know that real long knife that they cut off people's heads with back then. Seems as if you can't talk to the real people about having your cake and eating it without having to deal with the real Power of the People.

So King George encouraged his finance minister to keep looking for ways to raise more revenue.

I think he even used the word **"Investments."** Oh yeah, he
also had a problem with paying all of the expenses of keeping
English troops overseas. Yeah, kind of like our problem with
keeping troops in Japan, Europe, The Middle East and Further
East and Beyond.

Well, we fixed that problem, didn't we? Yeah, we had our own
George and we all pitched in and threw out the bums. You
know the bums that were taking our money and spending all of
it for something else. Seems as if that's what we should do now.
Just throw out the bums -- Come Next Election.

Wait a minute; we're not finished with our **History** lesson.
Don't you remember a real man by the name of FDR? Yeah,
there was a President before JFK and LBJ that all you had to say
was his initials and everybody knew whom you were talking
about.

Well, **FDR** had a really big problem back in the thirties. Seems
as if all of the banks and companies where people worked had
gone bust and nobody had a job. Seems as if they called that the
Great Depression. OK, not a **recession** when somebody you
know is out work.

A Depression is when You are out of work. FDR had this big
problem. Everybody was out of work and no extra taxes were
coming in. Well, there were some #1's and #2's that had jobs
and money but they hid theirs real well. FDR also knew that if
he raised taxes to pay for jobs that things would really get bad.

Why, the #1's and #2's might even move back to England or
down to Mexico.

So what did FDR do? He tried some things that at that time the
government normally didn't do unless there was a War going
on or a serious threat to our national interest.

He spent more money than we had coming in. Why did he do that? Because just like a race car driver who sees a big crash occurring right up ahead of him in a race and feels his car skidding and sliding, he tries something different and steers toward the crash hoping that by the time he gets there the crash will be going in another direction. In FDR's case he also had a pretty good idea that we were fixing to be involved in a pretty big war and a war always pulls you out of the crash.

So until that really big war came along he had to try something else. He decided to invest in our **Infrastructure**. Yeah, spend money on roads, bridges, schools and parks. A lot of people went to work.

Not big paying jobs, but as my mother would say. "When you are a #3 you take what you can get."

FDR also came up with the idea of the safety net. You know the net that was supposed to keep people from falling through to become a #4. One of his biggest nets was a little program called Social Security. Throughout all of his programs run a common theme. Government should play a bigger role in making sure that everything was Fair.

Did these programs work? According to your own point of view and remembering rule #1., his success can be viewed as either:

(A.) "FDR was the greatest President in our history. He really cared about the little guy. Just think about all of is good programs like Social Security; the jobs that put people back to work. He got the government caring about people."
(B.) "All FDR did was create a welfare class in this country. World War II was what got this country going again. He didn't do anything. All he did was to give into his wife on all of her social programs."

The truth is probably a combination of both **#A**. and **#B**. What happened was that FDR never got to see the end of the war and how his programs would deal with the new age coming for all of us in the fifties and sixties. Because in the language of the times all of those social programs were viewed as the Grand Experiment.

Just like that race car driver who has a crash in front of him, you also have to run the rest of the race when you survive the crash. But what's the fifties and sixties got to do with the **Great Depression** and especially now? You know our **Budget Problem** and **Fair Share**?

A lot, Bubba and even some more. You see, Bubba, a funny thing happened to us after we came out of the Great War. Yes, I know we won it, but some things happened that had never happened after a major war.

You see normally after a country comes out of spending a lot of money on fighting and winning a really big war there is at least a major **recession** or maybe even a big **Depression**. Not this time! The period of time from the end of the war through the sixties was one of the longest periods of prosperity in our History.

Now, why did this happen? You had economic change in this county like no other period in our history. Until the beginning of World War II, we were still a nation of unskilled labors and farm workers. A lot of this growth had to do with social events that took place during the war.

While we were fighting the evil Hitler and his cousins from Japan we sacrificed. How did we sacrifice? Everything went into fighting and winning the war. Even if you were a #1 and not overseas fighting the war, you still had a hard time buying a good steak or a new car.

Seems as if we had rationing and all of our efforts went into winning the war.

Women also found out that climbing telephone poles, working in factories and being police officers were not all that hard for them, but they did miss their guys. So what happened when the Boys came back? You guessed it. We had a boom in births.

We also had people spending a lot of money for all of the good things that they couldn't have during the war and some of the women didn't leave their jobs when the boys came back. Why is that important?

Simple, when women continued to work, they brought more money into the family to spend. The key to this increase in spending was that the spending was influenced by good old Self-interest. Self-interest driven by what people thought was important not what the Government thought needed to spend to get people to vote for theme in the next election.

What else happened when the Boys came back? For one thing the politicians had been taking economic classes and decided to do something for the Future. Instead of just giving all of the GI's some money for saving our country, they thought about it for a while and came up with the **GI Bill**.

This left the decision of going to College or building a new home for their family up to the ones who had fought in the war and saved this country. Some people did not choose to spend their money and some of the Government's money on either. I know my dad came back after almost losing his life on the last Japanese Island and didn't go back to College or buy a house.

His Choice. Others made their own choice. No harm Nor Foul. The reason that the **GI Bill** worked so well was that it was *Future Oriented*.

The **GI Bill** said simply that we will pay you to go to school to go from being#3 to become a #2. And the beautiful thing about this program was that none of the GI's counted as being unemployed which they would have been if the Government had just given them more money. Some of them had part time jobs to buy some things that thought that they needed.

Again, they choose not the Government. The other bright thing about this program was what it did for the **Future**. It helped a lot of people buy more things. You know when people get better paying jobs they have more money to spend on things and taxes.

What do they call it in **Economics**? The **Multiplier Effect**. Well, the **M** thing really worked well. In fact a lot better than anybody would have ever dreamed possible. What happened during this period of time? Just ask the People who worked in construction. Not only did we have more people in college than ever before, we also had a **GI Bill** for housing.

Yes, the government came up with a loan program that insured home loans for veterans. Housing construction exploded.

People were building houses all over the place and especially outside the cities. Remember women were still working and bringing in more money. What about the Deficit? Oh, it wasn't too big, remember more people working and paying taxes. Gee, sounds just like trickle down doesn't it? But most importantly people were working and spending more and more money. Multiply and multiply, why did it all have to stop?

Here the sixties come in and what happened then affects all of us now. It's called trying to fight two wars at the same time. You know the mistake that Hitler made when he invaded Russia before he had England beat.

Yeah, that problem. Well, for us it was a little more difficult. (It was called **Butter or Bullets**? Pick your war).

You see, we had a President during this time called **LBJ** who wanted everybody to like him. How does a politician make people like him? That's right he spends more money: Other people's money.

You see good old **LBJ** decided to declare war on an old enemy called Poverty. Yes, during his watch we would make sure that there were no more Poor people. Forget the rules about being wither a 1, 2, 3 or a 4. He was going to rid our country of **Poor People.**

He also forgot how the **GI bill** had worked and instead spent a lot of money. Kind of back to that negative meaning of that word **Fair.** A funny thing happened during this **War on Poverty**. You see we had another war going on called the Vietnam War and it was for real.

Very real and it took lots and lots of money. This is where the question of Bullets or Butter comes in. When I was in that old economics class, they talked a lot about how we lived in a world where we had a big conflict going on all the time.

Seems as if this was a world of limited resources with unlimited desires for those limited resources. You always have choices or options in how you spend those resources. You could spend them on buying bullets for war or you could spend them on butter to feed your people. But **LBJ** couldn't do that.

You see he had to spend money so everybody would like him. And the Vietnamese reminded him too much of the Mexicans that had always caused him problems down in Texas. No way was he going to give in to those little people. So we ran up a big deficit fighting both wars. Wars that we lost.

Okay, Mikey, I'll play **Fair**. I know that during the 1960's that our Gross National Debt went from $260 Billion to $366 Billion. The size of the increase in the National Debt is not the important point. The important thing to remember is that the federal government started believing that they could solve some of the **Fair** problems by spending more and more money. They also thought that running a deficit was not such a bad idea.

Now to be really **Fair**, we have to look at what happened in the seventies, eighties and nineties. Well, during the 1970's our National Debt went from $381 Billion to $829 Billion. Our National Debt went from $ 909 Billion to $ 2,867 Billion during the eighties. The 1993 Budget reconciliation bill estimates that the Gross Federal Debt will grow to $4.410 Billion by the end of 1993.

Sure, you are right Mikey, most of the $4.4 Trillion in National Debt did occur during the Reagan eighties. The point is that the public's demand that government try to fix their problems started during the 1930's and were continued during the 1960's and our concept of **The Great Society**.

We had forgotten that we only had limited resources to try to meet those unlimited desires for those resources. We continued to ask our leaders to keep spending the money. Sure, cutting the top tax rates from 70 % to almost 30% took away a lot of money from the Federal Government.

That definitely hurt the **Deficit Problem**. But what really hurt was continuing to fight a war that we could never win. The War on Poverty. How could we ever hope to win a war by sitting all of the successful people on the bench? How were we ever going to create a better world for anybody by taking the money away from the successful people?

Did that mean that we would only let people become successful to what we thought were an acceptable level? Once they reached that point, we were going to take from them and give to somebody else who had not been so successful?

Who was going to have enough money to pay for all of this? When was it going to be your turn to give up your money for somebody else? When would they come for you? Where will the government turn for more money when they have taken all of the money away from the **Rich People**?

Gee, this is starting to sound like some kind of war or something isn't it? Maybe we can't just keep listening to them give us somebody else to blame.

Maybe we need to ask ourselves if we are really that excited with those new programs that we would send them our own money. You know, be like Jerry and get everybody involved in solving a major problem.

"Wait, a minute, Richard, I work hard for my money and I pay too much in taxes as it is now. The Government needs to make all of those other **Rich People** pay their **Fair** share and leave me and Clem alone. We are just hard working people. They need to take the money from the people who can afford to pay their **Fair** share."

Let me get this straight, Bubba, you want the government to continue trying to make it **Fair** for everybody and to get the money to pay for all of these **Fair** programs from the people who have been more successful than you. What will the government do if all of the **Rich** people decide that it is better for them if they become **Poor** so that the government will help them?

You know it would only be **Fair**. What would the government do if everybody just quits making money and lets the

36

the government help them make a living for them and their family? What would we do then? Who would pay the bills? Sounds as if I fell off the back of the banana bus doesn't it?

Well, I have a friend of mine and he and his wife working together made over a Hundred Thousand dollars one year. Were they **Rich** people who had taken advantage of the other **Poor People**?

No, both of them were blue collar workers who worked a lot of overtime, gave up their vacations and worked a lot at night at second jobs so they would have that kind of money to spend on themselves. What do you think they will do if the government starts raising the taxes on people who are hardworking and successful?

Well, I know what they will do. As **AJ** told me, his ski boat is paid for and if the government will give everybody **some food, healthcare, housing and a little fooling around money** then he is going to quit working so hard and have a cool one on his boat.

There's no reason for him to work so hard if the Government is going to rob the **Rich** and give it to the **Poor**. "Hey, it will be fun being **Poor** if the government is going to make it **Fair** and take it away from the other guy."

Maybe we need to start thinking about another way if being **Fair** doesn't work. You know have another alternative plan to fall back on if the **Fair** thing fails like it has failed so many times before. Kind of reminds me of going on a diet to lose weight. Sometimes you have to have a backup plan when your first plan doesn't work.

3 OUR PROBLEMS
TODAY AND TOMORROW

Why can't the government listen to all of us? Why can't they just make everything right? You know every time you think that Billie, Ron, or Ross has it all right they turn their backs on all of the real people. You know just as Billie did. Yeah, you remember when he said, "The main issue is the Economy, Stupid and I'm going to give you a Tax Refund, too."

Yeah and what did he do right out of the blocks when he got elected. Yeah, he did that social thing. You know to pay them back. Why can't he just do what he said he would do?

Sounds like a broken record doesn't it? Well, that's the problem. We keep asking our leaders to do things that they can't in a million years do.
Maybe rather than asking for help like Virginia did with her father, we need to think about the problems.

Let's give Billie some credit. **It is the economy, stupid! Our number 1 problem is that people's standard of Living has declined from the sixties.**

How many people go to bed at night and say, "Lord just let me have another day like today?" You think that all of the **Rich Fat Cats** are going to bed at night and saying that. No, they are probably saying the same prayers that you're saying too. Make no mistake about it; we are all in a lot of trouble. We are starting to look real similar to what some other countries looked like before their declines. What countries? You know, just look in that good old history book of yours: Egypt, Greece, Rome, Spain, France, Germany, England and now probably us.

Is this something that we can change? You bet your good old US Dollar we can! Too many of our fathers and mothers paid a much higher price just so we had the opportunities. Maybe the opportunity to screw it up? But still, they gave us a chance, but first we have to understand what all of the problems are.

You see it is not just The Government, The Church, The Japanese, The Mexicans, The Fat Cats or any one thing that we can fix and it's back to good old times. You know the saying that everybody down in the Oil Country had on their car bumpers when the price of oil fell off the market. Yes, how did it go?

"Lord, let there be just one more oil boom just like it was in the Seventies and I promise I'll be good this time." Promising to be good is not the answer. The problem is all of the above. You know that answer that you always picked on that history exam because you hadn't paid a lot of attention to what the teacher was saying in class.

Yes, what has made our economic problem so hard to fix has been the complexity of the problems. There just isn't any one thing or group of people that we can blame. I wish there were. That would make everything kind of neat.

You know, just like in the movies, where you show the audience the danger and have just enough time for the hero to solve the problem before the end of the two hour movie. You also blend in some gaps in the action so that you can have plenty of good space for the movie theater to sell popcorn and soft drinks and the commercials when Television shows the movie.

Well, that is not the real world and the hero does have a real hard time saving the fair maiden. Heck, he even has a hard time in getting everyone to agree on who the fair maiden really is.

Yes, and he has to consider the effect of this group and that group and what will this do to the spotted owl and to that little snail that my daughter wishes would just leave her alone. It's become so complicated and turned around, that we can't even assume that any of our Institutions will act as we think that they should act. Maybe part of the problem is that everybody is just trying to be too considerate: Trying to be all things to all people and not step on anybody's toes.

You know, Clem, just like the gay problem in the Military. Yeah, X numbers of people thinks it is a good idea and Y numbers probably think that gays serving in the Military will ruin the country. If our only interest is to win a war, what should the question really be? **"Yeah, can you shoot straight?"**

We're trying to fight a hard War and we're debating what color the uniforms should be. Doesn't make a whole lot of sense does it?

But, that line of logic doesn't just go on in Politics. It's also true in our other Institutions. Take the Church for example. No, not your church or my church but any church. What should the major goal of this church be? Furthering the spread of its beliefs and how **God** has a plan for Man.

Right, but what is the current direction of most churches? What do you see on Television and in the Church that you attend? Let's take my church for a minute just so I don't make somebody mad. I was in church one day that was devoted to the celebration of the 4th of July.

Now, since you're not from **MY CHURCH** and I know that you're not, let me ask you why does the church care about the 4th of July?

Is that a special day in the Bible? Is it one of the Ten Commandments? No, but people like to hear the patriotic songs and hear about how out country has been a special place for **God** and it's easier to do a church program on the 4th of July than to really help somebody who has a serious problem.

Wait a minute, didn't the **Lord,** leave us with his last words: **To Love one another?** How does that relate to hearing the Star Spangle Banner in Church? Not a whole lot, especially if you were that person who walked into that church looking for some help with a personal tragedy such as burying your Three year old daughter because of cancer or losing your job and not being able to pay your bills.

Yeah, if you were that person looking for help with your problems, the last place you would want to be at that time would be in a church. It would kind of give you a bad attitude wouldn't it? But wait, hearing the Star Spangle Banner is not all. You probably could have walked in during a Clown service. You know, that's the service where all of the Ministers dress up as Clowns to make their service more fun and entertaining to people.

Well, just ask the guy who has been a drunk for Twenty years and finally he starts to ask himself if maybe he was wrong and he'll go see what the Church says to help him. Right, he'll find that bar if it takes him all day after **that service.**

Now, don't get me wrong. I don't have anything against clowns and I love music but I am not thinking about me. I'm thinking about that poor guy who just lost his daughter to Cancer. Explain it to him. What I am saying is that we are confusing a whole lot of people.

Our Government doesn't work as it should and look at what all of the Television ministers are getting into? Problems just like the problems that some of the movie stars and actress get into all of the time. You know the things that you read in that magazine when you're waiting for them to tell you how much you owe at the supermarket.

What I'm saying is not only does_____ happens it is not working either! Could there be anything else that's not working? Education! Now there's a really good mess. Everybody has a problem with the way them people are trying to educate our kids.

Yeah, up North they are even teaching them how to use Condoms for **"Safe Sex".** Why can't they just teach them the 3 R's? You know, just as we had when we were in school. How has Education changed in the last few years? Let's see, what has been the most dramatic change in education since the fifties? Have we developed new ways to improve the knowledge and abilities of our kids?

What important evolutions and modernization have been made in education? What! We've integrated the schools, introduced Busing and incorporated social agendas., Buy a House with a Really Good School and choose your favorite private Schools as new concepts.

We've watered down the curriculum to provide for "individual differences". We also got real concerned with kids' self-esteem and tried not to tell them that they were making bad grades and not succeeding when they made 20 's and 40's on their exams.

We invented a new phase called **Social Promotion**. If only the Japanese, Chinese and Germans would go along?

Yeah, all those strange looking people who couldn't speak English just worked and worked and they never think about the other guy. They just keep on studying and making good grades and acting as they were robots in those factories that make all the little cars. What's the World coming to?

Yeah, there have been a lot of real great improvements in Education. Test scores have been going down since the fifties. But that's not the whole problem. Just ask the Teachers about the problems. They are trying to teach kids without hurting their self-esteem. Well, not every teacher is. Just ask **Bobby Knight**, the Retired Basketball coach of the University of Indiana. He's tried to teach them about life. He also got into a whole lot of trouble too.

The point is that we're all working real hard. It's just not working real well. We've turned our education system into a version of Day Care. You know, let's not talk about test scores and achievement skills. It might look as if we are discriminating against_____.

How bad has it gotten in Education? Our public schools are so bad now that we even have to pay for kids to go to so called Technical Schools so they can learn some of the things that they didn't have time for in High School.

Right here in My Home State of Tennessee, we have an institution called Tennessee State Tech where kids go to school for a two year college degree. Now it's a nice looking degree, but what can you do with a Two year degree? I think they call it an Associate Degree. I'll tell you what you can do.

You can make a lot of money trying to teach kids things that they should have learned before they left High School. Go and talk to some of the teachers at the Two years schools who used to be public High School teachers and do you know what they will say?

"Let's see, I teach 3 classes a week with 20 in each class, have 6 hours of office duty and I am teaching the same curriculum that I taught in high school where I had 5 classes every day, with 35 in each class. This is the best job that I've ever had. Lord, please keep this School open!"

They also hope that the Government keeps giving ever body some type of Tax Credit for going To a 2 year school that tries to replace some of skills what were supposed to be learned in High School. "Just don't change the law not now. Wait until I can retire or move".

Are the kids better off? It depends on the opportunities that are available for two year graduates. But those people working at State Tech are sure glad that they are not trying to teach all of those students in High School.

Starting to see the problem? There is money to be made in offering alternatives to solving problems. It would look like that we could all agree on fixing our education problems. Let's see who all would we have to get into a room to talk about fixing the problems?

First we would have to get all of the parents to come to that room. Yeah, that's a good place to start. What do you mean; they don't come to the regular meetings? Are they working, laid off, run off, and dropped out or just not there? Well, that's not **Fair**. Every kid ought to have good parents.

Yeah, but what do you do? Well, let's give them good positive role models. No, not Michael Jordon, I mean a fine upstanding teacher right there in their school. But wait, a minute that's not the way it works. You see we have this little program called Integration where we bus white kids and black kids to other schools. We also make sure that white teachers teach in black schools and black teachers teach in white schools.

You know to make everything even and all. Does it work? No, not in your wildest dreams. Do you see a lot of black kids running around saying, "Did you hear the newest Donnie or Justine
record and isn't he so cool?" No, that's not being Racist, it is called being a Realist and there is a whole lot of difference.

My wife has taught school for several years in Inner City Public Schools. Schools where companies adopt the school. You know, give them supplies and things that the school board can't get the tax money for those items.

What works in those schools? It's common sense. It's called relating to people. The few teachers that are from the neighborhood and share some of the same experiences as the kids are the most effective. Are they better teachers? No, but they can get the attention of the kids and they can communicate in words that my little blond haired wife would never be able to pull off.

Now, back to the two R words. It's your choice. Do you call this racism or realism? It all depends on what your goals are. Do you care about giving the kids an opportunity for their life or you more interested in your own concerns?

I think for a long time we have been hung up on a lot of things that don't really matter in relation to helping other people. Probably at about this time, you're ready to start blaming somebody for this Education Thing. Wait don't fall into that trap. We're not looking for blame we're looking for solutions. So, education is a mess. Could it be that we tried to make it something else because educating everybody was just too hard?

You know, if Michael Jordon or Koby is too good, then we lower the hoop so everybody has the same chance. You know we make it **Fair**. There is another problem with lowering the oops because some people are too good for the rest of us. You miss the opportunity to see somebody overcome their physical limitations and succeed beyond your expectations. Yes, there was another Pro Basketball player called Mugsey Bogues who played for the Charlotte Hornets who later became the New Orleans Hornets.

Mugsey was also about Five Feet and some small change. Somebody that small is not supposed to be able to play basketball let alone Professional basketball.

How can that be? Does he know somebody? Yes, he knows himself. He has always outworked everybody else and concentrated on his strengths of quickness and speed. He didn't spend too much of his time worrying about his lack of size. He probably didn't even know how to say **Fair!**

Starting to get the picture? When we lower the goals to make it **Fair**, we take away from something that is special. In the case of Michael Jordon, if we lowered the basketball goal, then we wouldn't have all of those Nike commercials. Well, maybe there is some merit in that approach after all **no more** Nike commercials sounds kind of nice.

I wonder if we can do away with all of those stupid Phone Commercials. At about this point you're probably asking yourself, "What's Education and Michael Jordon got to do with my problem. You know, why don't I have more money to buy all those Basketball Shoes, Ping Golf Clubs, Big Screen Televisions, 5 Bed room Houses with swimming pools, Corvettes and not worrying about T-Mobile or AT&T!"

Bubba, it's all part of the problem! You see, our solution is answer # 4. It's all of the above. Everything has to change and improve. You see, what we have done is try to have it all. If you look at all of our major institutions, Churches, Schools, Business and Government you will see that they have changed in a big way.

They all have become too considerate of everybody's feelings? You know the **Fair Thing**.

Let's not make anybody mad or make anybody feel inferior. The only problem with that is that it is not the real world. It doesn't work. They are separate and different goals. But we've tried to make everything the same. Be **Fair**. Be Political Correct.

A while back, a Television newsman was interviewing Coach Bob Knight, the former Indiana Basketball Coach. During the interview the conversation turned to the change that had taken place in education and sports since the fifties. The interviewer was going on about how hard it must be now to motivate kids to learn. He asked Bob Knight about the difference with kids now versus when he grew up in the fifties.

Bob's point was a little different. Bob Knight thought that the kids hadn't changed. Kids were still kids. What had changed according to Bob were the adults. You know the ones who were supposed to be in charge. Bob felt that the adults were tolerating too much. Becoming lazy and letting the kids get away with too much. Sure kids will always try to get away with whatever we as adults will let them.

Too many times the adults just blamed the kids without trying to do anything to correct the kid's behavior. He felt that the adults were the ones who were lazy in not doing their jobs. Are we trying the wrong things because the right things are just too hard?

Another real radical thinker also wrote, "Children today are tyrants. They contradict their parents, gobble their food and tyrannize their teachers."
Who was the uncaring conservative that said that? No, President Ronald Reagan or President George Bush didn't dare say that. Thousands of years ago, one of the world's first great thinkers wrote that. His name was Socrates and he dared to look inside of man for solutions to the problems of his day.

Do you know how we beat the Russians to the Moon? I don't mean just beat them by a little bit but we are the only country to send our spaceship with people to the moon?

It started with President John F. Kennedy saying that our goal was to put a Man on the Moon before the end of the Sixties. He didn't say that we would go to the moon if Ralph Nader or Richard Nixon approved. Today we have to pay the Russians to send an American into space. Where is the vision in that?

No, we're not looking at some vision that we can all sink our teeth into. We're looking for someone else to blame and doing the **Fair** thing. The Russians probably told their people that they were doing the **Fair** thing. They also killed all of the **Rich** people and took all of their land and money.

Today when they tried to change they have **Rich** people, but you have to know somebody in the government in order to get rich or buy the assets that the government owned and sold to their Cronies at a very **Fair** price

I think that this is called   **CRONY CAPITALISION.**

All of that changed a little bit for a time when a chubby little Russian got in front of a Tank and said I have a vision follow me. That probably wasn't the politically correct thing to be doing right then. What's all of this got to do with us? A lot.

You see the Russians started their little experiment by saying that it was all the fault of the **Rich Russians**. You know the **Capitalists**. The ones that hadn't been paying their Fair share. Seems as if it took them about Seventy Five years to figure out that wasn't the solution to their problems.

"But we're different, we're, Americans." No, not really we're human beings and some things are inherent in the Breed. **Fair** doesn't always work. Just for a minute forget all of the really hard problems that we have and think back to a better time. No, not when you had a job and had money to spend. Think back to when you were a kid. Yeah, back then when someone else was paying all of your bills.

What did you do when you were young and growing up? That's right. You played a lot of games. And what kind of games were they? Kick the can, Annie Over, Simon Says, and Hide and Seek. How did those games go? Yeah, you had **Rules**. What else did you have? Well, you had **Winners and Losers**. And what usually determined who won and who lost those games that you played when you were a kid**?**

Skills. **Skills** that kids developed according to their physical abilities and most importantly to their interest in wanting to play and win **The Game.**

I remember when I was a kid, reading an article in *Boy's Life* about another kid that wanted to be the best at diving and staying under water for a long time. That summer he lost to all of the other boys and he was very upset at himself. No, not the other kids because they weren't being **Fair**.

He was upset with himself because he couldn't stay under water for more than thirty seconds. All the other kids could stay under water for a least one minute. You know what he did.

Well, he practiced all the next winter in a pool at the YMCA so he could train his body to stay under water for over ninety seconds and sometimes two minutes. Do you know how the story ended? Well, he went to camp that next summer and sure enough he could hold his breath for over ninety seconds. Something had changed though. While he had learned to hold his breath longer, the other boys had changed too.

They had discovered how to use Scuba Tanks and all of them could stay under water for over two hours. Was that **Fair**? Well, in this story the boy didn't complain about it not being **Fair**. He learned how to use Scuba Tanks and continued to play with the rest of the kids.

What's important in this look back at our childhood? When we were kids we didn't waste our time whining about it not being **Fair,** we learned how to **Win**. We didn't try to blame someone else. If we liked the game and we wanted to play the game, then we learned how to compete. Oh, sure there were some kids that went home to their mothers and cried about Johnny not letting them play, but you know what happened to them?

Yeah, they stayed inside a lot until they figured out how to play the **Game**. Or they remembered how to use that **Fair** word when they grew up or they kept using the **Fair** word and maybe moved to Russia or Cuba for a while.

Then the people who moved to Russia or Cuba saw how living in those countries was and they came back to the "**Good Old USA**". They also jumped off the plane real quick and kissed that first piece of **USA** ground when their plane landed. Looks like we are going to have to learn how To Play the Game. Seems as if Russia has even caught on and is learning how **To Play The Game**.

Clem, what do you mean, "I've left somebody out!" Yeah, I forgot the **B** word. You know, how does being **Fair** work in the business world. Well, it may come as a shock to most of you, but Business is probably the biggest users of the **Fair** word.

They can be downright crybabies sometime. I remember working for a large Hotel Corporation back in the Seventies. Okay, I'll "Fess Up" it was "Holiday Inns". You know when the **I** word was very important. **Inflation** would be the death of us all. Yeah, the government had to get **Inflation** under control.

Prices were going up to where a Businessman couldn't make a profit. Where and what were interest rates doing? Why Interest Rates were fixing to go to 20%. The government just had to get **their** act together and get **Inflation** under control. You know why it was important for us Hoteliers to get interest rates down?

Remember Rule #1. Everybody acts in their own best self-interest. Yeah, that one. Well, it sure runs true to form in the Business World.

You see we were raising our Hotel Rates about 15% a year and making a lot of good money. I mean **Real GOOD MONEY**. Like in Bonus and Promotions for a few good men and women. We wanted to build more hotels so we could make even more **REAL GOOD MONEY**.

The only problem was that high interest rates kind of put a kink in that little idea. You see, we had convinced ourselves that we were not the problem. We were not the ones that were raising our room rates. We were just passing on our cost increases. Cost increases that we planned on being around 8%. **"Why, it just wasn't Fair."**

Especially when President Jimmy Carter put in the Wage and Price Controls to keep us from raising our rates. Did President Carter's Wage and Price Controls work? Well, not really. You see you can always find someone to show you how to get around any system. Remember when you were a kid and how you got around rules that you didn't like.
Especially dumb ones like **Wage and Price Controls**.

Two things did happen during President Carter's Wage and Price Controls. First, the wage controls were a good reason for companies like my company to lower the amount of salary increases that they had been giving to their employees. So, see in this case, it was real easy just to say, "We are just following the President's Wage Control Program" and give some people less of a salary increase.

Did everybody get the same percentage wage increase? Are you kidding? Don't you remember how to play **The Game**? **Promotions**! Promotional increases do not count as wage increases. So, just like everything else in life the good and smart get the gold.

It's important to point out now, that I'm not bringing up this little story to stick a knife in the heart of **Holiday Inns** or any other business corporation. What I'm pointing out is that gimmicks do not work. Controls on Wages or Prices never stop talented and creative people.

All they do is give a false sense of reality and create shortages of the products and services that they were trying to control. What did happen was that Hotel companies continued to raise their rates and build more and more Hotels. Guess what happened next? Yeah, too many Hotels were built and rates came down. **The supply and demand thing,** but we'll hear more about how supply and demand works later.

Through all of the ups and downs of the Hotel Business, one thing that I heard over and over was how it was the government's fault. If interest rates were too high, it was the government's fault. If labor costs went up over 10% it was former Senator Edward "Ted" Kennedy's fault because he had sold out to the **Evil Unions**. It just wasn't **Fair**.

One of the concepts that you have heard in the 1990's along with the **Fair Thing** was the concept of making the people who made out in the Eighties pay their **Fair Share**.

Well, I hate to be the one to bring this up but there are a whole lot of people who were making it good in the Eighties that don't have a nickel now. To use the correct terminology. They have a **Big Hat But No Cattle**. Yes, I'm talking about some of the oil people or better yet the people who worked in the oil business.

You see, I went to Houston, Texas in 1981, right at the top of the oil boom. 1981 was a very good year in Houston, Texas. Everybody and his brother were coming to Houston to make their fortune. Why, you even had to take a number to get an apartment. "Gilley's" was cooking and "The Oilers" were almost in the "Super Bowl". Why, Ken Stabler was the new Quarterback and The Earl was the star running back on the team. Nothing could stop the "Oilers or Texas".

Oil was headed to $100 a barrel and the sky was the limit. You didn't hear anything about being **Fair** in Texas unless you were from Michigan or some other **Rust Belt** city?

So what happened next? Well, the oil people forgot that we could change if the money got right.

Yeah, a whole lot of things happened. People started conserving energy especially gasoline.
Everybody started finding more oil and selling it. All of a sudden we had a glut and prices went down. Now you started hearing the **Fair** word in Texas. It just wasn't **Fair**. Now, just like magic, everybody figured out that Houston had too many houses for sale, too many office spaces for rent and more oil field equipment than anybody would need for several years.

What happened next? Well, the banks jumped in and said it wasn't **Fair** that companies couldn't pay their bank loans and interest with all of those expensive people that they had working for them. The companies would just have to tighten their belts and cut the fat. Yeah, that would be **Fair**.

But why did the banks want companies to cut the fat? Remember rule number one: **Self-Interest**. "Don't spend your money on salaries; spend your money on paying your interest and principle that you owe us." **Did it work? Was it Fair**?

What do people do when they don't have a job or any money coming in each month? You got that right. They have a hard time paying their bills, especially Home loans on homes that drop 30% or more in value; Home loans that were financed at 10% or less down and 14% interest rates.

So you had a whole lot of people out of work and not being able to pay their home loans. What happens next? Well, even banks owe money to somebody. You guessed it: no more Houston Banks. Go to Houston, today and who owns the banks now? Yeah, a lot of other banks in places like North Carolina and New York. Was that **Fair**?

So what do we do with all of the people who lost their jobs and houses during the so called Roaring Eighties? Do we give them twice as much as everybody else? You know just to be **Fair**. Do we give them a big earned income credit?

Are we starting to get the picture? Blaming somebody else for your own problems is difficult and it doesn't work. Solutions are what are important. Something that will work. You see what we have done to ourselves is feel sorry for ourselves and try to put the blame on someone else. You know that old childhood game of let Mikey Try It.

We forgot how to win. We forgot how to learn and try. We've gotten stuck in the rut of it can't be me? It must be someone else.

Well, that can change. Haven't you heard of **The Dark Ages**? What was **The Dark Ages?** Well, simply put it was the period of time after the fall of the Roman Empire until we all got reeducated again and started to think and read again. The time when we all kind of went into a dark funk for a really long time. But what happened after **The Dark Ages**?

Everything started to look a lot brighter when men started asking difficult questions and looking at his world from a different angle. Yes that is where some of our solutions will be found; not in small minded repairs to a broken vehicle but in a **Whole New Vision**.

You remember the story about John F. Kennedy and his **Vision** about going to the Moon? That was a **Future Solution** We understood his **Vision** and we all wanted to come along. We also didn't look at blaming all our **Rich People** because the Russians had gotten the head start with sending up the first satellite called "**Sputnik**". No, we saw and understood JFK's **Vision** and we were willing to work toward that goal.

Some of our young people also took part in his other vision in the Jobs Corps. Yes, back then we were willing to compete with anybody.
We were Americans and we were willing to pay the price. What are we doing now?

We are even afraid to compete with **Little Old Mexico**. You remember Mexico that big bad country that invented that giant vacuum cleaner that is going to make that big sucking sound when we lose all of our jobs to them. Where we once had heroes who weren't afraid of the demons that existed in outer space, now we are afraid of having to compete with the Mexicans. What are we afraid of now?

Are we willing to look toward the **Future** now? Are we willing to look inside of ourselves and ask the tough questions? Are we ready for **Solutions?**

4 OUR SOLUTION TODAY AND TOMORROW:GOVERMENT

Any solution to our major problems has to start with Government. Why? Because we have become a Nation that believes that the Government can solve all of our problems. Government doesn't need to solve the problems of others; it needs to solve my problems. No, not their problems. **My** problems. So, the beginning has to be with Government and ourselves.

You see what has happened is that we have kept pushing all of our perceived problems up the line to where there were there is nowhere else to turn for our solutions. The buck has finally stopped unfortunately for all of us. So what will save us? What has always been there? **US.**

We can save ourselves if we really want to change for the better. Let's think about our government for a minute. Yeah, we have three branches of government: A legislative branch that makes all the laws, a judicial branch that interprets the laws and an executive branch that enforces all of the laws

But there's just one small problem. Remember rule number one about everybody acting in their own best **Self-Interest**? Yes, that one. Well, how come we keep paying people to work all the time to make more and more laws that people have a hard time obeying? If you don't agree with that, explain how come we can't keep enough prisons for all of the people who are convicted of breaking all of the laws.

Now, you see it don't you? We are trying to have it all. A perfect world ruled by laws. The only problem is that we pay people to keep coming up with more and more laws. I know that you don't believe me, Bubba, but our Congress's main job is to make laws.

That's what Legislation is. **LAWS.** They only got into the **Fair** business in recent years. Yes, Congress's reason for their existence is to make laws. Then we have to spend more and more of our money to put some people in jail after they break some of those laws.

A friend of mine who is a banker thinks that we need to be stronger on Law and Order. You know, start putting all of the law breakers behind bars and keep the lawbreakers off the streets. What else do you hear that sounds so good? Right, "Three times and you are out". Put them in prison for good if they get convicted of a Felony three times. Make this country safe for decent people. Why do we keep hearing that over and over but we still have the problems of people breaking the laws and not enough money for new prisons? Sounds like we ought to be able to fix that one. We are the ones who elect the people who make the laws.

Could part of the answer be that we are afraid that **We** could be the ones who break our own laws and we always want a way out? You know someday **you** might be the one who has to pay the price for breaking that law. Have we become so afraid of ourselves that we are willing to turn the other way when laws are broken? Is law and order just some concept that we all turn to just as college students turn to some pep rally slogan such as **Go War Eagle**?

Maybe, it's just gotten too big to manage. Maybe, it's time to give the country back to the people. Wait, don't you remember chapter one and the

Declaration of Independence and
The Constitution of the United States.

This country is supposed to be for all of us anyway. What's going on here anyway? What's going on is the problem. We keep asking the government to solve all of our problems. Yeah, the big government that has to make sure that it listens to everybody and doesn't make anybody mad.

We've tried electing Republicans, Democrats, Bull Moose's, Whigs, Federalists, Liberals, Conservatives and even Generals and Movie Actors. We still come up short of what we expected them to do for all of us. Maybe it's time to change things. No, not change that doesn't work like being Fair, I mean real change. No **Hope and Change** here. Change back to our own Rights and Responsibilities. Not the Change that some other Human Being says that is what they think we should have.

Where would the starting place be? Oh, let's look back in History real quick. How did the Romans do it? Well, the Romans started out with real limited government. In the beginning of the Roman Empire, government was voluntary. There were no Kings, everybody just followed a few simple laws and if a real emergency came up, then someone would put down his plow and go to save Rome. Romans didn't really trust government and military leaders. They were probably the first to figure out **Rule Number # 1**.

What happened to Rome anyway? Well, they got real lazy and **Rich** and started letting professional soldiers do their fighting and permanent leaders like Caesar rule them. Pretty soon, they got real lazy and the Barbarians came in and burned Rome. That's about the time that **The Dark Ages** set in. Well, maybe it's time for a new beginning for all of us. I wonder how someone would set up a really good government if they were starting from the beginning.

You know if we didn't have to worry about the past and trying to make sure that we didn't hurt anybody's feelings. I guess we should start small. Yeah, start real small. See that we got it right with a few things first. Maybe, the secret is just like in the ***Constitution* and *Declaration of Independence***. The Government is for and by the people. If that's true, then maybe I'd rethink having a full time paid branch of government to keep drawing up more and more laws. You know all of those laws that everybody keeps breaking. I wonder would that have an economic benefit.

Would that help to make the deficit go away? Whoa, I'm getting ahead of myself again. First things first. Let's see, rather than spending all of our money on Senators and Congressmen, I wonder how I could use that money. Right, I'd find a way to spend that money but first I have to change a few things.

Why not just have Congress elected for a real limited term? Say that each state got only one senator and one representative based on that state's population. We also would want to put a cap on the total number of Representatives that would be elected so that the House of Representatives didn't become another uncontrollable mess. Our cap could be a total of 200 Representatives elected across the whole country and not just in a specific State. If for just a minute we could make everybody stop having babies and that the population of the United States was 240 Million people then each of the Representatives would be elected in areas of the country that add up to 1.2 million people.

For example, if California had over 24 million people and there were 240 million people in the country then they would get 20 Representatives. If a state had less than 1.2 million people say in Wyoming then those Representatives would be elected over more than one state. In either case we would limit the number of Representatives to 200 and the number of Senators to 50.

Call it our Wise 250. Now, to make sure that it didn't get back to the way it was before, you would have to add some other touches. One of these new touches would be to limit the size of Congress's support staff.

There wouldn't be any. If any Congressperson needed a staff to help them do their job, then they would have to pay for it out of their own pockets. Congress would also only be in session for two months every five years. Yes, I did say in session for only two months every five years. Sound's Radical doesn't it? But does it? Stop and think for a minute.

Why do we need to keep making more and more laws that require more and more prisons for people who break those laws and spending more money that we don't have?

The Germans have sometimes used a simple concept on their highways. You see the German people are very respectful of authority. They also like to drive their cars very fast. So the German government came up with the concept of the Autobahn: a highway where there is no speed limit. If there was a speed limit then the German people would have a conflict. Do we break the law or do we not drive fast? Their solution was to leave it up to each person who gets on the Autobahn. That way there was no conflict. Seems as if the Germans figured out Rule Number One too.

So, in our solution, Less would be better. But would we stop here? No, you would have to carry this concept all the way down to the local level. This solution lets people truly decide how they want to live their lives. Little at the top and more added the closer you get to the people. This is called everything has a cost. You want to have a law for this and that. Fine. You make the law and guess who pays for that law? You do. That's who. Remember in our solution there are no villains and anybody to blame.

We don't even have to think about if it's **Fair**. It's fine with me. You want this law. You decide and you pay. Somewhere along the line some of our leaders thought that they really knew what was good for us and we didn't. You remember the concept of a wise government that saves the people from their own lack of decency and intelligence.

Yes, a government that would do the right thing even if the majority of the voters didn't agree with that law. Why, the government had to think about the future and save all of us from ourselves. There's only one little problem with that concept. Who really pays the bills? The government doesn't have any money of its own. All the government does is collect our money and spend it. Without us the government is broke.

Now, Mikey, I know you are fixing to tell me all about the concept of Economies of Scale and how smaller states couldn't afford to do some things on their own, but you have overlooked a major part of that logic. If the people in the small states don't have the money to spend on that, where do you think they will get the money? That's right, from somebody else. Just ask yourself how much money have you given to somebody else? I don't mean how much money have you given to the **ACLU** or the Friends of the Earth. I mean how much have you given to Jim or Jane.

That's like a friend of mine when you ask him how much he has given of his money to help people that he cares about and loves he always says the same thing. "Why I don't mind helping some needy person, but I am not going to give my hard earned money to somebody who won't even help themselves. Why should I help some lazy good for nothing person like that."

Oh, I didn't know that his friends and relatives were all lazy and good for nothing. You see that's his way of justifying not really spending his money to help somebody else. He comes up with a reason that it's them and not him. If individuals don't want to spend their money to help other people then how can we get the government to help those people? All of the government's money comes from those same people. Do you want to make up the shortage?

Let us get back to Congress for a minute. We also would not pay them to represent all of us. That's right not a dime, not even travel money or expenses. We want people who want to serve. We also want people who live in the real world and have to earn their living according to those laws. No more exemptions for Congress. You know how Congress writes a law, such as Social Security, and then puts in an exemption so that they don't have to obey the law.

Now is a good time to think about something else. Our solution cannot be a solution that is based on penalizing anybody or looking to fix the causes of problems of the past.

Remember Rule number one? Well, those Congressmen and Presidents have been trying to please us before and still remembering how rule number one affects them. You know the self-interest of Congress is in getting reelected. No, the solution is not in the people it is in the system.

What we want is a system of government that doesn't get in our way? Remember there are always at least two sides to every problem. One of the favorite approaches in dealing with the deficit problem used by politicians trying to get elected to Congress or become President has been to bring up all the wasteful spending that Congress does. One of the specific examples that keep coming up is **The $200 Hammer**.

Now, I don't know about you, but I don't spend that kind of money for my hammers. So that's wasteful, right? Well, what do we do? Let's stop buying all of those overpriced hammers. There's only one little problem. Yeah, all of those companies that make and sell $200 hammers have employees, especially employees that vote. Try to stop buying those hammers and lay off all those voters.

Think that's a problem? Look at all the difficulty we are having in closing military bases. Everybody knows that we don't need all those bases and all of the troops that we had during the Cold War. Right, but how did Congress and the President handle that one. Yeah, they formed a Commission to come up with a plan so that they didn't get the blame for closing all of those bases and making the voters mad.

Well, that's just as dumb as just continuing to blow out the matches in the baby's hands rather than taking the matches away from the baby. Think, I'm stretching? I have a friend of mine, who spent tons of money trying to get his three year old to do this and that. He finally took his kid to see a specialist in childhood psychology and told the good doctor all of his problems.

He related to the doctor all of junior's experiences, how junior would not eat his food, would not put on his clothes and would not do this or that. Finally, after the Doctor had patiently listened to all of his problems, the Doctor stood up. He said, "Look here and he raised his hand over my friend's head, this is you. You are the father, a big person. Then he put his hand about two feet from the floor and he said this is your child. This is a small person. What's your problem?"

See our problem is not so great. We are the big person. They all work for us. It's up to us. But do we want to be the big person or do we want someone to take care of us? Back to our solution again. Part of the solution has to involve shrinking the role of government. You see, there are two types of problems in our world. Man-made problems and problems that we have to look to God to solve.

Man-made problems are problems such as having to figure out how to fix a car that will not run. When we go to a mechanic to fix a problem that we are having with our car, he goes through all of his steps. He starts small and if that doesn't work he goes to the major systems of the car such as the transmission or engine. If that doesn't work he can always tell you that it's time to buy another car because this one is broke. Man-made problems can always be solved with combinations of two things. **Time and Money**.

How much time do you have and how much money are you willing to spend? Another good friend of mine is in the Car Business and sums it up best. When confronted with any problems, Rick always asks, "How much will it cost to make the problem go away?"

What he is doing is looking at all of his alternatives and then trying to pick the best alternatives that he has. He starts out with his most expensive alternative and works from there to his solution. All man made problems have alternatives. We may not always like the alternatives but they are there to solve the problem. It always comes down to how much time we have and how much money do we have to fix the problem when we are dealing with man-made problems.

Problems in **God's** world are a lot different.

They don't offer us any alternatives. They may involve our health. In the case of problems in **God's** world the mechanic could be a Doctor. The Doctor still goes through an objective approach of checking for simple problems to major systems such as kidneys, lungs, hearts and brains. He has one major problem. When he gets to the end of his analysis there is no buying another human body. That's in **God's Hands.**

Any solution to our problems with Government has to involve this concept. The best that we can do is to try to pick the best alternative that we have. This alternative will always involve time and money. We also have to remember that there are limits to our abilities to pay for our solutions. Remember the conversation with Virginia about living on an allowance? The choice that we pick will not work if it just means looking for someone else to pick up the tab.

A Capitalist friend of mine has a solution to the **Welfare Problem**. To him the solution is real simple. He thinks that we should do what some of the European countries do with this problem. According to him, in some countries in Europe, the government gives everybody a little amount of **Welfare** even if you are working. That way a poor person can work at a low paying job and not lose their welfare benefits. Yeah, in Europe, they are handling **Welfare** a lot better.

There are some problems with this concept. Who pays for all of this benefit? Well, according to my friend, everybody pays.
He doesn't have a problem with that because he probably thinks that it wouldn't cost him that much. Didn't Social Security start that same way?

Small at first then people started asking for more and more benefits. Yeah, it is not real hard to ask for more of something if you do not have to pay the cost. You also start to run out of people to pay for that benefit. No, I don't think that is where we will find our solutions.

So back to our new government. We must change the rules about how and why we give power to our government. If we keep paying people to spend money that we don't have, we will continue this problem until we run over the side of the cliff like so many little rats and lemmings going blindly to our demise. My little girl doesn't deserve that and neither does yours.

So the starting point in our solution is to shrink the government's ability to make new laws and spend money, money that we don't have.

Now **Michael**, before you start coming up with a lot of statistics and figures showing why this won't work hear me out. This is not a version of trickle down or voodoo economics. There are several parts to this solution that will address some of your **social concerns**. Just be patient they will be there.

Just remember this. We are not going to blame anybody and the solution comes in giving everybody an opportunity to be part of the action. We also will use rule number one a lot. Remember that everybody acts in their **Own Best Self-Interest**.

Oh, okay. I will explain a little early, just because I know that is your nature to interrupt and try to out **Word** holler me to death? Stop and think for a minute about how we have been going on the **Thing Fair**. Do you know what people do with the money that they work hard to make?

There are only two things that you can do with your money. Two things and I don't care if you have $200 million dollars or Two cents.

You can either spend or save that money.

Let's look at what happens when that evil **Rich Person** who has $2 million dollars spends that money. He may buy a really nice car that we can't even pronounce or a really large house. Well, the money for those things that we all envy only has one place to go.

Right, it goes into somebody else's pocket. Now, we may wish that it was our pockets, but it does end up in some working person's pocket.

Remember, when we tried to put a tax on Yachts? You remember we were going to raise a lot of new taxes from all of those greedy **Rich** people especially the ones that had the nerve to spend all of their money on things that we couldn't have or understand.

Why, it was only **Fair**. "How dare those **Rich** people spend money that should have been ours, it was only **Fair**. If I don't have a Yacht then they don't deserve to have one. What could they possibly use a Yacht for anyway? Nobody that I hang around with has even ever seen a yacht.

Go ahead and tax them. Tax them some more. All right by me and it will serve them right too." How did we say it when we were kids? Hit them again. Hit them again. Harder. Harder. What happened? That's right; all of the people who worked at making those tacky Yachts lost their jobs because people stopped buying yachts. Wasn't that really tacky of all those people to stop buying Yachts?

What else can a person do with his money? Well, he can save that money for a rainy day. Remember that concept from your childhood about putting aside something for the future? Yeah, we forgot that one didn't we? Well, that has to be really bad doesn't it?

Remember that cartoon about Donald Duck's uncle Scrooge and how he just wallowed in all of that money in his bank vault. That's not the real world. When somebody saves their money, that money goes into things like bank loans for houses, cars and other things. It also goes into investments in the business world.

Investments that do create jobs. Real jobs not jobs that last until the next public swimming pool gets built. So why would you be angry if somebody was successful? Regardless of how he uses his money, we will all benefit.

I know, Mikey that just does not fit in with what we have been told about being **Fair**. There's just got to be a **Villain**. Somebody that we can take their money away from them and give it to the **Poor People.** There is just got to be a way. If there's no **Villain** who do we blame?

Now, that you stopped me, I guess we need to think about what Barry said about the Gay issue. Yeah, that Barry that everybody just knew was a solid conservative. Yeah, he would really set those Gay people straight about what it took to be in our military. Well, surprise surprise, what did he say? Something about being more important to be able to shoot straight than being straight.

Barry has been in combat. **Barry knows**. When you are at war and risking your life and the person next to you in that foxhole, you don't think about blaming people or anything else but shooting straight. If you have ever been in the Military, you also know how horrible war really is. You know that going to war is always your last resort. War is about killing and not being killed. War is not about playing games and pep rallies.

Wars will always get nasty. Rules? Have you ever heard any rules about being in a knife fight? No, there are no rules except kill them before they kill you. What was it that Clem told me about being in Combat?

"Throw all of your rocks real hard and if they keep coming after you then you throw down everything that you are holding and head for the hills."

So let's forget about judging other people and what they have. Let's start thinking about how we can improve our situation without taking away from somebody else. Forget about trying to be **Fair** by taking away from somebody else.

We need to figure out how all of those **Rich People** got to be so successful and see if we can be successful too. The government can't do that for us.

Only we can make ourselves successful.

Our new Congress would only be in session for two months every five years. They would consider the needs of the government and pass a budget for the next five years. But how could that deal with all of the spending needs that the Government has now? That's part of the solution. We are going to really change the Government and what we ask the Government to do for all of us.

When we are through, what we will really need the government to do, will cost us very little. What's a little?

Well probably less than 10 % of everybody's income. It's also real important to agree on the concept first of what we want the Government to do for all of us. If we can get the government out of all of our lives then the cost of that government will be very small. But more on that later, first let's look at what that Government would do and how it would work.

5 OUR SOLUTION
WHAT GOVEREMENT WOULD
DO TOMORROW

Think back to when you first got out on your own and away from your parents. Yeah, those parents who always made you eat all those greens and yellows and made you walk straight and look right. Them! What did you want them to do for you when you were finally out on your own for the first time?

Well, if you were like me and everybody else you wanted them as far away as you could get them but for them to still be there if you really got into something that you couldn't handle on your own. But you definitely didn't want them dropping in on you on a Saturday night.

I remember when I had just come back from Vietnam and was going to College on the GI Bill. I could never quite explain to my mother why I was out on Saturday night till 1:00 AM in the morning. She always said "that there was nothing that was going on at that hour". At least nothing that she was interested in doing. I think maybe she forgot what was going on at that time of night.

Well, what do we really want out of our lives? Do we want to have an opportunity to live it our way or do we want to live in our mother's house and live by her rules.

You see that's what our Government has become. It's become everybody's **Mother**. Anytime that you take a lot of money away from people you set up different expectations about what that government should do for you. Unfortunately there's just not enough to go around if everybody takes the biggest slice that they can get their hands on at the moment. And the Government is starting to get real hungry and they are just not interested in a *Kid's Meal* to go.

Our future government would not be our mother, father, uncle or even a kissing cousin. Our new government would be just like the Government that our founders envisioned in the **Constitution**. It would give everybody a chance to live their life as they wanted to live it.

(Maybe not like everybody else but an opportunity to live as they choose.) We also would remember: **Truth Number One:**

The Government has no money of its own.
All of the government's money has to come
from somebody else who has to earn that
money first.

Without us the government has no money. We are the customers of the Government. The government needs us for its source of money. It cannot spend any money that we don't have or don't want to spend on our own.

So what do we really need for the Government to do for us? Now, think back to that Movie that we all watch on Television at Christmas every year. Yes, I'm talking about; *it's a Wonderful Life* **with Jimmy Stewart**. What does the Jimmy Stewart character ask all of the people who are trying to get their money out of his Savings and Loan when they think that his Savings and Loan is fixing to fail?

Yes, he asks, **"What do you really need, what can you get by on?"** Well, what can we really get by on for the Government doing for us? Remember that the government is like my mother and yours. If you stay in her house you have to go by her rules. The government's rules are a lot harder. They have to try to be **Fair** and please everybody. Well, they at least have to try to please **their** voters.

Another important concept that we better deal with is how and who pays for what the government does for us. In our **Future Solution** the answer is that we all pay for that government. Everyone pays. No progressive or an oppressive scale but the same portion of whatever base we use. It can be a percentage of income or it can be a percentage of what we spend, but it has to be the same for everyone. Now, why would I come up with such a dumb idea as that?

That just wouldn't be **Fair**. Everybody knows that my mother cannot

71

afford to pay the same percentage of her income in taxes as Donald Trump. Why it just wouldn't be **Fair.** **Fair** is not the main thing. When you have one group of people paying the taxes that fund those programs and another group of people using the programs you will have problems. Demand goes up and supply goes down. It is real easy to keep asking for more services when you don't have to pay for any of the services. It's real close to the same dilemma that you have on Sin Taxes.

Yes, Sin Taxes. The tax that everybody is always too quick to put on some human action or habit that all of us think is so bad. Well, my mother has lived her whole life opposing alcohol in any form. Why, she was even against Restaurants and Bars serving liquor by the drink even when it meant that people would buy smaller amounts. She didn't care.

She was against alcohol in any form or fashion. A tax on alcohol? Good idea with her. "Why those people need to pay the taxes. It's not right for people to drink. It's definitely not **Fair.**"

But what happens when you tax something that you don't agree with? Two things can happen. People still keep their habit that you don't agree with or they stop because of the extra cost to them. What have you done if they still keep the habit and pay the taxes?

Now you have a habit that you don't like or agree with and you are depending on them to keep that habit to pay those taxes. If they quit the habit you would have an even bigger problem.

How do you replace the taxes that the government has gotten used to spending? If they stop the habit right away, taxes are not coming in to the government. Reminds you of the Yacht problem doesn't it? The Government has a really difficult problem on Tobacco. Since the 1960's medical facts have shown that smoking will kill you. That's right it will kill you. Has the government stepped in to protect American lives by abolishing the growing of Tobacco and put the cigarette makers out of business?

No, the government has used cigarettes to bring in more taxes. Just as the Pharmacy stores have used selling cigarettes to bring in more customers for their other products that they sell to the public. The government has also continued to give Tax money to farmers for growing tobacco. If smoking is that bad for you, why doesn't the government just make it go away?

No, that would be too hard and would affect too many people. The government just uses an indirect approach and uses Tobacco as a giant whipping boy to get People to support additional taxes: taxes that are on the other guy. To avoid these and other problems, we want our Government to be out in the open and everybody paying the same percentage regardless. It may not be **Fair** but it will work and work to all of our benefits.

Back to the Jimmy Stewart question, how much do you really need and what can you get by with? Remembering when we first got out of our mother's house, what do we really need the government to do for us? We need to have the security that we can live our lives as we choose to live them as long as we don't hurt somebody else's ability to live his or her life. That's the main purpose of government, not in making sure that it is **Fair**.

That is up to us. We need the opportunity. **Fairness** will be covered later, but right now we need to have the opportunity to make it on our own. Before anybody calls Mr. Nader, think about how we do it now. Everybody knows that stealing and murder are against the law. Why, it's a Federal Law? Wrong, it's not a Federal Law, it's a state law and according to where you live, there are different punishments for stealing and murder.

Of course if you are a might too quick in telling somebody that you have a romantic interest in them, you could go to jail or have to spend a long summer in explaining how you didn't say that. Now, I know that sexual discrimination isn't on the same level as murder or stealing. That's the point. Our Federal government has spent a lot of our money trying to make everything **Fair** and has forgotten about some real important **Rights**. Yes, our **Right** to live our lives!

Doesn't it seem that we have gone a bit too far? Maybe we need to start over at square one. Why not come up with some simple laws that we could all agree should be respected by everybody who lives here? Try to get everybody to start agreeing with those laws first. If we can get people to respect those laws then we can start dealing with the other ones. Remember the Germans and the **Autobahn**? Probably a good start would be in the **Ten Commandments**. You know the ten laws that Moses brought down from that mountain.

Now, hold on a minute, I'm not suggesting a religious government like what they tried in Iran and some other Bad Place. I'm just saying look to the **Bible** for a starting point. Men have been using The Bible for examples for years. Just ask the Military how they came up with some of their ideas on organization.

What I am saying is that let's pick say the top twenty things that relate to how we all want to live in this country. We don't want to be lied to, cheated, robbed or Killed. Make those things against the Federal Law. Now, for other things, let the states, counties and cities write those laws. That way people can have more freedom in how to live their lives and can vote for the amount of freedom that they are willing to give to a government.

They also can vote for the Taxes to pay for those laws. People could even have a choice on living in a state where they all agree on that state's laws. What would be wrong with that?

Didn't our original founders of this country believe in the rights of people to live as they wanted and that state rights were important? What would be wrong with giving people the right to decide how they want to live their lives in their own cities and towns? Oh, I know it wouldn't be **Fair**.

No, Mikey what that really means is that you don't want to see them living their lives in a way that disagrees with how **You** think that they should live their lives. You know we have to make sure that everybody lives by the same rules. Even if they don't agree with them or wouldn't be willing to pay the taxes to enforce those laws.

With this concept the Federal Government starts to look a lot smaller. This couldn't happen could it? Well, before you start saying can't happen, look at what's going on in the old USSR.

74

Right, they are shrinking their government. Do we want to wait and see what happens just as we did with the Japanese and Germans?

We leveled all of their old factories and then helped them build brand new ones that could out manufacture anything that we could with our old factories. Right, let's wait and see if the Russians start building those cheap looking toys like the Japanese did or will they figure out how to use their Oil as the Arabs did?

What do you think? You know that they do have a lot more oil and other natural resources than even the Arabs Think about it. Russia may end up being our biggest Competitor in Business.

Do you want to hide and see what happens? So, our new federal government would be responsible for our defense and Security. Will that still cost a lot of money? It will if we still keep holding on to the defense jobs and World War II military as the old Viking looking at his army being defeated with tomorrow's technology. But we're not going to fall into that trap.

Our military will not still prepare to fight the Russians or to fight World War II. again. The military that we will need will prepare to fight the future battles and for all of that we all need to pay. Not our **Fair** share but an **Equal** share in paying. You see it is important that everybody shares in paying the same percentage as the next guy for our **Future Government**.

If we convince ourselves that some people have to pay a higher percentage of taxes than other people, we start having problems, such as the people that are getting the government services at no cost to them for those services demanding more and more of those services. All the while the people who are paying those taxes and receiving little of the services are getting more and more frustrated.

You see government does not have any of its own money. All of the money that the government spends comes from somebody else. Somebody first has to make that money. Now, I know that will come as a shock to most people, especially the people who are getting the government benefits and not paying a lot of taxes but that is the real world. Government is only a middle man. It takes money from some and gives money to others. We would change that. We would also want our Federal government to enforce the laws inside our country. For this kind of task you need a national force. Okay, I'll use a term that will probably cause a lot of flak: **A National Police Force**. But, keep in mind we make the laws and there's not going to be a lot of laws that people will say that they didn't understand. Oops I forgot about Healthcare and Homeland Security.

Oh, never mind; just make sure they always read the Laws before they vote. Those laws and penalties are left up to us. What I'm trying to avoid is the **C** word. Yes, we need to make some hard choices. What laws do we want to write that say that for committing some crimes you will no longer be with us? Sounds harsh I know, but that is a choice that we have to make. And Mikey, wait till we get to the **Future of Education** before you start saying that it's Not **Fair.** Get a life and give us a chance.

"Wait a minute, you forgot the courts and especially those guys and gals that don't have to run for reelection and have a life time job. No, I've not forgotten them. You see this is a manmade problem. We can solve this kind of problem. We're going to take the matches away from the Courts also. You see if we can agree on a few simple laws then we will not need a lot of people sitting around to see if all of it is **Fair**.

We are making our choices to define how we want to live our lives and if that is not how you want to live your life then you go to court.   If the laws are simple and the punishment goes with the crime we will not have a lot of courts.

We will have a choice on building more prisons or applying Capital punishment. This forces you to think out simple laws, doesn't it? No, in our **Future Solution**, we would reduce the amount of money that we spend on The Judicial Branch too. We would still pay judges to be judges, but we would have a lot fewer judges. We are going to have fewer laws and we will expect to spend less money on that branch of our government too.

I have a brother-in-law who has a real hard time with this concept.

Oh, yes he is always for some extreme measure like capital punishment. Right, Capital punishment, when it wouldn't apply to him. He keeps telling me about some new program that he has heard such as **Tuff Love**

or something that gives somebody another chance. More programs for people who still don't want to live by the laws that almost everybody else agrees with and goes by.

Maybe we have made too many laws and too many exceptions. At some point you are forced to deal with your problems. We have run out of alternative approaches to dealing with people who won't go to school and people who won't respect our laws. Let's try simple laws and simple penalties for people who violate those laws.

Before we enact more laws and keep trying to kick all of our problems up to Congress and The President we need to ask ourselves two important questions.

1. Is the law that we want Congress to pass and make everybody else go by a law that all of the people in our family are abiding by now?
2. Is everybody in our family paying for all of the cost of enforcing that law?
3. Will the new law cover everybody including all of the Government?
4. I Mean Everybody. With a whole lots of periods and no Question Marks.

If we cannot even get our own family to follow that law, why do we think that the government can make it work for everybody else in this country? Remember the phrase of "Start out small first". The family is the first organization of government. We have to start first with ourselves and our Family if we want to see other people change.

Haven't we heard all of the Republicans talk about **"Family Values"** before? Yeah, I know this was just as meaningless as the Democrats talking about being **Fair**? Both of these concepts have to start with all of us first. Let go back to Law and Order and Prisons again. Let's think about the concept of "Three Strikes and You are Out". You remember that concept of putting people who commit a Felony for a third time in Jail and throwing away the Key. Well, Mikey, I know this will shock you, but I agree with you this is a really dumb idea.

The reason that it is such a dumb idea is that this will really cost a lot of money and I know a lot of people will resist paying the taxes to fund this program. Yes, it is a program when the government tries to pretend that it is a magician and can pull a rabbit out of a hat. Well, think about what it would cost to put somebody away with all of our laws that protect their rights.

Remember the part in the **Constitution** about the government not being able to use Cruel and Inhuman Punishment? Right that one. Well, it would cost all of us a lot of money to provide those people in jail with all of the basic needs that have become associated with humane treatment.

To most of us, Humane Treatment means a lot of things. It means good housing, heating, air-conditioning (Except in some public schools in Memphis, Tennessee), good food, enjoyable recreation (This has come to mean Color Television and Tennis Courts), security and Healthcare. All of those things can get real expensive. Could we end up with people inside of Prison having better Healthcare and Televisions than the people that are on the outside and maybe even the people who were hurt by those people in prison?

Doesn't make a lot of sense to put somebody away and end up costing us over $30,000 per year for each prisoner that we put away. Do you want to pay the bill at $30,000 a year to put somebody away for thirty years or the rest of their natural life?

Could there be another way? Could we really put them away for good? Forget making them change for the better. Could we really put them away so they could not hurt somebody again? Could we do this and not cost all of us over $30,000 a year per prisoner?

Yes, we can but we have to use our imagination and not get hung up on what we have done in the past. In fact we need to look to our past and ask ourselves what we did with the kind of people who wouldn't follow the rules in our family that everybody else in our family followed. What did we do with these people when we first came out of the garden and lived together as families and tribes? We made them leave our family. We made them go someplace far away from the rest of the family. Why can't we do that now?

Make them go away. Some place where they couldn't hurt any of us again and putting them away from all of us wouldn't cost us all of our money that they were probably trying to take from us in the first place. Maybe we could come up with some place like they had in those:
Superman Comics that I used to read when I was a little boy.
Could we come up with our version of the **Phantom Zone**?

You remember that place where they sent all of the really bad people who broke all of their laws on **Superman's** home planet.

Somewhere there's got to be an island that the government owns that we could send really bad people who had killed or hurt somebody. Why couldn't we come up with an isolated island to send those people? Now, Mikey, I know this sounds a lot like what the French tried with their Desert Island, but think about it and give it a chance. We have to come up with an inexpensive way to make these bad people go away.

Let's say that there is an island in the Pacific that is isolated and under US control. Remember some of those islands that the government used to test Atomic weapons. Yes, those islands. Well, what if we used some of those islands to put people who had committed crimes like Rape and Murder and just put them there to live their lives as best they could away from all of us.

Now, Mikey I know this sounds harsh, but we are talking about people who don't really care how you or I feel. These people have raped our children and daughters. They have taken away our husbands, wives and brothers. We don't want them around anymore. Forget Revenge or changing them for the better. We don't want them around and we don't want to pay for keeping them in prison. We want a low cost way to make them all go away and not come back and hurt somebody else.

79

You know our other brothers, sisters, sons, daughters, husbands and wives. Our biggest expense in keeping these bad people away from all of us would be to prevent them from escaping and coming back. For that we would use our Navy.

Yes, I did say our Navy and not spend a lot of money on prison guards. No, the island that we picked to place these bad people would be self-contained. What I mean by that is that the only people who would be on the island would be **Bad People**.

No guards. No doctors. No Television. No prisons. You have the whole island to yourself. You make the rules. This is your home and you will never, never leave. You have killed somebody. You have raped one of our daughters. For this you will never come back to us. Our main expense will be in transporting you there and paying our Navy to make sure that you don't hire somebody to help you leave that island. This is what you wanted. **This is your home.**

Now, I know that all of Mikey's friends will talk about how some of the prisoners will take advantage of some of the weaker prisoners especially the younger prisoners. That's right. You will not want to live here. It will be rough. You won't reach down and pick up your soap when you drop it in the shower. Heck, there won't even be a shower. It's up to you. This is your home. This is the home that you have made.

You did not want to go by our rules and killing somebody or raping somebody is against our rules. We would have to use this new method real carefully. What I mean by that is that Mikey has a good point. We would still want to make sure that everybody got the benefit of any reasonable doubt. We would not send anybody away to this island for the rest of their lives until they had exhausted all of the appeal process that we currently have.

Where would they stay until they got that final answer? Would they get to live at home or in some nice new prison? No, once a killer or rapist had been convicted by a court, then they would get to spend some time in a military jail cell. Nothing real complicated or expensive. Just a good old temporary holding tank like Paris Island.

Put that place to some real good use. They might not be real men but the Marines could put them away from us for a while. That is until the last jury had agreed with the first jury about sending them to that island. I wonder if we could use the part of Cuba that we still control. You know it's some type of Bay. I heard that it is real secure and would be perfect for that. **Nah, the Liberals would never go for that.**

What about the people who committed other crimes? What would we do with people who broke Laws other than murder or rape? We would come up with other islands that people could come back and join us if they truly wanted to go by our rules. There would have to be some major changes. Those changes would involve giving those people a chance to prove that they had learned their lesson and were willing to join us as a family again.

Okay, Mikey, I agree with you, we would have to deal with some of the reasons why they had broken our laws in the first place. You know, why does somebody feel that they have to rob somebody else or break some other law below murder or rape. Part of it could be that they didn't have the opportunities that other people had. Part of it could be that they didn't want to have to do the hard things that other people had to do in order to overcome their own short comings.

I heard a very experienced Judge talk about this issue. He was part of a round table discussion on the problems with the criminal justice system and what should be done about the lack of prison space and education for prison inmates. Someone asked him about what you should do with a criminal who had an unhappy childhood.

Do you know what this Judge with over 20 years of experience said? He said that every convicted criminal had a story. They all want to tell you why it is not their fault. They had bad parents. They had a bad education. Their mother didn't love them. They didn't eat right as a kid. They didn't have cable Television. They all have a story.

So, they didn't go by our rules and laws. That is why they were in his court. They did not want to follow our rules. But what about some other people who had shortcomings, what did they do to deal with their situation? Remember what the short basketball player did to overcome his lack of height.

Yes, he outworked everybody else. No, some people would be there because they didn't want to play by any rules. Some would be there because they had made mistakes. We would have to make allowances for both.

These islands that we would use for the people who committed crimes other than murder or rape would also be self-contained. This would be your home and you would be on your own. There would be a few differences between these islands and the island that housed murders and rapists. If you didn't commit murder or rape, you would only stay on the island for the time of your sentence. You would leave this island someday.

You also could have the chance to learn a new skill or trade. There would be education and training available for you if you chose to work at it. This Education and training would be offered through the few Television sets that were available on the island. The Television sets would only carry educational programs for those people living on the island that wanted to really change.

My wife, the teacher, wanted me to point out to everybody that her school has Televisions in her class rooms now. The problem is that somebody keeps stealing all of them and breaking them all the time. If they remain in the classrooms, obsolescence takes over and they become useless.

Well, it's their choice; if they really want an opportunity then it will be there. It's up to them. These islands for the lesser crimes would be similar to the islands for murder in some ways. There would not be any guards and we wouldn't spend any money on the islands that kept the people who broke the laws. We would spend money on sending them there and making sure that they didn't come back to commit more crimes.

It would be real tough living on those islands. Probably not as tough as it would be on some of the victims of the people who broke our laws. It also probably wouldn't be **Fair** but we're not interested in trying to use the correct wording, we are interested in making this country safe for all of us that don't break the laws.

No, Mikey, I am not a Lawyer, I am a CPA. Lawyers sometimes, use words to hide the numbers and to give them a way to make money on both sides of an issue. Heck, we Accountants even tried that with our own little **APB's** and **FASB's** before that made us turn to the Government for help with **SOX** laws. See, I can talk like some lawyers if I have to.

We can't keep on using those words in Government that can mean almost anything. All that does is disappoint a whole lot of people. We have to go to our own room and ask ourselves some really hard questions. Questions like what are we doing about some of the problems that we think should be corrected by government.

Problems that deal with how we handle natural disasters like floods and earthquakes. Once, I would like to see the following on Television. You know when the President, a congressman or some political writer starts telling us about some national problem that will cause us to pay more taxes or increase the National Debt to solve that problem.

Let's take the example of all of the flooding that took place in the Midwest a while back. Now, everybody will agree that it is horrible what happened to all of those people. Forget about who's at fault. The scene that I want to see on Television would go like this:

"My Fellow Americans, I address you tonight to tell you about a National Tragedy that has occurred in the heart of our country. Some of our fellow Americans have suffered as few Americans have in the past. Some of them have lost their homes and some of them have lost their children. Their plight is beyond our belief.

I am calling on all Americans to send your money to help them in their hour of need. I also will establish a Federal Fund to aid these victims of this horrible disaster and all federal relief efforts will be paid out of this fund.

In order to establish this fund and start the process of helping all of these Americans, I am donating 5% of my yearly salary into this fund. I call on all Americans to match my donation to help their fellow Americans in this their time of need."

That's at the heart of how we have to start handling all of our problems. If we think that something needs to be done, then we are the ones that have to lead the charge. We can't just ask the Government to handle the problem and then not want to pay the bill. We have to change our attitudes about what we want the government to do. Let's look at how the numbers work on the cost of repairing the damage that the last Earthquake caused in California.

Do you remember the President flying out to California to show all of us that he cared? Do you remember him rolling up his shirtsleeves and going around and looking at all of the human suffering?

I remember something else. I remember him going on National Television and signing a bill to get California some financial help. I also remember him making the comment that he and his budget director would have to go back to Washington and try to figure out how to pay for what he had just signed. Is that the way that you handle your money?

Do you just go ahead and get something that you want first and then figure out how to pay for it later? Will the banks let you buy all that you want that way? Now, Mikey, be nice don't call me all those unkind names. I do care about people. I just want you to think about how to pay for it. Caring and paying are two separate concepts. Almost every human being hurts for the people who have lost their homes, business and love ones.

We all feel for them as fellow human beings. My concern is how we will pay for that piece of paper that the President signed and all of the other bills that will follow.

For just a minute (That's another way to say be quiet until I have had a chance to say what I want to, Mikey) let's assume that the total cost of repairing all of the damage that the Earthquake did in California will cost 50 Billion dollars. It may be more and it may be less, but let's run with the 50 Billion figure for a minute. If there are 50 million taxpayers (It could be a little less or a little more) then that Works out to only to $1,000 per taxpayer. Is everybody ready to send them a check for $1,000 right now? If not now when?

Do we just put that cost off into the future? Do we just continue to devalue our Future earnings for something that is just too costly to pay for now? Do we continue to make holding the value of Government debt worth less and less? How will we pay for helping those people in California? Where will the money come from?

Now, some Conservative friends of mine (Except the ones who live in California) will say that the people who lived in California should pay for all of the cost themselves. Heck, they knew that they were taking a big risk in building their Homes in such a dangerous area. Don't you remember that house that was built on the side of a tall hill top overlooking the ocean? Now, it really had a breathtaking view of the Pacific Ocean, but who in his right mind would want to build a house in such a risky place. Would you take that kind of risk?

Hold on Mikey, I am not through. As **Paul Harvey** would say, You haven't heard *The Rest of the Story*. For another minute think about what we would do if a really big meteorite were to come at us out of the blue (Really out of the Black of Space). Let's also say that this really big meteorite and some of its relatives destroyed our entire major cities. Really did a lot of damage. Let's also assume that the cost to repair all of that damage was 10,000 times the cost of repairing the damage that this last California earthquake did. How would we pay for all of that damage?

Could the government just start printing money so the President could fly around to all of those cities and roll up his sleeves and sign some more pieces of paper? How would it get paid?

The answer is that we would all have to help out. We are the answer not the government. How did we come up with the money to fight World War II? We all pitched in and did what we could. Whatever the size of the current Deficit, it is not the result of fighting that war. That cost has already been paid. Why do we keep falling into the trap of wanting things and not wanting to pay for them? What's wrong with our own **self-interest**?

You see, everybody has a different point of reference. We all look at things from how those things affect us. Yes, we all have our own point of view or **self-interest**. If we think that something needs to be done, then we need to do it.

Don't just ask the government to do it and then run away from paying the bills. Sure, I know that our current laws and Constitution would not allow us to do this. Why that would not be **Fair**. But remember laws are made by man and men and women can change those laws and the *Constitution*. Remember how all of this started in the *Declaration of Independence* and the *Constitution*? Just be a little more patient and I promise we will talk about how to change our laws and the *Constitution*.

Hold on Mikey, I haven't talked about what would happen to the Executive Branch in our new government. We wouldn't want to reduce the size of the Congress and The Courts only to end up with another **King or worst yet a Queen.**

There would have to be major changes in the Executive branch as well. For starters, if the Federal government is getting out of the **Fair Business** it would need to reduce the level of government employees in the Executive branch

"Now, hold on Richard, don't you realize that getting the Federal Government out of the **Fair Business** would throw a lot people out of work and cost us even more money in unemployment benefits? Wrong, Mikey, you really need to wait until we start talking about the Fair Corporation to see how that is handled, but for now yes, that would mean that we reduced the size of the government in federal agencies. How much of a reduction? All of them. They would all go away. The only federal agencies that would remain would be the agencies that related to preserving our Security.

The Government would get out the **Fair Business**. What we are talking about is real close to what our cousins over in England have as a form of government. No, Bubba, you cannot go back to sleep. I'm not talking about having a Queen or King and definitely no room for any Knights or Ladies in waiting. I'm talking about the party in Congress electing one of their own party members to be the President. Only one party would be in control. Yes, we would still want to have separate branches of government to:

1. Make the laws,
2. Judge those laws and
3. Execute and carryout those laws.

We just want it to cost a lot less and all work together. Why keep a system that can create a conflict between the branches when one party controls the congress and the other party controls the Presidency. That's how you really get into trouble. It's kind of like the situation that you have when a husband and wife break up and still share the task of raising their kids.

The kids will play each parent against the other to get what they want. Yes, young children learn real quick how to use **The Fair Word.**

No, we have enough safeguards now or we could create some more of them to keep our government from becoming too powerful that we couldn't control that government. We want the system to work and we don't want our government to control everything that we do. We just want our own lives back.

How would this new system work? Well, if you haven't followed how the English do it here is how it would work. We would still elect people to congress as we discussed before. There would be 200 Representatives and 50 Senators. The party that had a majority in both the House of Representatives and Senate would get to form an Executive Team that would run the executive branch. This branch would be administrative in nature and the head of each department of the executive branch would be elected in this manner.

What would we do if no one party had a majority in both houses of Congress? Simple, then there would have to be a compromise between the parties or a new election to get a majority in one party to carry out the laws.

How would these wise people be paid? They would be paid just like the members of Congress. They would volunteer their time for the good of the country.

Again, we want people whose **self-interest** is truly in serving their country. We don't want Professional government leaders. We want people who want to serve. Remember that the Congress has a limited term and the executive leaders would also have those same limed terms.

We want to have a continued wave of new ideas and leaders who want to serve. What about the department heads and other government workers that would still be needed, say for our security? Would they be volunteer workers? No, for the people that we needed for those purposes, they would be paid for the use of their services. How much would they be paid? They would be paid what the market was paying other people with similar skills and doing similar work.

What I am trying to avoid is some artificial dollar level on what those skills should be worth. I don't want to get back into the trap of writing into law what we will pay. Remember what we pay the President and Congress now. Don't you remember how Congress keeps raising their salary for the next Congress?

I bet you haven't heard a lot of talk by any of our Presidents about raising their salaries. There must be something that Presidents get that is worth more than money. Right, the President can still get that. Whatever that is and it could be the honor of going down in history or it could be some other **self-interest**.

You are right Mikey; I know I also didn't talk about what and how the states and cities would make their laws. There is a real important reason for that. We need to leave that to them to decide. This probably really makes you mad that you can't tell all of these people how to live their lives. You know, show the uneducated people how to really live and make somebody other than you pay for those laws, but that is part of our solution for Government.

A few years ago, I lived and worked in Louisiana. The whole time that I lived in Louisiana; I thought that those people had lost their minds. Why did they all like those little things that looked like deformed lobsters? Why did they all talk so funny and go crazy over **LSU** and anything **Cajun**? Why didn't they like Barbecue and the other good things in life? Why did they have such strange laws and customs?

For a long time, I thought that they had been responsible for my bad experiences when I lived in their state. Why if they had been more accepting of me it would have been different. I was wrong. I was trying to get them to change for me. I was the one that was not being realistic.

I wanted them to be just like me. In our **Future Solution**, we have to allow people to be themselves. If we live somewhere and we find ourselves in the minority then maybe we need to leave and go someplace where we are more comfortable. Now don't get me wrong on this, I not saying that everybody should run over the minorities but think about me and what was happening to me in Louisiana.

I was the perfect minority. I was one person surrounded by millions and millions of Cajuns who didn't like me or Barbecue. Should the government have passed a law to protect my rights? No, the best thing that I could have done would have been to become a little more Cajun. I might have even learned to like those little orange things. Right, with a lot of hot spices and beer.

If you are like Mikey, about right now, you have made a whole list of problems with this. Top on your list would be the social programs and what to do with the Deficit. Before you start trying to deal with the Deficit, you have to deal with the problems that caused the Deficit in the first place.

You see, we have run up a real large Deficit because we have tried to make everything **Fair**. Now, I know Mikey will start talking about all of the military spending that we did under the Republican Presidents but he will be wrong. Sure the spending on National Defense grew during both President Ronald Regean and President George Bush but spending on **Fair** programs grew even faster.

There is also a major difference in spending money on Bullets or Butter. You can reduce the amount of money that you spend on Bullets when the action cools off as it has in the case of the end of the Cold War. Just try to stop spending money on somebody who has come to believe that they are entitled to receive that money from the Federal Government.

No, in order to solve the Deficit problem, you have to deal with the reasons that people are demanding that the Government spend money on those programs.

"Wait a minute, Richard; I was quiet while you were talking. What about some of my problems with what you have said? I don't believe you understand why we have separate branches of government. The people who wrote the **Constitution** were afraid of the government becoming too powerful and not attuned to the needs of the people. They wanted to make sure the government didn't become too powerful and forget the people that they served."

Good point, Mikey, there is just one little problem with that. The government already had become that powerful. It needs to take more and more of our money in order to try to give the voters more and more of the things that they don't want to spend their money for. Right now, the minorities that are getting trampled are the people who the government thinks are **Rich.** When will they start looking at you for their money?

By making the government smaller and making it a part time volunteer profession, you take away the incentive to spend money that we don't have. You also let people decide how to use their abilities and their money. People should be able to enjoy the fruits of their labor. That's real freedom. Enjoying what you have produced.

Sure, we could spend a lot of time debating the numbers but we would miss the main point. There is not enough money in this country to pay for all of the things that we think that we need the government to do for us. We have to first start with what those needs should be if we want to have an opportunity to buy the things that we really want.

So let's take the social programs first. Just turn the page and grab on to your seat. Better yet, go to the refrigerator and get another cold one. You'll need Several.

6 Our Solution
The Fair Corporation

Hey, Bubba, did you know that some of the **Muligrubbers** moved off to Washington. Yeah, you remember some of those people that we knew down in Louisiana who were always complaining about how things were changing too quickly. You remember the ones who kept complaining about how all of the boys at **LSU** weren't playing as a team.

Why, as I remember it, they wanted the team to be composed of only the good old boys from the State of Louisiana. Right, they thought that there should be a federal law that you had to play college football in the state where you were born and played High School Football. Why it would only be **Fair**.

I think that they even invented the **Fair** word. Yes, they must have moved to some other states and got elected to Congress. You see them all of the time now on C-Span. You've seen them before when you watch C-Span and see them come out of the woodwork and start telling everybody on Television how that we can't reduce the money that is going to some of their favorite programs.

The Muligrubbers.

You remember them don't you? Every state in the Union has a few. They are all for balancing the budget. Just don't cut the federal money going To one of their programs and their state.

Don't you remember some of the debate that they had in the House of Representatives on how to pay for the disaster relief for the Earthquake damage that occurred in California? Yes, they were all for helping out their fellow man; they just didn't want to see some of their programs cut.

No, leave my little deal alone. We're not going to balance the budgets on the backs of the American people. Where do they think that the money will come from to balance the American Budget?

Are we going to get the money from the backs of the Mexican people or do we want to try to out negotiate the Japanese?

What they are talking about is funding for Social programs. Yes, those programs that passes some benefits on to somebody else. Now it can be a great sounding program like Feed the Homeless or Giving a Child the chance to overcome poverty, but it is still a Social program and it is taking money from somebody who has made that money and giving it to somebody who can't generate that money on their own.

It is charity. No, it is not charity. Charity comes from the heart and is voluntary. What the government does is rob from the haves and give to the have nots. Rob from **the Rich** and give to **the Poor**. The government is also finding it harder and harder to come up with the money to meet those expectations.

So how do our **Muligrubbers** deal with this continuing problem of increasing public expectations for the government meeting their needs and the declining source of money to pay for these needs? **They Muligrubb**.

They talk about all of the damage that will be done to this program if we cut anything from their program. And at the same time, the Federal government continues to give farmers money for growing Tobacco and another part of the Federal government tells us using Tobacco will kill you. Have they lost their minds? No, they are giving us what they heard us ask them to do. Keep spending money that we don't have to try to deal with problems that we as individuals cannot solve.

They also know that we wouldn't pay for solving these problems when we were trying to deal with them on our own. So the giant shell game continues. Will the magic coin be under this shell this time?

Most people would agree with helping all of the needy people that need our help. Helping out these groups of people is not the problem; the problem with all of the good social programs is that our government spends money that it doesn't have. There are few people that would disagree with the problems. Everybody is for helping his

92

fellow man.

I have a Dentist that probably pays a ton of money in taxes. He doesn't mind since he thinks that the money goes to help the homeless and provide for the poor. He goes home every night feeling as if he has done something really good with his money. That is **Fair**. He does have a problem with seeing his money go down the drain when it is sent to people that don't want to work for a living. "Why, that's just not **Fair**."

That is our major dilemma. **Fair** is a purely personal and subjective word. You can't measure it. You can't count it and it can mean almost anything that you want. So what are we to do? We do have major problems with poor people and People who need our help.

No, I don't believe in trickle down or in business or individuals acting in any way other than people's own best **self-interest**. I also know that the government cannot keep going on spending all of the money that it spends now. Government will also find it hard to reduce or eliminate social programs that voters want but do not want to have to pay taxes to fund.

Maybe there is a solution out there. I just wish there was a company that was in the business of taking care of people that can't help themselves. What do you mean Bubba, that there are tons of Companies that are supposed to help people? What are they called? **Churches!**

Don't we have to worry about the separation of church and state? Yes, but our federal government has been acting like some type of **Church** for several years. You don't have to pray to them. All you have to do is to reelect them. And remember, it's not them that are the villain, it's us. They just figured out how to give us what they thought we said we wanted.

So how would all of this work? Do we just tell the homeless and the unwed mothers with five kids to go down the street and see her local padre? No, it involves a whole lot of new steps. One of the problems that we have had for several years is what I call **"Compassion Myopia"**

We are very near sighted when it comes to feeling for our fellowman. We also like to use the **Fair** word a lot. We look at our compassion to our fellowman in terms of **Fairness**.

You know we are willing to help somebody as long as they meet our own definition of who needs help. We also have a problem with "Latecomers." You know those people who don't really have a right to our compassion. The people who don't have a lot of money and seem to work all of the time and still don't seem to be making any progress in making their lives any better have a problem with people on Welfare.

You know people who have not worked as hard as we have. People who have had money for a long time also have problems with **"Latecomers"**. You know them; they are the **Old Rich People** who go to the Opera and wear those tweed coats with the patches on the elbows. They always have problems with people who have just recently come into some money. The problems of the **"New Rich"**. They can never be just like us. Why, they are not like us.

Hold on for a minute, Bubba, think about what this means. Do you remember all of those bad riots that we have had in Los Angeles?
Yeah, I'm talking about all of the burning and looting that we saw on Television. Every time it happened, a liberal came on Television and told us about how they were just working out their frustrations about being in the **Poor** underclass.

A **Conservative** would come on Television and talk about how this showed the failure of the welfare system and the lack of law enforcement. When all of this starts breaking out what do most of our large churches do? Nothing! Oh, you might get a sermon about might doesn't mean right or something like that but no real help for the people who needed help. So you see those people burning and looting are hurting. They are hurting in not being able to live the American Dream.

How did they learn about the American Dream? From Television, that's where. They saw all of the commercials on Television that showed real Americans living the good life. They saw great looking Basketball shoes, expensive cars, televisions, DVD's, watches and the experiences that you could have if you owned a major credit card and had a real good paying job.

They believed the hype. They could be happy if only they could buy more stuff. Yeah, the stuff that they saw all of the successful people enjoying on television, but they didn't have good paying jobs or the tools to get those things. They knew that and they were frustrated. For some of them, it reached a boiling point and they exploded. They burned and they rioted. They felt that life had not been **Fair**.

Has there ever been a program any program, federal, state, local or private that has tried to help these people and really worked at getting these people some help that would enable them to try to meet their expectations? No. We have tried block grants and a ton of money. These programs usually result in frustrating them even more. They still can't get any more stuff. What are the major churches doing during this time? Are they out there in the trenches trying to deal with these and other social problems?

Well, I can't speak for you but I can tell you a little about my home town of Memphis, Tennessee. In Memphis, we used to have two major Protestant Churches. Bellevue Baptist Church and Central Church. During the last fifteen years, both churches have had major fund raising drives.

Have these fund raising drives resulted in some programs that deal with the poor, homeless or people without jobs? Most of these fund raising drives have resulted in big new churches. Churches that look like basketball stadiums or coliseums for some type of major sports attraction. Maybe they are just trying to be like Mike.

Now **Pastor**, don't let your hair catch on fire, you don't have enough of it left to see it go up in smoke. Give me a chance with this. I'm not trying to blame the churches for all of the problems in the cities. We will really try to end up with a great opportunity for all of you if you will just let me have a chance to finish. I will come back to churches.

You see, the government has gotten into the church business **"Big Time"** as my friend **Rick the Car Man** would say.
Real "Big Time". Why the government is taking so much money from business and the working men and women that nobody can give a dime to their churches. Forget giving 10% to my church. The Federal Government took that and more.

When was the last time that there was a major social problem like a whole factory or company going out of business or moving out of town? Did you see any churches jumping in to help all of the people that lost their jobs? Again, I can't speak about any place but where I live in Memphis, Tennessee. We did have a couple of major companies either lay off a lot of people or just leave town.
A lot of people lost their jobs.

One of the largest employers in Memphis, Tennessee was Holiday Inns. They were even developed and created here in Memphis. Well, for whatever reason they moved to Atlanta, Georgia. A lot of people lost their jobs. The Mayor of Memphis even lost his job when he couldn't convince Holiday Inns to stay in Memphis. Was there a major thrust by the Memphis churches to help these people.

There wasn't a lot of help coming from the churches unless you count some of the seminars that the churches developed to show the people who were out of work how to call companies and ask for a job. That did a lot of good for all of those People who had lost their means of providing for their family.

The problem wasn't in knowing how to ask, the problem was in a lack of jobs for those people who had Lost their jobs. They did help some of the people putting on the seminars think that they had done something good for the people who didn't have any jobs. No, you don't see the churches getting involved in that kind of problem. You do see them having their annual fund raising drive for church expenses and new Buildings. That they do **"Big Time"**!

The churches also have gotten involved in the political process. We even have had ministers running for President. Yeah, but when they ran for President, they told everybody that they were in the Communication Business not in the Religious Business. Watch your words just like the other politicians. Don't make anybody mad or uncomfortable

I remember sitting in church one morning back when Jimmy Carter was President and hearing the Minister tell everybody how dumb he thought that Jimmy was acting. During his sermon he went on to say that he had gone to an important meeting in Washington for concerned fundamentalists and if we came back on Sunday night he would tell us about what they had been keeping from all of us good Christians. Well, you know, with that kind of advertisement I just had to go.

I went and what did I hear? Oh, more about how all of them liberals were trying to do this and that and how we all should support people who believed as we did and pass the collection plate The churches have also been real good at sidestepping the abortion issue.

You know they believe that both sides have a good point. Sounds like the Big Tent theory of the Republicans doesn't it?

What was it that the head of all the Protestant churches said when he was here the last time? No, we don't have anything like the Pope; I'm talking about **Jesus Christ**. Did he tell all of us to go out and raise a lot money to build more brick and mortar churches? No, I think that he didn't spend a lot of time on that. I even think that he went into the church and drove out the people who were trying to make a lot of money in the church without telling people about **God**.

I think that he spent all of his time trying to help people. What were his last words to all of us? **In the Gospel according to St. John, Chapter 21 verse 17 – 18**

> 17. He saithe unto him the third time, **Simon, son of Jonas, lovest thou me?** Peter was grieved because he Said unto him the third time, Lovest thou me? And he said Unto him, Lord, thou knowest all things; thou knowest that I love thee. *Jesus* saith unto him, **Feed my sheep**.

18. Verily, verily, I say unto thee, When thou wast young, thou girdesdst thyself, and walkedst wither thou wouldest: but when thou shalt be old, thou shalt stretch forth thy hands, and another shall gird thee, and carry thee whither thou wouldest not.

Sounds like helping everybody that needs help. There are not a whole lot of qualifiers in those statements. Nothing about if they have worked real hard or this doesn't count if they are all a bunch of bums. It seems as if **My Lord** wanted all of us to love our fellow man and help them.

He didn't mention anything about Race, Religion, Sex, national origin or anything else. Just help them. He didn't care how somebody got in trouble just help them get out of trouble. It reminds me of some of the solutions to people's problems, that I saw when I was an important businessman. You know the problem that occurs when Jim has been caught drinking at work.

Well, he would invariably get called into explain his problem to **The Boss**. The Boss would kind of him and haw a lot and look down at the floor a lot. Pretty soon he would have to make eye contact with good old Jim and after a few moments of icy silence he would tell Jim to just get a grip on himself. Yeah, that would really help solve the problem. It did make **The Boss** feel as if he was a great leader. You know, that would have been what Coach Vince would have done.

Another time, I was called in to help a company prepare their Financial Statements. This company had recently fired their Company Controller because he was drinking on the job. Well, the first thing that I did was talk to the Controller who had been fired for drinking on the job. After a few minutes of conversation on the company's accounting policies, I asked him why he had been drinking on the job and risked losing his job.

Do you know what his answer was? The reason that he Had started drinking was that he had not been paid by the company for over three months? The company was in such bad shape that it couldn't even afford to pay its Employees. The boss had made some bad decisions and was real short of money. Things were so bad that the Controller had started drinking at work just to try to forget all of the problems and get through the day.

"Now, Richard, why have you gone and brought up all of that Religious stuff. You were always too much of a Christian when you worked for me. You have to learn to live in the real world. Don't you know that in the real world you can't go round talking about Religion? Why, you might offend somebody. You know, make some other person feel slighted that you mentioned a Religious name. Don't you remember what happened at Holiday Inns a while back?"

Yes, Bubba, as I remember it was me that told you the story in the first place. You will never change. Always looking for something to pick at me. I remember that it was always you that would break wind when you got off of the elevator and left me with those total strangers who gave me the evil eyes. Yeah, that was real funny. Go ahead go back to your office close the door, sit down, pick your nose and start thinking about your latest deal. I know why they always you called Digger.

I remember a major meeting that we had when I was at Holiday Inns that was concerning a major problem that we faced in the Hotel business. After we had gone all around the block trying to come up with solutions to this problem, somebody said that maybe we ought to say a prayer and ask for **God'**s help. Well, somebody jumped up and said that really showed how desperate that we had gotten. Just think about having to say that we needed some help from above.

Well, we need his help. When will we realize that we can't be our own **God** and savior? We can't create false idols and look to them to solve our problems. We do need help in trying to help our fellow men and women. Let's try to solve some of the troubles of the Jim's and Jean's.

You know our fellow men and women. Worry about what Coach Vince would have done later. Let's listen to the real **Coach** and get them some real help. If you took a big survey right now on how effective the Government was in helping People deal with their problems, you would get a lot of "No Way, Jose" answers. You probably would get all kind of solutions to what they should do and who to take the money from to fund the programs. Would it work?

No, we've tried that. Now let's try something that will work. Let's get the Government out of the **Fair** Business. Let's turn the business of helping people over to the organizations that should be in that business in the first place. Yes, **the churches**.

I know I should have warned you to sit down, go get a cold one or something, but it will work. Remember Rule number one. Everybody acts in **Their Own Self-Interest.** Right, that one. It is in all of our self-interest to help our fellow man. Yes, help our fellow man even if he is not in our same class.

Wait a minute, Mikey just woke up again. Why do you have so many problems with getting the Government out of the **Fair** business? I know it would be really great if we could have a government that could solve all of **Our** problems. Why do you keep thinking that the Government has all of the answers? Do you still really believe that the Government has a secret source of money? A money tree or has the Government figured out how to spin Gold out of straw?

Oh, the government could even out everything and take from the successful people and give to the people who have not been as successful with their lives. No, I am not going to use your slogan about taking from the evil **Rich** who have stepped over the **Poor** people in order to become **Rich. That's Muligrubbing**.

You are looking for a villain to blame again. Sure it is right to help our fellow men and women. That's what I've been trying to tell you all along. That's what **Jesus** was talking about when he came here the first time. He didn't try to overthrow all of the government or to change the government. He tried to get us to change and See that it was important to help all of our fellow men and women. No, being right has not been the problem. Coming up with the money has been the problem. So let's put up or shut up. Let's create the opportunity for all of us to help our fellow man. Now, remember that we have shrunk the government Down to where the Government's main job is our security.

Security does not mean being **Fair**. We now have several new companies that will be called the **FAIR CORPORATION** that will take the place of the government. How will it work?

The **FAIR CORPORATIONS** would be chartered by the federal government to spend all of their money on whatever needy social causes that were defined by their charter. Let's say that we have a corporation that has the charter for providing shelter for the homeless. Then that company could advertise that they were: **The Help The Homeless, Fair Corporation, Inc.**

Fair Corporations would even have divisions to offer different kind of help to different people   They would also be able to solicit funding from the public just as companies are able to sell stock and raise financing.   Instead of being regulated by the Security and Exchange Commission, Fair corporations would be regulated by the Fair Exchange Commission.

The regulation of Fair Corporations would be very simple and straightforward. They would be required to develop business plans that explained why they were asking the public to send them money. They would also be required to furnish Financial Statement Certified by Certified Public Accountants and reviewed by the FEC. They would disclose how much they gave to the people that they were trying to help. They would also have to disclose how much money they paid their employees and where the major dollars went, just as a public company tells its stockholders.

All of the money raised by the Fair Corporation would be exempt from taxation as long as the money was being spent according to the cause that was designated in their charter. Any money that was invested and was earning interest or income of Any kind would be taxed just like any other business corporation. The goal of the **Fair Corporation** would be to spend money in support of their causes defined in the **Fair Corporation's** charter and business plan.

This probably would cause some problems for some charitable organizations that hold stock, real estate and other investments. That's too bad, because that isn't **Fair**. We want those companies spending their money on helping people not in helping business corporations.

They would also have to spend 100% of their contributions that they receive less their normal business expenses each year. No, holding back for another rainy day, we want them to have to go to the people each year for what they would spend.

What did you say Mikey, how about people that don't believe in **God** or other religions? Well, personally I will pray for them, but they can still have their organization to give to. I'm more interested in helping people who need our help than deciding who was wrong or how did they get there in the first place. If they want to give to the "Pet Rock Society", that's fine with me as long as the money goes to help people.

See, we can't start this whole thing all over again with debating this and that. The most important thing is in helping people and believe me, I hear enough about this from my brother.

See my brother is a very good person. He also is a born again **Christian** who is a devout member of the **Baptist Church**. He followed the views of the Preacher in his **Church** who talked about how some of us are just a bunch of materialist sinners who are trying to satisfy ourselves with worldly possessions.

"Everywhere you look there are greedy sinful people who need to be saved from their sins. Why, the problem with all those people out in California who riot is that they are giving into their lust it's just like Sodom and Gomorra. They are all humanistic sinners."

Somewhere, I think that some of his logic misses the point. That is a **God** problem and if I remember it He solved that problem once before and I really think that **He** could take care of that problem now if **He** wanted to solve it.

I think that **He** wants us to try to help our fellow man first. Leave the judging to him. **He** also wanted my brother to lead a Church and He created an Opportunity for my Brother to be a real Brother and Minister. See what can happen when you leave **God Things to Him** and you only try to solve manmade problems and don't try **To Legislate Morality.**

So the main regulation of the **Fair corporations** would be how they helped people. The government's main responsibility would be to let everybody know how and for what purposes The Fair Corporation had spent their money. We are starting to match benefits with the cost of those benefits. One other wrinkle that we would have to add would involve advertising. You know all of those commercials that make **Poor People** feel as if they were not real people for not having the money to buy all those nice watches, cars, houses, clothes and basketball shoes.

Well, we are going to help the **Fair Corporation** out a little bit. Every business company that advertises would have to send 5% of every dollar it spent on advertising to the Federal Government. The money would be used to finance a special 8% Federal Jobs Credit.

Now, slow down Mikey, you will have to wait until we talk about Jobs and more Jobs for more details. The program would be very simple. All Advertising sources like Television, radio, newspapers, magazines and etc., would be required to collect this amount when they collected their advertising fee and spend the money to create the advertising.

All money spent on advertising in any fashion would be subject to this tax. Money spent on High **"Q"** factor spokespersons would also be included in the amounts subject to taxation. Money spent inside the company advertising for staff costs would also be taxed. All money spent on developing and creating the desire of people to buy a company's product would be subject to this tax.

If companies are going to try to make people want their products even if they cannot afford those products, then they should help people to get the jobs that can pay for those products. It would work very much as a sales tax. They would then Send these moneys to the Federal Government each month.

Now we would make a special exception for the **Home Shopping Network** and all of those stupid Long Distance Commercials. For them there would be a flat rate of $10,000,000 every time that they ran an advertisement or each day that they were on Television.

Just kidding!! I won't get into the **Fair** Trap. No, getting even here by me for all of those stupid commercials that I have been forced to sit through.

Wait a minute, Mikey stop all of your questions about exemptions for Groups like Friends of the Earth and even advertising by churches to get people to send money to them. And forget about the Preachers that come on Television and ask for our money with tears on their faces.

I have a simple answer for you. Anybody or any Organization that uses Advertising to get people to give them their money has to pay this tax. It doesn't matter if it is some fast food company showing you a **"Magic Moment** "that only occurs when you buy their product or some fine charity that shows you the magic feeling that you get when you send your money to help some needy person.

If they are creating those impulses to send them money then they will have to share in creating the ability for those people who send them the money to earn that money.

End of story here, just like the teaser on the local news. Has it ever happened to you where you see or hear something real exciting that is about to come on Television. You know some of those local Television stations that give you just a little controversial information on some topic and then they tell you to stay tuned for the News at 11:00. Well, in this case, you will have to wait until we start talking about Jobs and more Jobs.

You can wait like the rest of us. The main thing that we want the Fair companies to do is help people. It would all be voluntary and **Fair**. One major benefit would be the absence of the Federal Government and most of our taxes would go down. We couldn't use the excuse of having to pay taxes to the federal government instead of helping our fellowman. No more saying that we gave at the Office. We would all get to help people. We would also get to choose how and what organization we wanted to support.

What do you mean Richard; most of our taxes would go down? Are you pulling the same trick that the Liberal politicians have pulled on all of us for so long? I thought that you were headed in the right direction until I heard that little modifier. Why couldn't everybody's taxes go down? What about the flat tax approach? Wouldn't that really help?

Well, **Pat**, this conversation is about how to help people. Can't you wait until we get to the part about the budget? When will you learn that this is a very difficult problem that first starts with trying to meet everybody's idea of their needs? Sure, most of our people would pay a whole lot less taxes. Taxes going to the Federal government would go down drastically in **Total**.

But to avoid the **Fair Trap** that we have been stuck in for so long, we would have to have everybody pay for what they want Government to do for them.

Just be a little more patient and we will get into the Budget. It's real important for us to realize that the Government can't keep trying to help everybody overcome problems that they face in living their lives. For that we will create the opportunity for everybody to really help them. It also will give them the opportunity to truly give to those people of their own free will. Sounds **Fair**? Doesn't it?

Hold on Bubba, do you really understand what this would all mean? I'm talking about all of the Social Programs that the Federal Government has tried to force down all of the taxpayers' throats. **All of Them**.

They would be sold to **The Fair Corporations**. I'm also talking about all of the subsidies that the federal government gives to some group or another. Money that flows to that group from our Federal Government because they have an important special need.

You remember all of the programs that the Federal Government has for something that you might or might not agree with. No, it's not just the subsidy that goes to the Bee Keepers or the Subsidy that goes to farmers who raise Tobacco. I know that you hate people who smoke and you lost your sense of taste a long time ago.

The problem that we have had with trying to cut our Budget Deficit revolves around so many of these subsidies. Sure, I know that it would only involve a little money for this program and that program. All together they add up to some real serious money. We have failed in the past because we couldn't see the forest for the trees.

Any program on its own didn't hurt, but together they did. There never was a program that could get eliminated. Why, we even kept subsidies for people to grow a certain type of wool. We kept subsidies for people who raised silk worms and we kept subsidies for people who ran target Ranges.

Even when everybody and his brother in Congress were trying to enact Gun Control to show the voters that they supported Law and Order. No, this type of spending is charity of the worst kind. This is forced charity. That will change. Yeah, the Churches and some other Organizations that do good things and the Federal Government would be making a new deal. The Churches wouldn't tax people and the Federal Government wouldn't preach to people. Sound's Revolutionary doesn't it?

Well, that's a lot closer to our original idea of what Government should do than what we have now. What we are trying to do now doesn't work too well. You see as part of this new deal, the Government would stop taking so much of our Money. They would let us keep that money and we could pick the charities that we believed should receive our Money. Sound **Fair**? I hope so because it would work. Let's take a closer look at how this would work.

One of the problems that we have today is how to help people who have lost their jobs? How do we provide them with Healthcare when they have no jobs or money to pay for the Healthcare? The government's answer in the past has been to talk about how **Rich** People have all of the money and how that this is not **Fair**. Once, they have our attention, they come up with a federal program that tries to help people that cannot afford Healthcare.

Once the government has developed a program they turn the program over to government employees. Those government employees then start spending government funds for the purpose of the government program. The government also spends a lot of money on government employees, buildings and things other than helping people.

You see the government employees' main **self-interest** is not in helping people; it is in continuing the program. Yes, keeping their jobs. Kind of like a friend of mine that wanted to sell cars for a local auto dealer here in Memphis, Tennessee. Well, my good buddy, Clay went and interviewed with the Automobile Sales Manager. The car man looked at good old Clay and said, "Clay I have only one question for you, Why Do you want to work here?"

Clay said very quickly, "Because I love cars." Clay didn't get the job. You know why? The Sales Manager wanted people who wanted to sell cars not people who liked cars. There is a big difference in the two. In the case of Government programs, government employees want those programs to continue. Continuing the government program is in their own **self-interest.** Sure, I know that there are a lot of fine government employees that do a lot of good, but their **self-interest** is still in continuing the program not in the individual.

Have you ever had to go and apply for Unemployment? Lots of fun isn't it? From the first minute that you enter the Unemployment Office (I know that the government likes to call it the Employment Security Office or some other positive sounding name, but for all of us who have been there, it is the Unemployment Office to **Us**.) you know that helping you is the last thing on their minds.

Why, you can only come in for a first time claim during certain hours. When you finally do come in at the right time, the lines begin. Line up to get the initial form. Sit down and wait. Do not eat, drink or smoke. If you get up to go to the Rest Room and they call your name you go back to the end of the line. There are Rules for this and Rules for that.

Does anybody every smile at you and talk to you as a real person? No, you are always Mr. Smith or Mrs. Jones and remember to follow the rules. Do you find work here? No, but if you follow the rules you will get some money and you will feel like a loser. Does anybody think that this system is great? If you do, go through the lines and answer all of the questions. Wait in line and wait and wait. No, you don't get much help here, not if you do want to work and provide for your family. This is a rut and the end of the line. No happy faces here. I know, I have been there too.

Back to our **Future Solution** and how it would work. A **Fair Corporation** would provide Healthcare for people who didn't have a job or didn't have a job that paid them enough to afford Healthcare. Our **Fair Corporation** for Healthcare would be staffed by people who really wanted to help people.

That's right volunteers. We want people whose main **self-interest** is in helping people not in continuing their job. Where would all of these volunteers come? It would be staffed by retired Healthcare professionals, who have retired from the rat race of making money and supporting themselves and their family.

People who have valuable skills and most of importantly, people that care about other people and have the time and talents that are needed. In a few years retired people will be one of the largest age classes that we have. Let's maximize that valuable resource.

I'm not talking about good old Uncle Jim putting in a full 40 or 50 hour week. I am talking about creating an organization that people can truly give their time and money. The people who have retired can donate their time and talent. The people who are still working can give their money. The key is that they give in their own **self-interest** whether it is their money or their time.

Now hold on Mikey, what you mean it will not work. It's happening like this already. Do you play golf by chance? The next time you go to a golf course you will see a lot of retired people working part time at a golf course. They work for Free or very little wages. They work for the right to play golf on that golf course in exchange for the use of their time.

They have traded their time for the right to play golf. It is in their **self-interest** to trade some of their time so that they can play Golf. We could use this same principle. People could trade their time and talents to help people instead of seeing all of their life savings eaten up in more taxes to support the Government Programs. They would even get to pick the **Fair** programs that they wanted to support.

In the case of Healthcare, I know that there are a lot of Retired Doctors who would rather volunteer some time each week than pay more and more taxes. What about you? Wouldn't you rather give some of your time than see your savings go away or the Government continues to tax more and more of your social security? I thought so.

Remember the key is **self-interest**. But what about all of the buildings, people and assets that the Federal Government has tied up in spending money on charity. That's right it is charity when you take it from somebody and give it to someone else.

Well, the Government would sell those assets to a **Fair Corporation**. Yes, as part of their Federal Charter to be a **Fair Corporation** they would get to purchase the Government assets. Okay, everybody stop complaining, we will talk about how those assets would be financed when we talk about: **The Deficit**.

Our **Future Solution's** main key is looking for people's **self-interest** and increasing the supply of items and services needed by our people. What do you mean, what would we do if there were not enough people who wanted to give their time or their money to help other people? That's a good point. What would we do if people wouldn't volunteer either their time or money? Well, to use a slogan from the past, "The people would be voting with their feet".

In this case it would be with their true feelings. We have gone too long trying to get the government to do things that the majority of people wouldn't support with either their time or money.
This will be a good test to see if some of those programs were really supported by the majority of our people.

Sure, you are right; we should always look out for the rights of the minority. We just can't continue taking from one group of people and giving to some other group. You know taking from the haves and giving to the have nots by force of government. People should want to help other people. The key is that this wanting to help somebody else should come from individuals. Not the Government taking away from them and giving to somebody else. If you continue to do that, sooner or later you run out of the people that you are taking from in the first place.

Don't you know that when you don't raise taxes to support these programs, that you think are needed, you are slowly drowning this Country in debt that someday will drown out all of our creative efforts to improve our lives? Can't you see how deep that sea of red ink has become? Who wants to jump into where it is really deep?

Let's jump into the real deep part of the pool. Let's look at how the government has tried to handle the Double **A's**. I mean **Abortion and Adoption**. The two are linked together.

You see when the Supreme Court told all of us that Abortion was Okay, it did two things. The first thing it did was to allow women to get an abortion on their own terms. This is called the choice issue and a lot of women decided not to have babies. The other thing that occurred at the same time was a shortage of babies to adopt. This is called life. The babies died because they didn't have a choice.

Either way at the same time more and more abortions being performed at more cost to us and adoption is getting more and more expensive because of the shortage of Babies. What if I told you there was a **Future Solution** that answers both sides of the issue? No, Mikey, I'm not going to split the baby. I am going to deal with **self-interest** and supply and demand. When the government starts talking about social programs they never really talk about helping the **Rich**.

They always talk about helping the **Poor**. So let's really talk about helping the **Poor**. Let's think about a poor 14 year old girl from a family of 10 other brothers and sisters. She's found her someone who makes her feel special. Yes, she has found her a **Man**. She also is pregnant, 14 still in school and doesn't have a job. What choices does she have in that situation? None, too good, are what her choices are. She can go down to the local clinic and have it killed. Yes, let's not even use the clean Medical word.

She has it Killed. She can decide to be a mother and live off Welfare or she can try to find a Church to place the child for adoption. She doesn't have too many good choices. A lot of times she makes the quick choice and goes down to the clinic. It's quick and maybe she won't remember.

Except, when that day on the calendar comes around each year. Yeah, that date when she had her baby killed. Then she will remember and it will be hard for her. So, do you care about that little girl? The little girl who could be your daughter or sister.

Is there another way? A way that deals with her **self-interest**, the baby's and the rest of us. Yes, there is just, think for a minute. What is there a shortage of that might present her with another option? Yes, there is a shortage of babies for people to adopt.

Yes, women can put their children up for adoption now but the big difference is the **self-interest**.

You see women cannot sell their babies for their own self-interest. They cannot sell them for money. Oh, they can give up their flesh and blood to satisfy some church's concept of adoption, but they cannot receive any cash or profit from giving up their babies. Think about that for a minute. Winos and bums can go down and sell their blood for a few dollars but a Woman cannot sell her baby. We have always had a real big problem with this concept. Yeah, it just isn't human to let women sell their babies.

So what do we do? We let them kill them. That's their choice but the baby is still dead. Why not let them sell their babies and then the baby truly has a choice. Now, I'm not talking about a system where the majority of the money goes to some middleman, I'm talking about the money going to the mother. Of course the government would have to establish a few rules to protect all parties but they would be simple and easy to follow. The goal would be to help some poor girl and to help some family have children that couldn't have on their own.

We also don't want to see the government grow. We want to see people act in their own **self-interest**. We also hope that some of those babies would get to grow up and dream. To dream of the time in their Future when they could go back and talk to that poor girl who may have taken the money for selling her baby.

What do you think that Baby will tell that little girl that sold her? I think that she will say, "Thank you for giving me my life." If it was you that had that opportunity to talk to that little girl, What would you say? No, not what some of your friends and other people in your group would say if they were looking at it from afar. What would you say?

Now, come on wipe that frown off your face. It would work out for the best. What do you mean, "what would we do if some poor girls decided to make a living having babies?" That happens now: it's called **Welfare**.

The only thing that would be different in our solution is that supply and demand would help solve the problem. What problem? **The double "A" problem**. **Abortion and Adoption**.

Get the Government out of the issue and let the people involved decide that one. Why do you have a problem with somebody paying $20,000 to some poor girl for having a Baby? Isn't that better than paying taxes to help her and complaining about it all the time. Look at what would happen. If a baby was sold it would live. Isn't life better than death?

What about all of the money that we are spending now to try to deal with this problem with our current solutions? We are taking money from some of our people who don't believe in killing babies and they are acting just as some of the people who didn't believe in taking their money to get young Americans killed in Vietnam acted. Do we want to continue this conflict over abortion until we finally have to surrender in the dark of night?

Do we want to force that 14 year old girl to give birth to that baby and then see that baby grow up with other poor kids that cannot live the American Dream and live on Welfare?

Yes, Welfare that great Federal Program that people keep complaining is wasting the tax payers' money. It keeps growing and growing and still there are a lot of poor people.

Or do we really want to help that little 14 year old girl and her little baby who has not had the opportunity to dream and to make choices? You see the best that we can do in this life is to make good choices. Let's make a good one on this one. Let's try to help our fellow men and women. Sure, I know that there are a lot of good people who want to help their fellow man now. The problem has been in how to pay for that help. We have truly believed that we could keep throwing that responsibility up to the Government and the Government would take care of the problem.

Yes, the Government could come up with programs to deal with **that** problem. Unfortunately we did not want to pay for the cost of the programs. In our Future Solution we have the opportunity to put our money where our words have been. Let's make helping our fellow man our job. Let's get the Government out of that problem.

We will all benefit and pay a whole lot less. If you really believe that something is a major problem then you will have the opportunity to really act and Help the people who you think are in need of your help. You can either give your time or your money.

The choice will always be yours and mine. A choice to act. Not a choice to make somebody else pay for something that you want done but are not willing to pay for yourself. What's more important helping the individual who has a problem or your problem with an ideal?

7 OUR SOLUTION
EDUCATION

My mother taught school in one of those little old one room schoolhouses several years ago. She was one of the low paid respected members of her small rural Tennessee Town. She didn't make a lot of money but everybody sure did think that she was neat. My wife has several degrees in education, doesn't make a lot of money, when you consider all of her years of experience and she wishes that she could get more respect in the classroom.

Times sure have changed!

When you look very deeply at education you can come up with several problems according to your own point of view. If you are a teacher, you may sight low pay, lack of discipline, lack of security in the classroom and lack of respect by the community. Your solution may be to put some cops in the classroom and to go back to a true pass and fail system.

If you are a parent, you're not too happy with what your kids are learning and you also don't like them having to be bused all over the city. You also don't feel that the teachers are tuned into your kid's special needs. You may not like having your eight year old being out of school at 3:00 PM when you get off work at 5:30 PM.

Your solution may be longer school hours, say until you get off work and more individual instruction according to each kid's needs. If you are interested in other Social causes you think that the schools are not teaching the kids according to your concerns for those causes. The causes run the range of sex, race, religion and politics. Part of your solution would involve teaching kids more about sex, race, religion and politics.

If you are a kid in this system you may think that the schools are not teaching you the skills that you need in our current work force.

Why should you have to take algebra and Latin? It just isn't **Fair**. Your solution may involve more classes in sports, video games and how to get a job.

If you are an employer, you may think that the school system isn't turning out people who have skills for your company. "Why those kids can't even read and write. What are the schools doing anyway?" You don't have a solution but you Adopt schools and give them a lot of supplies that have your company's name on it and send some of your executives to school board meetings.

If your kids are out of school, you may think that your property taxes are too high. "Why do I have to pay so much when those kids aren't learning anything?" One of your solutions is for the Government to tax somebody else. "Why, my kids are grown. Why do I have to pay taxes for their education?"

If you are a rock solid conservative, you may think that the schools have become too bureaucratic and they are wasting the tax payer's money. "Why do we have to pay for Dwarf Music and all of those other social programs that the schools keep coming up with? Why do the school boards have such a high number of people in staff jobs? They're wasting my money." Your solution may be the use of vouchers. "Let everybody choose where they want to send their kids. Let the market place work."

If you are a well-educated Liberal, you may think that the school systems are too biased toward "White Kids" and the sons and daughters of "Rich People" and those minorities don't have a chance competing with all of those other kids given their upbringing. You probably use the **Fair** word a lot. If you are a Mayor, Governor, Congressman or the President you have a problem. It's getting more expensive to fund Education and those tests and achievement scores are still going down.

With all of those problems what can we do? The very first thing that we can do, is ask ourselves what kind of problem is this? Who causes this problem in the first place?

No, not the liberals, conservatives or anybody like that. Is this a manmade problem or is this something that we have to look to **God** for a solution? Yes, regardless of who and how the problem was caused, this is a manmade problem. We can fix this problem if we start small and if we are looking for solutions and don't try to find villains to blame.

You see no one thinks that Education is living up to our expectations except those people working in those Two year special Technical Schools. Those teachers are working there and they hope that the school where they are working will continue on forever. They probably get up in the morning and pray "Lord, let me keep on teaching here. I have 3 classes every week for a total class load of around 70. I have an additional 10 hours of 'Office' duty!

When I was teaching in a public high school I taught 5 classes every day and I had one hour a day for conferences. This two year school is so much easier and I am teaching the same curriculum! Please, Lord, let this continue until I can retire!"

But our solution has to be a broad solution. A solution that looks at our whole society's needs. Not just the kids, parents, educators, employers or retired people—**All of US.**

If you look at this problem long enough and in simple and basic concepts, you see a big problem with how it is organized. What I mean by this is that Education has become too big: a huge black hole that we have allowed to get side tracked into other issues that we couldn't solve on their own. We have allowed Education to become a large dumping ground for the problems that we could not solve. We have also let it become a huge Monopoly.

"Richard, there you go just popping off again, trying to blame us hard working Businessmen. Don't you know that education is really controlled at the local level? How could that be a Monopoly? Don't you remember what the definition of a Monopoly is from all of your old economics classes?

Yes, Bubba, I do remember what the definition of a Monopoly is. **According to *Webster's New World Dictionary* (1984 by Simon &**

Schuster, Inc.), Monopoly. Exclusive control of a commodity or service in a given market, or control that Makes possible the fixing of prices and the virtual elimination of free competition.

What did you do, Bubba? Look up the word Monopoly in that old Dictionary that you used to argue with me on what words really meant? Sure, the public system doesn't control education in Louisiana. All of you guys send your kids to private church schools. Maybe the churches there have the Monopoly? Look back to that definition again. Do you see the part about the exclusive control of a service in a Given Market?

Well, what do you think that means when people are either forced to pay taxes to support public schools or they get brow beatings in their church to support church schools? And sure some of you guys even support Bingo and raise a lot of money that way. Why do you think that some of the churches were so against Casino gambling in your state for so long? Why, we have to protect our Bingo operations that raise money for Our Schools. Sounds like a Monopoly to me. Yes, there is a monopoly now and it is at the local level.

Education is primarily funded and controlled at the local level. Budgets are designed around the needs of that local school system each and every year. States also kick in some funds to try to balance out the education funds across their state. The federal government also kicks in funds for free lunches and other problems that are deemed necessary to educate the kids. The courts jump in when the schools are not acting according to: **The Constitution**. Local school boards draw up the rules for classroom instruction.

They respond to the local views of their citizens and the requirements of state and federal government. Sounds like a lot of people saying how to and how much? Can it be made simpler? Most importantly can we make it work?

"Wait a minute, Richard, there is nothing wrong with **our** schools. Why, the School where I send my kids is great. They get a great education there. Don't you know that there will always be different levels of education based upon the abilities of different local areas to fund their education needs. It's not my fault that the other areas of the country can't afford to pay for quality education.

Don't you know that you can't rob from the **Rich** and give to the **Poor**? There always will be winners and losers. Isn't that what you have been saying all along? Your wife was right; you have fallen in Love with Jane Fonda. Or worst yet, maybe you have been paying too much attention to Hillary?"

No, Bubba, you are wrong. I haven't been paying too much attention to either of those people. Those people may have just been listening to a lot of us who believe that our current education system needs a major overhaul. We cannot just continue to argue for our own little deal and forget about everybody else. No, we have to make sure that we look at all of our **self-interests**.

We can't just make it work for **our** kids and then leave the other kids out in the cold. If we do that we are just waiting to send more and more people to another island. And at some point you end up on that island yourself.

You see, education is the key to the future for our kids. If we don't offer **All** of them a way to provide for themselves then somebody else has to pick up the tab. That tab gets real expensive when you consider the cost of being robbed or killed. Our kids mean all of them. Not just yours or mine, but every little kid who wants to dream of growing up to be something and somebody. Those kids are in your town and mine.

All of our Kids.

"But Richard, what about your idea for an island. Won't that take care of the problem? You know, put them away for good. Far away from decent people so they can't cause us any more problems."

No, Bubba, you have to offer people a way to avoid the island. Don't you remember that we are talking about people? People who could be your son or your daughter. Don't you remember how hard some of your kids were to raise and try to get them to follow your education plans for them? Didn't you have a real hard time getting them to follow the rules? What would you have done if one of your kids had really messed up and broken one of the major laws?

Would you want them to be sent to an island forever? No, you would not. They are your kids and you love them. The same is true for all of our kids. We should love all of them. And for all of them we need to make education work. Also remember that if you send all of the people to the island, then where you are becomes the island.

You will be alone on your own island. Yes, we can make it work. Remember this is a manmade problem. Problems of this type can always be solved with time and money.

Our first part of the solution is recognition of the problem. This is a problem that we have all across the county. It is not a problem only in California or New York or Arkansas. It is a national problem. Why are we still trying to try to fix a broken car? How can we make the problem go away?

Let the federal government collect all of the money that we need to educate our next generation of workers. Yes, I said this problem is too big to be left to local solutions. Now, Pat, be nice. Just give me a minute and I think you might agree with me. Remember our solution does not only reflex a Conservative or Liberal solution. It is a solution that will work.

Now that we have gotten the Government out of the **Fair** business, we have left them with the responsibility for our security. Part of this security is in developing Well-educated citizens that can provide for themselves. If we do a real good job of educating all of our kids, then there will be smaller number of customers for either: **The Islands or The Fair Corporations.**

So what if the federal government will have to collect all of the funds for Education. If we truly believe that it is in our best **self-interest** to have educated citizens, then the funding will have to be at the Federal level. Now, how will the Federal government assess and collect this tax for this new and improved education system? For a minute let's look at the world of professional sports. How does Baseball develop its future baseball players?

Right, professional baseball has a system of Minor League ball teams that are part owned by the Major League teams and funded by them to develop into Major League ball players.

"Wait a minute, Richard, I was following you up to this point, but what do a bunch of money hungry ball payers got to do with education. I agree with Pat. You have fallen in love with Madonna now. What could we possible learn from Professional Baseball? Don't you know that all of the owners in Professional Baseball are just a bunch of power mad capitalists?"

No, Mikey, you missed the main point, didn't you? We are looking at how they develop a team. A team that wins. How do they do it? They start from the Beginning with raw talent and train and develop them into a winning team. A lot of teams tried to just throw money at buying a World Series and what did that get them?

This may be real familiar to you, but all that did was to cost them a lot of money and a bunch of headaches with overpaid ballplayers that complained all of the time and didn't win. What did work was starting with young talent and developing them into a real Team that understood what it took to win.

Well, let's use something like that for our team. Where do the kids in our education system go after they have graduated? Right, they go to work somewhere. Let us fund our Education system from business. This is not just a tax that we pass on to some villain, especially a villain that has had the nerve to make a lot of money. This is all business. Business needs future workers so let's let them pay for developing that talent.

What do you mean, Mikey, that's not **Fair**? "Why if business funds education, it will have too much influence on education. You know, business will only be Interested in training people to make more money for them. They'll probably not want to see us spending money on social issues. You don't want us to end up like Japan or Germany do you?"

But why do we want to educate people anyway? If we want to educate people so that they have a means of providing for themselves, then this would be a good approach. It matches the benefit with the cost.

Business needs well-trained workers and the cost of this education should be a part of the cost of doing business. For years, we have tried to hide the cost of our needs. You know, put them in sin taxes or, better yet, a

Wheel Tax.

Okay for everybody other than my mother I'll explain what a "Wheel Tax" means. States and local governments have started using this concept in order to be **Fair** and raise more taxes. The logic is that if you have more than one car that has four wheels then you should have to pay more taxes.

Taxes based on the number of cars that you own. If you have more money and more cars with wheels, then you pay more taxes than my mother who is lucky to have four wheels on her car that don't have holes in them. (My mother also tried to get by without a spare tire, but they were too smart for her. They said that this didn't count because the wheel tax was based upon everybody having just 4 tires on their car.)

This is just some other way to get money to continue the programs.
Keep putting money into that old car. "The car that has 100,000 miles on it and every system in the car is breaking. You know new cars are just too expensive. It doesn't matter that repairs are expensive too. We'll just keep avoiding having to buy a new car."

How much will this new tax cost? "Why, we can't afford to pay all of those taxes." That's the point. We would only pay one tax for education and it would be included in all of the products and services that we buy.

"You mean to say that we would do away with all of the property taxes and wheel taxes that we currently pay?" Yes, all of the local, state and federal governments would no longer collect taxes for education. All of the money for education would be funded by a tax on business.

A tax that all of us would pay when we bought Goods and services from business that employed people to make those products and services. This is what is happening to the cost of developing minor league Baseball teams now. This cost is included in the ticket price to watch Major League Baseball. It would be a simple tax. Every five years Congress would develop an education funding plan for all of our public schools from kindergarten to College. Based on these needs, a cost budget would be developed to totally fund this education.

The Congress would then at the same time develop an estimate of Revenue that would be generated by all businesses including foreign corporations doing business in The United States.

"Wait a minute, Richard, why are you just picking on Business. What about some of the Government that employs workers. How would **they** pay for the cost of educating **their** workers? There you go again, sticking it to Business.

Another version of tax and spend."

No, Bubba, you are wrong. For one thing, we wouldn't be sending a lot of our money to the Government in **Our Future**. You are starting to argue what words Mean again. Don't you remember that we are all in business to some degree? In the case of the Government their taxes are just like your Revenue. If a government, any government receives taxes from their customers, then that is revenue that will be subject to the same education tax that you and the other business pay.

"Ugh Oh! I think I know what is coming next." What does this mean for my church Bingo operations?"

What this means is that any organization that is receiving money from anybody will pay this tax for education. That means all of the **Churches** and other members of the **Fair Corporation**. We are not going to leave any organization out of this process. Even if you try to argue that you don't have any employees you will pay this education tax.

Some worker had to make all of those machines that you are using in your organization. And forget it if you aren't making any profits. You still have to pay for educating the people who will buy your products or services. Why, the schools and other members of the education system will also have to share in the process.

Nobody gets left at home without taking part. End of story and now on to how it would work. Based on the cost of the projected education and the projections of business revenue to be produced in the next five years, Congress would establish a tax percentage to be charged to all businesses.

This tax would be collected each month based on sales reports submitted by all businesses. It would resemble a **National Sales Tax.**

Distributing the funding to education would be another matter. Here we are going to use some more competition. The funding for education would be similar to how the **GI Bill** provides education funds for Veterans who go to College or other educational institutions.

The individuals going to the schools would pay for their education directly or in the case of minors it would be their parents. All schools would develop tuition charges for attending their school.

The cost of this education would be driven by competition and the quality level of education that each school was providing for the cost that they were charging. Competition and supply and demand would force schools to offer similar education for the money charged to attend those schools. Most schools would charge a certain percentage of the tuition cost when the student enrolled for that school year.

The balance owed for this education could be paid on a monthly basis. The parents would receive their standard education check each month similar to how veterans are reimbursed at present. The tuition reimbursement would be the same for all people and would not be increased due to the cost of the school where the student attended. Regional cost differences would be considered in the reimbursement.

In order to receive this tuition reimbursement, the schools would send a form to the federal government certifying that the student was enrolled at their school for the specified education. They would also send quarterly attendance records showing that the student was still attending their school. Parents and non-minor individuals would receive their tuition reimbursement on a monthly basis as long as they were still meeting the standards of the school that they were attending.

"Hold on, Richard what was that phrase that you tried to just drop on all of us. What does meeting the standards of the school that they were at meeting mean?

Does this mean that you are not going to allow for individual Differences and social and ethnic differences? I just knew that sooner or later you were going to start picking on disadvantaged kids. Try to make them compete with all of your suburban blond haired Beemer Wieners. Don't you know that you have to make allowances for the kids from a disadvantaged background? Give them a chance?"

Well, Mikey that is what I am trying to do. I am trying to give them a real good chance of avoiding the island. You haven't been there when some of those disadvantaged kids call their principal have you? Kids that had allowances made for them all through public schools until they finally got in trouble.

What do they do, then? Well, some of them use their only quarter to call their old high school principal and tell him about what all of the other prisoners are doing to him when he bends over in the shower to pick up the soap. Where are you when that disadvantaged kid finally ends up with all of the other disadvantaged kids in the only place that we have for them now.

What do you say to them at that point? How can you make allowances for one of those kids when they are surrounded by other disadvantaged kids? What do you say then? Oh, so sorry it is not your fault.

You are right it is our fault if we don't try to give these kids a chance. A chance to either succeed or fail. No, our new education system would offer kids a lot of new chances. The key would be that they get to make choices. Here is what I mean by choices.

One of our major goals for education has always been to prepare our young people to enter our society as **self-sustaining** and productive members of society. We wanted all of our kids to be able to earn a decent living and be able to take care of themselves in an adult world. Later in the process, we started to make allowances for kids that weren't able for whatever reason to learn and develop in this process.

Okay, I will talk to you like a teacher. They were difficult to teach. They would not pay attention in class. They threw spit balls at the other kids. They called each other and me names that sounded as if they had been in the **Navy** for twenty years.

They brought guns to school. They stole the Televisions and Computers that we begged some corporate citizen to donate to my school. They didn't do their homework. They made 20's on my exams. Even when I reviewed the material before the test. Sometimes they even missed the questions that they asked me before the exam that I had answered for them.

They also got pregnant and couldn't stay after class and do the makeup work that I knew would help them learn the **Concept** of what I was trying to teach them. They got thrown in jail for stealing somebody's car. They couldn't take my exams because they had excused absences due to being in that jail. Their fathers had left their mothers. Their mothers had given up on them and couldn't help me control them. They were disruptive in class and when I sent them to the office, back they came. Too many problem kids and not enough money for solutions?

So, what do we do about kids that due to their surroundings and lack of fathers or mothers or whatever have a hard time learning in our Future schools? Well, for one thing, we listen to what Coach Bobby Knight had to say. We remember that we are the adults and we are in charge. If we are afraid to tackle this problem now when they are small, what do you think will happen when they are really big?

That island will get real crowded if we just use it as our only solution. No, we are going to have a new beginning now. We will not let that **Island** take all of kids. We love all of them too much for that.

In School Suspension.

That big loud cheer that you heard was from all of the teachers that have been saying this for years. Before I explain this to you Bubba, do you know why that this approach to the problems of lack of discipline and lack of effort for some kids in our schools has not been tried on a large scale before?

Money! It costs money to do this. It also takes a lot of time too. Money and time that our schools have not had. We also will have Air-conditioning. Another loud cheer went up for over half of the Memphis Schools. In School Suspension means that we develop a system of really dealing with kids that don't follow our programs of education. A system that will increase in a force of wills.

The adult's will to educate kids over some of the kids wills to resist that force. Our first step is to: Now repeat after me.

We will win in the force of wills.
We will win.
We are going to save you from the Island.

Because if we fail, that is where you will end up. **The island is not fun**. **The island is not cool**. There you will find a lot of people who didn't believe us.

They now get to make their own rules that allow for individual differences as long as you know how to avoid the other person's rules on that island. It will not be nice, but we will try to offer you another alternative to that island. But if you don't care about yourself and don't want to learn by our rules then you will get the chance to make your own rules on that island.

That is if you are bigger and meaner than the other people on that island. Remember the call to the principal about the bar of soap?

Okay, this is how our In School Suspension would work. We will have rules on what is expected of students in our classrooms. Now, for all of you school administrators, this is not the end of the story. Just having rules of conduct is not the answer. Have you ever been in some of the teacher's classrooms in our public Schools? Why, they have rules for everything. My wife even uses my computer and word processing system to make the letters so big that even **Bubba** without

126

his glasses could read them. No, rules would only be the starting point. What would come next when you didn't follow those rules would be the main thing.

Every classroom would have rules of conduct that all students would be required to follow. Each grade from kindergarten to college would have their own set of Rules that students would be expected to follow. What happened if they didn't follow those rules? The school's force of will would increase in their level of force to each student's lack of respect for those rules.

For example let's take the situation of a student that is talking in class. Now, this student is not only talking, he also is talking just like a sailor back from a two year cruise around the world. Yes, he has learned a whole lot of new words and he is more interested in impressing the rest of the class with his new vocabulary than in listening to what the teacher is saying.

Now hear this, after one (only 1!) warning, This fine sailor of the seven seas goes to In School Suspension.

What does he find when he gets there for the first time. He gets to spend some of his time in something that resembles the concept of **Time Out** that some of us use on our Eight year olds. He goes into a room with no other means of entertainment. He will be alone with his thoughts. The only items of interest and entertainment in that room will be some pictures of islands with some of the unsuccessful former students going by somebody else's rules.

It will not be fun. He will have time to think about what he wants to do when he grows up. Hopefully he will not decide to continue his cruise to that island and he will go back to the classroom and use his chance.

When he goes back to that classroom, he will forget all of those words that the other future sailors taught him. At least he will know that he can't use those words in the classroom. What about the kid that doesn't learn from this little form of force. What will we do? The force continues. There is another level. Now for students that are starting to use not only their voices to be disruptive, we have another room. This room is staffed by a former football coach who couldn't win enough football games. We may have used him in the past as a school bus driver or he may have worked down at the old board of education before.

We have a new job for him. That old former football coach may be thinking about all of those football games that he listened to the crowd and went for it on fourth down. He wishes that he had punted the ball instead. He is remembering how he got here in the first place. He is there to help you. How will he help you? He will help you learn to communicate. What we have here is a failure to communicate. A failure to communicate! He is going to help you to get your mind right.

"Wait a minute, Richard; you are sounding like some kind of uncaring Calvinist. All you want to do is hurt somebody. Don't you know that people only respond to positive reinforcement? All this does is use the stick and appeal to their worst instincts. Don't you know that we changed that a long time back in our past? Why, we are all civilized now. Nobody uses that approach anymore."

Gee wheeze, lookie here all of you teachers, we now has another volunteer to sit in that room and get that disruptive student to change their attitudes. Come on down, Mikey it's your turn to sit in that room and try to turn that person around before the last boat leaves for that island. We'll let you deal with those kinds of problems.

Gee, dead silence.

Somebody must have been looking for the easy way out. A way to sound like you cared and wanted to be **Fair**. What will we do?
No, we will not take the easy course of action and put our problems off on somebody else. We will always have an open room for you to come on down and see if you can do better than we can. Do you want to try your luck? That's what In School Suspension is all about. If you don't follow our rules the force and pressure will only increase to turn you around.

Hopefully few students will not need to go farther than the room with the old football coach. It will get harder on you the more that you don't want to change and learn something. We love all of you and we don't want to see you go away to some island. We want you to learn to be part of our family. A family that has rules and expects you to follow them.

"But Richard, aren't you going to have some things that these students can work on when they are in that room? You know offer them another teacher that can do a better job of communicating with those problem students."

No, they didn't do that when they had the opportunity in their classroom. There is only one way back, and that is, accept our rules. Do they want to wait and see how it works on the island? Sure, I know that there will be some that will go the whole Nine yards and what will we do with them? You know those young kids that continue to fight the rules and end up stealing and killing people. What will we do with them?

Unfortunately for them and for us, they get to catch the early boat to the island. You have to design your system with that in mind. You start out slow and increase your pressure in degrees. At some point you reach a point of no return. For whatever reason it is not working. That's when the early boat leaves for the island.

We cannot lose sight of what we are trying to do. We are trying to give our kids a chance to have a better future. We cannot keep spending all of our time on the few students that don't want to have that chance. At some point we have to go on with the others.--the ones that want that future.

"Okay, Richard, I'd be willing to give that program a shot if you were flexible in the approach to who went into those rooms. I also wouldn't want to see a lot of minorities and other disadvantaged kids end up in those rooms. You know the kids that don't have a strong father figure to lead them down the right path. What would you do for the kids that came from a broken home? How would you handle all of those kids that didn't have good parents?"

Okay, Mikey, here's your opportunity. Are you ready to have some of those kids that you are talking about come and live with you? Are you willing to take the place of the father that they don't have? Can they come and live with you? Are you prepared to be their father for the rest of their lives? Will you be there for them when they come home from school? Will you be there to tell them how much you love them and take them to the movies and to the swimming pool? What are you prepared to do for them?

Gee, I just heard a door closing and it sounds like a car engine starting up. I guess I got my answer, didn't I?

No, that is not the way to solve the problem of kids that don't have good parents. This country will never want to take on the role of being that parent. It may not be **Fair** but that is a fact that we must deal with or we are doomed to fail these kids. All of the temporary father figures don't work if they are not there all of the time when that kid needs them. We will have to take another approach.

That approach involves caring teachers and yes even caring old football coaches that don't want to see those kids fail and end up on that island. You haven't seen some of those teachers try everything that they can to reach those kids now. You haven't seen those teachers that stay after school to go over the lesson plan with those kids. You haven't seen those teachers try to call the parents of those kids only to end up talking to a male who is not the kid's father but is just sleeping with the mother.

You haven't seen that teacher who falls asleep in her chair at 1:00 AM in the morning grading papers and coming up with lesson plans.

Teachers don't care? Where have you been? You've not been there in the arena. We will give all of our teacher more of our support. We will also give them more of our money too. Support will mean teachers having good air-conditioning, heating, lighting and supplies in all of their classrooms.

Support means giving the administrative support that they need to do the job. It means addition support people to grade papers and to do all of the clerical work that is now done at night by those teachers who limp into their classrooms each morning hoping for no problem children to deal with that day. Teachers will spend their time trying to Teach, encourage and develop our kids.

Teachers care and we care about them too. And for all of that we will pay. What will we pay? A lot. Don't you know how the market works?

I'll tell you how it works. Everything is based on supply and demand. If we give education the best tools to educate and pay teachers for those skills, then we will start attracting the best minds to education. No more counting the days until June comes around even if it is just the 1st of September. No, we will raise the money that we need through our new Revenue Tax approach. Changing our funding for education from local property based taxes to a National Revenue Tax sounds real complicated doesn't it?

Do you know how local governments are funding their schools now? It's a real mess! Most public schools are primarily funded by taxes that are raised by taxing the property of individuals and business. Property is taxed at the county and city level.

Why, in Houston, Texas there are even separate School Districts that collect a specific tax just for their schools. If you live in Houston, Texas you also pay property taxes to your city, county and water District. This process for collecting taxes from property starts by first determining the current Market value of the property such as individual homes and business property. It can be a real struggle just to come up with a **Fair Market Value**. Why? Don't you remember all of those words that can describe **Fair**?

Well, in the case of **Fair Market Value** being applied to somebody's home, it can get real complicated. Complicated because this is the base from which taxes are assessed. The higher your Fair **Market Value** the more taxes that you pay. People tend to get real involved in this issue. Why, they even go down to their local Equalization Board and protest the value that was placed on their homes. They use the **Fair** word a lot.

Local governments try to waffle a little on this issue and come up with some interesting concepts. Some states even grant their citizens what they call a **Homestead Exemption.** They may exempt 25% of this **Fair Market Value** from any taxation. It is only **Fair**.

Here in Memphis, Tennessee we have had a lot of problems with citizens and businesses successfully getting their **Fair Market Value** assessment lowered due to several factors. It has gotten so bad that our Mayor has even suggested that we hire a full time expert to show the city how to successfully defend the assessments. Guess what his candidate's qualifications were? He was one of the consultants who were very successful in helping business get a lower assessment and pay a lot less taxes.

Yeah, it is real complicated right now and it's not working either! You see the federal government doesn't have a patent on using the **Fair** word. State and local governments annually tell their citizens that the new sales taxes and increased Property taxes are going to Education. The money comes in and still there is not enough to pay teachers' salaries and the other needs of the school systems.

Why, in Memphis, Tennessee where I live, we even have some schools that don't have air conditioners. Some of you have probably seen The St. Jude Federal Express Golf tournament on Television during our Hot Summer. You have probably heard the announcers talk about how hard it is for the Professional Golfers to concentrate in all of that heat.

Well, what do you think the teachers and students are doing in Memphis during this time? Yes, they are trying to teach and learn in the schools that do not have air conditioning. We had a real big tax increase this year but still air conditioning is too expensive. The board of education is air conditioned but not some of the Schools. Why, our current Mayor was once the Superintendent of education and we still have schools that don't have air-conditioning. It just doesn't seem **Fair**.

Know why education loses out? There are other local problems too: how to pay for police, firemen and other social programs. Education always loses. Seems as if we have really hidden that cost too well.

Who would draw up the curricula for all of the students? A few good men and women, that's who, a small voluntary board would be established by Congress or the President that would be responsible for developing the Criteria for all schools. They would have a lot of people from business. You know the ones that are paying the taxes.

What would happen to local school boards? They would go away. If we truly believe that it is in our best **self-interest** to educate our kids, then we need to establish standards for all of our kids. No, not for their kids. All of our kids. We tried other ways and they haven't worked. We are looking for solutions. One more thing on funding.

As part of this solution, taxes would have to be reduced by all the local and state governments that justified their taxes that were supposed to go to Education. We wouldn't let those governments get to fund other programs with those tax dollars.

What about standards? How would our schools look? Again, we're looking to educate our future citizens not to right a past wrong. Standards would be established for all grade levels. Those standards would also involve student conduct in a class room.

It's kind of hard to teach someone something when they are trying to out **Word** holler Jim. As part of these standards, we have to come back to reality. Not everybody has the same abilities. Not everybody can just say, "I am somebody and I will be somebody." You can, if you are willing to pay the price. If, for whatever reason, you don't have the same abilities as the guy next to you, then you have to work harder than he does.

Just ask Coach Bobby Knight of the Indiana Hoosiers, he's been doing it for years: taking kids that don't have all of the abilities and teaching them how to win. It's hard but that's your only choice to work harder if you are not as talented as the other guys. It may not be **Fair**, but it's true. So, we now have some improved standards for education. How would these standards work? Simple, follow the standards and rules and you get to go to the next level.

The opportunity will be there for you to follow. It's starting to sound as if we have a real competition isn't it? Yes, it is. Just like all of the simple things in life: the talented guy gets the pretty girl. That may not be **Fair,** if you are not talented or highly intelligent, but it's the real world. Now, I'm not going to go on and on with all of these standards, but they would have to be developed around what we expect students to learn at various grade levels.

If you don't learn these skills you don't go on to the next level. There will be no more social promotions. Business is paying the freight and people need to have the skills for their jobs. What's the self interest in this? Well, simply said, if people don't have the ability to pay their own way then guess who pays.

Yes, all of us. Just think back to the problems that we have had in Los Angeles and some other big cities. Yeah, I'm talking about all of the riots, looting and burning that we have had. Know why we have all of those problems?

The people doing all of the rioting are having a hard time meeting their needs. All of the Zone Grants and other social programs will never work if we don't deal with their problems. They cannot meet their expectations of what their needs are. Education has to offer a way for people to develop and meet realistic human expectations. It also must offer several tracks for people to develop.

Now I know that this is a hard concept. A concept that has caused all kind of **Fair** problems, but reality does not care about being **Fair**. There are all kinds of talents and skills. Said simply, not everybody can be a Rocket Scientist. What we can do is offer everybody the chance to try to be one.

What happens to the little kid whose talent is not suited for being a Doctor, Lawyer or Accountant? We have to offer him a chance to be the best that he can be at whatever his talents are. Why have we believed that everybody has to go to college when some people do not have that talent or ability?

By tracking, I mean we have to establish jobs training for kids where they can have a chance of attaining what's taught. You know, teach at a level that a kid can see himself succeeding. At the same time, you have to allow a kid to have an opportunity to fail, but have another plan there so he can become a success at something. What do we do with the ones that will not follow the rules?

Well, the answers that we have tried before haven't worked. We have to have a system to offer alternatives to kids as they develop. So if you don't like the program in this school that is training people for college, then here is a program that trains people who don't get to go to college. If you don't like that one, then here is another one until you prove that you don't want to live in our society. What do we do then?

First off, we would hope that a lot of people didn't get to that point but some would. That's the hard part. What do you do with people who don't want to be part of our system and won't follow our rules? Well, the one thing that you don't do is keep them in the schools and try to baby sit them. That's what we have been doing before. At some point you say, "Here's a broom, try this."

Either way, you will come down to that problem somewhere. Education and all of the money in the world will still not solve all of the problems in society. Somewhere along the line you have to deal with these problems. Our schools just are not the place. We have gone through different approaches to this problem. We tried sending them off to the army. We've tried putting them in prisons. Let's just try not to keep dumping them in education because we don't have any place else to send them.

Do you remember what we are doing with most of those two year colleges? You know those Junior College and Technical schools that every state has. The schools that are supposed to be for the kids that do not want to go to college. Yeah, the ones that are trying to deal with kids that didn't try to learn anything in grade school and high school and couldn't pass the ACT if the only question on the test was how to spell Boy and you spotted them **BO**. Yeah, those **Schools**.

Could there be any benefit to us and them if we just abolish all of those schools right now, and take all of the money that we were spending on kids that didn't get an education in grade and high school and put all of that money back into grade and high schools? Could those teachers and administrators use that money to help educate those kids? Could we also bring back Vocational Schools in High School for those kids that want to be tradesmen? You know plumbers, electricians, and other skilled labors.

I know we thought that is was not **Fair** and that everybody should go to College but it didn't work. All that did was frustrate a lot of people and cost a lot of money. Could the people who manage our public schools also start looking at all of our schools at how effective they are in educating kids for the cost involved?

You know rate all of the schools as either **keepers** or **throwbacks.** They better start now because that will be what people will do when they truly have a choice of where to send their kids to be educated and it's their own money that they are spending. But what about some of the schools that will lose out in this plan? You know those schools that are in deprived areas.

What will happen to all of those schools? We can't let those schools fall through the cracks. You know, I went to that school and my child deserves to go to the same school that I went to when I was a kid. Be true to your school.

Well, my wife worked at some of those schools and dealt with the lack of discipline, supplies, no security, and lack of parent and supervisor support. Do you really want our kids going to school where?

1. The kids have more guns than the Policemen
2. High School students have their own kids in grade school.
3. Televisions are stolen as soon as they are put up.
4. Kids talk as sailors and nobody notices.
5. Parole officers try to keep kids in school so that they don't go back to Jail.
6. Drug dealers stay in school so that they are close to their Customers.
7. Everybody teaching is just counting days till the end of the School year.
8. You cannot stay after school and help students that need your help because security people go home and they will lock you in if you are still dumb enough to be there.

No, for those kinds of schools, we need to close them and build some really good schools for educating our kids. Give them something to be proud of and want to educate them. We especially want to use **Air**

Conditioning. Let's get real for a change. Why have schools that don't offer kids a real chance? What would we do with all of those schools that are not in good enough shape to educate our kids?

Why, let's turn them into places that hold those people before they get sent off to **the island**? If they are in that bad shape they would do great for putting bad people away from all of us until they are sent to the island. Now, hold on Mikey, I know that would be Cruel and Inhumane Punishment. Good, that's what people deserve that break our laws. They should hurt. Maybe when they get out they will change. And I know what the Constitution says on that subject, but that will be something else that we will have to change. Just think about it for a minute. Those schools that are not fit for criminals are where we continue to put our kids to try and learn how to have a future. That's our Future we are talking about and those same schools would not be fit to put people who have thumbed up their noses at us and our Laws.

When will it ever change? What is more important to us? Do we care more about people who have broken our laws or the future of all of our kids? Where are our priorities? Our solution tries to give everybody one thing: **A chance: a good Chance**.

It also matches the cost with where it should have been all along. It is a cost of doing business to educate our future workers. Most importantly, there must be something in it for everybody's Own self-interest: the self-interest of the kids, the self-interest of the parents, the self-interest of the teachers and educators and something in the self-interest of the business that will pay the cost of the system. If we go looking for villains and people to blame, then the system will break down.

8 OUR SOLUTION
HEALTHCARE

In today's world, one of our most difficult problems is Healthcare. The Conservatives say that the problem is caused by too much government regulation. If we just let the market place work, then the market place would solve this Healthcare problem. The government just tries to spend too much money on taking from the Rich and giving to the Poor.

The Liberals say that the problem is caused by all the Greedy Doctors and Drug companies that over charge the public. "If we just took the money away from all of the **Rich** people then we would have plenty to spend on the **Poor** people."

Who's right? Neither group has an inside track on the truth or solutions to this problem. The solution to our Healthcare Problems will be based on the way that other products and services are distributed in our market, not just supply or demand but supply **and** demand.

You see, in our country **Price** is determined by **Supply and Demand** working together. If the supply of an item or service is short and the demand is high, then the prices for those items and services that are scarce go up. If the supply is high and demand is low then prices will fall. The prices for all goods and services are determined in this fashion.

The only exception is for goods and services such as Farm products that the government has decided to support artificially, due to political concerns, like getting reelected. Farm products like sugar, corn and wheat are price supported by the Federal Government. If farmers produce too much corn or wheat for what is required by the market, the Government steps in and supports the prices that the farmers need for their effort. Who pays for this? You got that right.

We do every time we go to the grocery store and buy farm products. The government has increased the prices and farmers produce more and more food--food that the Government buys and stores, gives away or let it rot. The government is even demonstrating how supply and demand works. When you increase the price of an item or service, Demand will drop and Supply will try to increase. When you lower the price, Demand will increase and Supply will drop in relation to the price. Simple isn't it? Most of the government programs so far have attempted to deal with the price of Healthcare without any concern for the supply.

The demand side of the Healthcare issue has been increased with most government officials saying that all Americans have a Constitutional right to adequate Healthcare. They have also created government programs like Medicare and Medicaid to show the voters that the government really cared about them.

Why, "it was only **Fair**." They also created different rules in how they got their Healthcare. Have you ever compared the Healthcare insurance that Congress and the Federal government has to your Healthcare insurance?

All of the efforts of the government overlooked a few points. First, Healthcare is just another commodity that people can buy and sell. The market place sets the price of Healthcare based on the supply and demand for healthcare services. Just passing a law saying everybody has rights does not change **Supply and Demand**.

What would you think if the Federal Government pasted a law saying that every American had a Right to own a **Corvette**? This would sound kind of nice, but how could the government make Chevrolet produce more **Corvettes** and force them to sell all of those **Corvettes** for a price that everyone could afford. The same thing is true for commodities like **Gold**.

The reason that **Gold** is more expensive than copper is that there is a whole lot less **Gold** in the world than copper. The price for both copper and **Gold** reflect the supply of both metals. Now, everybody could also agree that having a nice **Gold Chain** looks a lot better than a copper one. Heck, the copper chain will even turn your skin kind of green when it gets wet. Yes, **Gold** definitely is a lot more valuable than copper. For a minute, think about what would happen if everybody had to have a gold chain. Let's say that they wanted **Gold Chains** so much that they demanded that the government do something about the price of **Gold Chains**. What could the government do about making **Gold Chains** cheaper for the public?

Could they go on Television and talk about how greedy all of the people who sold **Gold Chains** were being and how that it just wasn't **Fair**? Could they try to come up with programs to lower the price of **Gold** so every American could be assured of having a **Gold Chain**?

If they tried that, know what would happen next? We would have a big shortage of **Gold**. You see there is only so much **Gold** in the World. If you try to lower the price of a commodity to less than what the market will pay in a fair exchange you create shortages. No, the solution is to increase the supply of the Commodity.

In the case of **Gold** this means either encouraging people to either find more **Gold** or developing a way to manufacture artificial **Gold.** You have to increase the supply. Any other approach just creates shortages. Why is Healthcare so different? Because it is an emotional issue and people want to believe that the government can give them things that they could not afford on their own.

Where does the Government get that money? **From somebody else, that's where**.

Remember the Catastrophic Health Care Act of 1990 that Congress passed for Senior Citizens? Well, this act would have provided an insurance policy for senior Citizens having to pay for sickness that could have bankrupted elderly people. It would also have paid for Drugs and some other Healthcare that had not been covered by Medicare. The only stipulation to this program was that the elderly People would have to pay a small insurance premium for this coverage.

The program would be paid by the people who received the benefits. What happened to this program? Well, this program was repealed when all of the people who would have benefited from the program complained about having to pay the premiums. Seems as if they expected somebody else to pay for the cost of providing them those benefits. They still believed that the government had this secret source of money. You know—

Magic Money!

They were looking for something that was **Fair**. Right, somebody else to pick up the tab. Unfortunately it just doesn't work like that. For a minute let's think about the whole Healthcare Industry in simple terms. Right now we have X number of doctors, nurses, dentists, hospitals, drug companies and other Healthcare providers servicing Y number of patients.

It's a simple equation like 2 +2 = 4.

Do you think that the government can come up with programs that take more money away from somebody else to put more money icanto the pie so everybody gets good Healthcare? **No, that would be like 2 + 2 = 5.** Surely the Government can remember basic Math the government did not change the supply It just changed the demand and the prices went up. That is what we have been doing for over 30 years.

Trying to change the math without thinking out the process. If we try to change the price, say lower the price of Healthcare, we run the risk of lowering the supply of Healthcare.

Let's think about the supply of Healthcare for a minute. For years we have said that we wanted only the brightest and most talented people to be Doctors and Healthcare providers. How many people have dreamed of their child growing up to be a Doctor? Yeah, Healthcare got the best people. If you don't believe me just watch your favorite Television Soap Opera. They always show Doctors as being the smartest and richest.

What can talented people do? That's right they can adjust. They have a lot of talents. They can do other things. Well, this may come as a surprise to you but there are a lot of Doctors that have given up on filling out Medicare, Medicaid and other insurance forms. They have gone into other professions. Some have even gone into developing Computer programs to show other Doctors how to bill Medicare and get the most for their services.

They are talented and resourceful people. They have a lot of options.

Have you seen the Movie *Jurassic Park* about Dinosaurs or *Rising Sun*? Did you know that the author of *Jurassic Park* And *Rising Sun* once was in Medical School studying to be a Doctor? Yes, **Michael Crichton** at one time wanted to be a Doctor. A funny thing happened to him. He wrote a very successful book called *The Andromeda Strain* that became a popular movie. **Michael we sure need you now**.

Unfortunately, Michael passed away and is no longer able to help us. Thank you Michael for writing so many books to make us think about our world and to rethink our concepts with books like "**State of Fear**".

You made me think.

Yeah, Doctors do have a lot of talent and talented people will always get rewarded. Why would you want it any other way? If we try to set the Prices for Healthcare we will end up with a shortage of Healthcare providers. They will go into something else. Then it is back to the lines. Remember the Gas lines in the Seventies? Those kinds of lines and probably worse.

One other point about Healthcare needs to be made. Just letting the Market Place do it won't work. I know because in the Mid-Eighties, I was in Healthcare as the Chief Financial Officer of a successful Pharmacy company. Healthcare providers have **self-interests** and their **self-interest** is in maximizing the wealth of their stockholders. This is only **Fair**. That's their job.

The problem is that, the Government has tried to pay for several healthcare services without thinking through the equation. They will always be behind the corporate Healthcare providers because they are paid to make money for their stockholders. Any program that the federal government tries will always cost more than they budget. The reason is that business people are good at figuring out how to provide a service when the federal government picks up the tab and the customer doesn't have to pay.

The company that I worked for was averaging over 20% profit growth over a five year period. The majority of this growth was coming from Medicare and Medicaid programs. We were a very honest company and we were not doing anything that was against the law. Why, we even spent thousands of dollars each year to have Healthcare lawyers watch over our shoulders and make sure.

We did know how to maximize our profit and provide more and more services to the public and then get the Federal government to pay us more and more, all within the rules. An example of this was in what we developed in a program called Enteral Feeding. You see we serviced several Nursing Homes. Some of these Nursing Homes had patients who could not take food by eating food like you and me. These patients had to be fed with a tube through their throats into their stomachs. This was called Enteral Feeding.

Now, we discovered an opportunity to provide the billing services for nursing homes that up to this point had had a hard time billing the government for the service. We would bill the government and save all of the Nursing Homes the time and trouble for this service.

We estimated that we would generate over $5 million in revenues in our start-up year. On this revenue of $5 million, we budgeted to make over a million dollars in profits. Sounds **Fair** doesn't it? Well, maybe not **Fair** but our little company would pull in an additional $1 million in profits from the federal government from our efforts to provide this service. Nothing had changed. No new revenue was being raised by the government. We were going to generate more money for our company and our stockholders.

That's how the Healthcare game works. The Government creates a program to provide Healthcare services for people who can't afford to pay for them and somebody comes along and figures out how to use it to make a lot of money. There's nothing wrong with that, but it does cost a lot of money. Remember how the price of gold works? Same principle applies here.

Healthcare costs keep going up at a rate of inflation above other products and services. Can we stop this animal that is threatening to take all of our money? Yes, we can but we have to look at it from the basis of supply and demand. We can't just look to reducing the profit that goes to the companies that provide the services. If we do that, then we are just waiting to stand in lines, that is, if there is a line to stand in.

What tools does the government have or should have to win this battle and believe me it is more than a battle? It is a **War**. What about on the supply side? No, Mikey, this is not a conservative solution, just wait a little and I think you will like this solution. Pat, I 'm a little concerned about you but maybe you will understand too.

Our main problem is that Healthcare is too expensive for the majority of Americans because there is a shortage of Healthcare already. Yes, I did say that there is a shortage of Healthcare providers. Just like Gold chains, price does follow the laws of supply and demand.

Now Bubba, think about it for a minute. What happens every time you get a pretty bad cold and you think that this is the time. You know the time when you really are sick and it's time to start writing the will, especially if you haven't been eating right, exercising and you are still smoking.

Yes, that time. What do you do? Right, you somehow get up out of bed, clean up, get dressed and struggle to the phone to call your Doctor. If you are real lucky that day, your doctor is in that day. You talk to someone who sounds as if you are the last person on this earth that she wants to have a conversation with at that time, but you have to talk with her and get an appointment to see your Doctor.

If you are real lucky the real friendly person on the phone in the Doctor's office lets you come in at 3:00 PM. "Yes, Doctor John Luke is booked solid today, but we'll try to work you in somehow."

You get in your car and somehow limp into the Doctor's office after you drive all over the earth looking for a parking space. You also find out a lot about how people are not real **Fair** when it comes to parking their cars at Doctor's offices, but you want to get well, so you park your car over by the Drug Store- you know that place where you are going to end up anyway. What if there is a sign by the parking place "For Customers Only"? You are sick and you and "The Terminator" will be back.

So you finally get into the Doctor's office. Is everybody in the Doctor's office just waiting to make you feel better? Guess again. You sign your name on a long list of people trying to see Doctor John Luke. You also look around and see a lot of sick people. Everybody looks like the same people trying to get their electricity turned on or paying for their car tags. Yeah, everybody looks real happy.

The whole time you have been writing your name, address and insurance information on the Doctor's list of patients, no one from the other side of the Doctor's office has even made eye contact with you. They are always filling out Insurance forms and talking on the phone and telling people "to come in and we will work you in somehow."

You spend the next hour looking at magazines that are over four months old and thinking about how you are going to give that Doctor John Luke a piece of your mind for making you wait so long. About this time something magical happens.

Yes, an angel opens the door and calls your name. You are going to see Doctor John Luke. Your Doctor is not the reason for your wait. Why, he probably had to go to the Hospital and save the life of the President. Yes, he is a fine person. Then what happens next? Yes, you wait again. This time in a sterile office that

Has nothing for you to read. That is if you don't count all of Doctor John Luke's Degrees that he has hanging on the walls. Now, it's about 4:30 PM and your Doctor has changed from Marcus Welby to Doctor Strangelove. Where is he? Is he lost? Doesn't he know that you are sick? Why, you will give him a piece of your mind, when he finally has the nerve to come see you.

Then something magical happens again. The door opens and there is Doctor John Luke. What a guy! What a Doctor and he is going to make it all right! You are going to be fine. The Doctor is there to make you well. Doctor John Luke listens to you describe your problems and asks you a few questions. He listens to your heart and your chest. He makes you open your mouth and he looks down your throat. He looks inside your ears. Finally he picks up a white pad and starts to write something that only he can read.

He tells you that there is a lot of this going around and hands you the slip that he has written on in a strange language. You will be all right in a few days if only you go to the Drug store and buy these drugs. He tells you to come back in week if you are not any better. He tells you to take your file to the secretary and quickly he is gone.

You walk slowly back toward the door that you first walked in to see the Doctor and give your file to the secretary. She says, "That will be $90.00 and we only take checks, "Visa" or "Master Card"."

Sorry, no money comes back to you. This Doc does not take the "Discovery Card". You say a little prayer that you are going to be okay and forget all of the time. You look at your watch and it is 5:30 PM.

But what about the other time? The time that you wake up one morning and you cannot see. You open your eyes for your first look at the world and the world is not there. Instead of all of the beautiful colors that you have taken for granted, there is only cloudiness and shades of gray.

This time you make the phone call and you don't even hear that they are crowded. All you hear is that the Doctor is in. You get into your car and will your eyes to see the road and all of the cars that are coming at you. You strain and strain and somehow make it to that one parking place that you somehow find. You don't even notice that you have to walk hundreds of yards from your car to the Doctor's office.

You don't see the secretary or the crowd in the office. You don't see the clock on the wall that still ticks away. You don't see those degrees on the colorless walls. You don't see your Doctor open the door and come in to your room. You don't even see him flash that light in your eyes or see his eyes go round and round. You answer all his questions but still you don't understand. You don't see him pick up the phone and order some tests that you cannot even pronounce. You don't see him call other Doctors and try to get you some help.

But after all of these tests, they are all certain that you will see again. They give you some more Drugs and tell you to trust and pray. You go home and Pray and Pray.

Then just as they all said you can see. You can see so well that you don't even mind when that big bill comes in. You can see. You can see. But wait a minute, that's how it would end if this was a Two Hour Television Movie. You know the healing hands of Medicine work another miracle again. Does it happen just like this every time in the real world?

Do we have all of the solutions to the bad things that happen to people? Is it just a question of time and money? Do the Doctors have all the answers to our health problems? Is this how that visit to the Doctor really turned out?

No, they didn't say that they were certain that you would see again. No, they didn't tell you to trust and pray. They kept giving you more and more tests. They didn't answer your questions when you asked them when you would get your vision back in your left eye. They just said that you would have to wait and see. They don't know! For all of our progress in Medicine, there are still a lot of things that they don't know. Sure, there are breakthroughs each and every day. There are many dedicated professionals out there now looking and looking for solutions

To problems like mine and yours. They are looking for solutions to Aids, Cancer and even a cure for the common cold. They are searching and searching. How does that make you feel if you are one of the other people with Aids, Cancer or if they can't figure out how to get your vision back?

It hurts. You want your good health back again. You want to live. You want to work and run and play. You want it to be all right. Make it go away. What can they do? What can you do? What did you do?

147

You do what you wanted them to do. You turn it over to the ultimate Doctor. Yes, you pray each and every day. You ask God and Jesus to hear your payers. You trust and pray.

You identify with people who have Aids and Cancer. You pray for them too. You cry when you see Movies like *Philadelphia* that shows a little of the pain and suffering that people go through that have that horrible disease. You pray when you hear about young mothers who get breast cancer.

You realize that it is not just them. They could be you and someday you will be like them. You don't remember when you were not sick and could blame them for all of the problems that caused them to get sick. Yes, it was their fault that they got Aids or the cancer that could take their lives. You also remember that there always has been something that could take our lives. You think back to the past and the Problems that those people had with Leprosy and the Plague.

There has always been something there to harm us. There always will.

What can we do? Do we just shut our eyes and hope it will go away? No, we keep trying and hope and pray. We all should pray when we see or hear about someone fighting those kinds of battles. We should not try to blame.

That's what is different with Healthcare. Yes, it is a commodity. It is subject to the laws of supply and demand. But there is one thing that is different. It involves lives--your life and mine. Healthcare is different. We must make it right even though we may not find all of the cures right now. We must expand the supply of healthcare for all us--not just for you and for me--for all of us.

Where do we get more Doctors?

Future Doctors must go to College for four years and then they must attend Medical School for four more years. Doctors then spend time as Interns and spend some more time in residency for whatever specialty that they wish to practice.

They must be very smart, make very excellent grades and be very patient. The colleges and Medical Schools are all under the supervision of the States. States also license Doctors and set the standards for entering State Medical Schools. Private Schools such as Harvard set their own standards that are very hard standards. This concept was developed around having only the best and the brightest people go into Medicine and are similar for Dentistry and other forms of Healthcare. You have to be really smart to become a Doctor but if you do you will be rewarded handsomely.

Well, that system of only the top people becoming Doctors would work real well if we let the market alone and if we could tolerate having a shortage of Doctors and people who couldn't afford their services. Over time the price for healthcare would stabilize around the supply and demand. However, this is not a perfect world and we believe that everybody has the right to affordable Healthcare.

What's the solution? **It's supply, Dummy! It's supply!**

"I knew it. I just knew that sooner or later you would try to bring up that phrase. Trying to sound like those old supply siders that we finally proved were wrong. Don't you remember what happened in the Eighties when you guys tried to blame it all on the lack of **Supply**? Is this just another version of **"Trickle Down"** supply side economics? When will all of you guys learn?"

No, Mikey, mistakes were made in the Eighties for sure. The biggest mistake that we make was in assuming that the Government could just sit on the sidelines and watch the supply grow. No, the government has a role but that role is not to decide who wins and who loses. The government's role has to be one of structure and then to make sure that the game is being played by the rules.

Call it the ultimate referee. You know the Zebra's that make sure that there are not a lot of holding and pass interference going on all of the time. They also wouldn't use instant replay all of the time to make sure that everything was **Fair.** Just try to keep it going in the right direction. No, if the Federal government is intent on making sure everybody has access to affordable Healthcare it must increase the Supply. Here is how.

At present, Doctors are licensed by each state where they provide their services. They also apply to Colleges, Medical Schools and Residency based upon how well they perform on Entry Exams and prior school grades. Let's let the Federal Government regulate how people get into the business of becoming Doctors.

Wait a minute; let us say that the Federal Government is going to grow more Doctors. Rather than trying to attack Doctors for making too much money and having too much stuff, the government is going to help create a larger supply of Doctors. Now here, I have to give somebody some credit for this idea. Do any of you remember a little red headed guy named **ZIG ZIGLAR**?

Yeah, that guy from Mississippi that made all of those inspirational talks to businessmen. Yeah, that guy. Unfortunately **Zig** is no longer with us.

Well, I was a big **Zig** fan. One of the concepts that I learned from **Zig** is where to look for my solutions. First, **Zig** believed that being successful was not a crime. **Zig** thought that if you had a hard problem, you always first looked at how Successful people solved it. In other words, don't steal from the **Rich**, learn how they got to be so **Rich**.

We're not going to tear down the Healthcare system and take all of the money from the doctors or the insurance companies. We are going to create more Doctors and we are going to use the Federal Government to do it. This is how it would work. The Federal government would develop and budget a Strategic Plan for the number of Doctors that would be needed over the next ten years based on population and healthcare trends.

The government would then develop new standards for all of the people who wanted to get into Medical Schools. I am not saying that everybody would get in but you wouldn't have to be a straight A student and have an IQ of 140.

Getting in wouldn't be the problem. The problem would be in being able to stay in and absorb the knowledge to do the work of a Doctor. What do you mean -- where would we put all of these students?

We would still have to have medical colleges and hospitals to train these doctors. Where would all of the facilities come from and we couldn't afford that!

Well, the solution is right under your nose. We already have some of those facilities and we are not using them very well and they could be made available to training new doctors. These facilities are called Federal Government Hospitals. Hospitals like VA Hospitals and Army and Navy Hospitals that are being considered to be closed as part of the Defense cuts. We could use some of these facilities as Medical Colleges and places for Internships and Residency.
Kind of like killing two birds with one stone.

With this kind of approach we probably could even come up with a new version of the Student Loan Program. Give somebody the chance to become a Doctor through this program if they agree to set up their practice in certain areas of the Country that need Doctors. Would it work? Ask yourself would it be in their and our **self-interest**? Yes, it would work if we planned it right.

What about Drugs? That's a very hard one. I know from first-hand experience that drug companies have to have an incentive to develop new drugs. My favorite example is a Drug called Augmentin. It is a true wonder drug that fights infections. It is so effective that it is only used for very serious infections like Pneumonia and Strep Throat. It is a true wonder drug.

Whenever I hear somebody talking about this drug it is always the price. It used to cost about $50 for a ten day supply. I always remind the person who is complaining that he forgot one thing. His son or daughter got a lot better quicker for taking this drug. Did he forget that? No, he is thinking about the price even though twenty years ago he would have paid a lot more than $50 to cure his child.

I just wish that Augmentin could be a true miracle drug and give people back their vision in their eyes. Yes, I would not complain about how much it costs. Fine by me. How do most people look at that drug if they are paying their money? They forget. They have forgotten about some of the other expenses.

They also would have saved all of the expense of having their child's tonsils taken out. Nobody talks about how some of these new wonder drugs have saved money by treating conditions that used to call for surgery. Think about that for a minute. Do we want to stop the incentives for Drug companies to develop new drugs and end up spending more money somewhere else in the Healthcare chain? Those kinds of drugs do not get developed with a small payoff to the drug companies.

If we cut back on the amount of profit that Drug companies make, we cut back on the amount of money that they can invest in research. We also cut back on the number of Drug companies that are looking for the new drugs.

How much money could be saved if somebody discovered a Drug that would cure Aids or Cancer? Why worry about their side of the deal and the money that would go to them? We would still be better off and all of the expense that these horrible diseases are costing us now. Remember Augmentin and the next Wonder Drug?

Does anybody remember what Richard Nixon said about Healthcare over twenty years ago? Yeah, that conservative Republican President declared war on Cancer. He said that it was one of our most serious problems and committed the Federal Government to finding a cure for Cancer. We are still waiting. Cancer must not be a man-made problem.

No, we are kind of in a deep dilemma on this one. The last thing that we want to do is take the incentive away from discovering new drugs. We also don't want to shorten the time that a Drug company has to license the drug that they have discovered. Our best bet here may be to try to improve the education of our people and train more people to look for those new drugs. We definitely don't want the government trying to discover new drugs. Remember the war on cancer?

What about the other parts of Healthcare such as hospitals, other healthcare services and insurance? The answer to all of these lies in supply. If the government can encourage the increase in supply then the cost will come down.

We have a separate problem on insurance. Here is an area of our economy that begs for major changes. No, I don't mean doing away with insurance and letting the Government act as the insurance, I mean regulation. Why is insurance regulated by state governments that all have different laws and requirements? (I don't know the answer other than it's not too smart.)

Why not let the Federal government regulate all insurance in the United States? Have one set of regulations that all Insurance Companies have to go by, and I do mean **All** forms of Insurance. What would be wrong with this? It would probably cut out a lot of money going to the Lawyers.

You know the people that we keep electing to give us benefits and laws. Laws that allow Lawyers to either be our advocate in court or to be the bad guy on the other side.

Whatever the form of Healthcare, the answer lies in creating more sources of healthcare not the regulation of price for the Healthcare. If we increase the supply of Healthcare then we will lower the cost and bring healthcare to more people.

But wait a minute, Richard; you have forgotten the **Poor** people. What about the people that cannot afford to buy adequate Healthcare? Well, Bubba, you have to understand that the first solution is to increase the supply of Healthcare. If we don't do that first then everybody is in big trouble. The issue of people that can't afford that cost even if it is reasonable for the other 80 % of the people is a different issue. You need to remember what we talked about on dealing with that problem in **The Fair Corporation** for that one.

One part of our insurance solution would be improving and lowering the cost of healthcare insurance for working people. Because we are going to have the Federal government to regulate all insurance, we can make insurance policies for healthcare standard for all people.

Here is how it would work. All of the major Healthcare Insurance companies would have three months to draw up a standard healthcare policy that they would offer to sell to any person in America. This policy would establish standard levels of reimbursement that the insurance company would reimburse each person for healthcare that they had incurred under their healthcare policy.

The key here would be that Insurance would be offered to Individuals. The supply would go with the demand. No entity would stand between people who want this service and are willing to pay for the service. Now, Bubba, we could spend the rest of our time together going into all of the details but we would miss the good part. Yes, we are going to make the laws of supply and demand work. Yeah, and we are going to be smart too! You see, Healthcare has become something that we think we can get for nothing.

Yeah, just pass it on to the employer and make them include it as part of the benefits of being employed by that company. Well, for several years Healthcare Insurance was paid by most employers. The cost to the employer was small in comparison to the amount of wages and salaries that was paid by the employer and everybody felt real good. Heck, the employee even got a break by having this benefit be nontaxable to him. Everybody made out.

A few years ago, things started to change. Healthcare started getting to be real expensive. Maybe it had something to do with the demand for Healthcare without the supply increasing. Yeah, you guessed it. Prices really went up. Business saw their Healthcare costs going through the roof. They tried to change their insurance so that they could get control over these costs. Healthcare costs were going up more than the Revenues that the Businesses were earning.

They changed their Healthcare Insurance from one form to another. They came up with Peer Review, Cost Containment, Self-Funding and anything that might slow the increases in Healthcare Costs. They also reduced the amount of Healthcare that their insurance policies provided.

Nothing worked. Healthcare costs put some companies out of business. Who could afford this mess? In our Future Solution we have to change how Healthcare Insurance works. We have to put the laws of Supply and Demand back into the action. Let Business pay employees for their labor and let Employees purchase Healthcare Insurance with that compensation.

In our **Future Solution** the Federal Government would review the Insurance policies submitted by the major Insurance Companies and make sure that the consumers were offered sufficient Healthcare service for the premiums that the Insurance companies would charge. After the Federal Government had approved the Insurance policies, they could be offered to the public with disclosures similar to what companies have to disclose when they offer Stock for sale to the Public. The Government would regulate the performance of Healthcare Insurance companies very much as they regulate Securities. You know The **SEC**. In the case of Insurance it would be called The **IEC:** Insurance Exchange Commission.

To be effective all healthcare insurance would have to:

1. Be offered to all people regardless without any exceptions (No exclusion for preexisting conditions or medical conditions).
2. Be priced to all people for the same standard coverage in the policy (No special pricing if you don't smoke or any other conditions. No more Cherry Picking of the people with excellent Health and leaving the sick people out in the cold).
3. Allow for additional coverage with additional cost above the basic policy.
4. Be reimbursed to the individual policy holder and not to the healthcare provider. The individual would pay the provider directly. Just like the VA college program.
5. All paperwork would be submitted by individuals and no administrative cost to providers of Healthcare.
6. Cover all healthcare costs after an annual deductible.
7. No cancelations except for Fraud.
8. Different levels of care for different cost. Just like buy a Chevy or a Cadillac.
9. All health insurance policies to be allowed to be sold over State Lines.
10. Dollar limits to be established for Pain and Suffering and Attorney Fees to be capped at a specific amount similar to Fee levels in Social Security Disability Claims.

What else would happen in this solution? Well, what about the entire healthcare costs that business has been paying? Yeah, that cost. In our solution, all employers would have to increase the wages and salaries of all of their workers by the exact amount of the Healthcare that they would no longer have to pay.

Now, Healthcare cost is an individual issue not hidden in the wage and salary issue. But the government has to make sure that money is passed on to the employees and Business doesn't just reduce their costs and leave employees out in the cold. We just can't focus on one group of people as the villains and another group as the good guys. The solutions have to work for all of us.

"Come on Richard, haven't you heard about the work that Billie's wife Hillary is doing on the Healthcare problem? What about Managed Care and getting all of the waste and inefficiencies out of Healthcare? Won't that work?"

Well, Bubba, do you really think that there is a magic solution out there that will just make it all go away? Think about managed care for a minute. Isn't that just another way for some company or somebody else to not pay the bills? Passing laws that say that everybody should have Healthcare will never be the answer to helping people obtain the help that they need. If any future President tried to use that approach, we would just end up with another version of COBRA. That really expensive Government Law that says Business has to allow employees to continue their coverage on their Employers Healthcare Plans when they lose their job.

Very few people take out COBRA coverage when they find out what the employer is really paying for that Healthcare. The law says that employees are entitled to continue COBRA coverage. The employee just has to pay the employer for the cost. No magic money tree here. Whey if some future President tried that one He would be lucky to find a job working for one of Mac's eye glass stores. We always have to look at the Supply.

How does that affect the Supply of Healthcare? Think about how Insurance companies work now with big medical expenses. Remember that time when I had all of those problems with my left eye

156

and I couldn't even see my wife with that left eye.

Yeah, remember how I went to the best eye Doctor that I could find and that fine Doctor told me that I needed to have a Magnetic Resolution Image **(MRI)** to make sure that I didn't have something real serious. So I finally got up the nerve to sit in that machine that felt like a coffin for over 60 minutes and what happened next?

You remember what my great Insurance Company did, don't you? Why, they did a **Utilization Review** on my claim. That's Insurance company talk for we'll ask a lot of questions and try to stall for as long as we can and maybe we won't have to even pay this claim. Wasn't that a lot of fun! They kept sending me more and more forms to fill out and what happened when I finally called them and tried to Explain that my Doctor had ordered those tests only after I had gotten a second opinion?

Did the Insurance Company ask me about my left eye and had I gotten back my vision? No, they told me that they had the right to do this utilization review and if I didn't fill out the form and return it to them my claim would not be paid. They also used that real friendly tone of voice that they train the people who answer the phone in Doctor's offices.

No, Managed Care is just another way to avoid paying for Healthcare. The answer has to be in increasing the supply of Healthcare. That way prices will drop. All Managed Care, The Government and Insurance companies can do is to say **"No"**, a lot and try to avoid paying the bills. Our solution for insurance comes from putting insurance back into a market situation. Somebody needs the service and they pay for the service. We will create customers for Healthcare Insurance.

"But Richard, what about the other parts of President Hillary's, Whoops, I meant Mrs. Clinton's Healthcare Plan? Is the entire Plan just so many useless words that wouldn't do anything positive about Healthcare Cost?"

No, Bubba, there are some real good points in Ms. Clinton's Healthcare Plan. The best part is the part about Insurance conditions. You know where Insurance companies would have to offer standard policies and wouldn't be able to cop out of paying a claim due to preexisting conditions and the part about not covering people who have had certain medical conditions. Those are some improvements that should have been made a long time ago.

They are being made now as prospective federal law because they were ignored by business for so long. It just like the complaints that business has with the Federal Cobra Law. You know the federal law that says that companies have to offer continued Healthcare Insurance to Employees that they have fired.

Well, the reason that the government stepped into that one was that Businesses ignored the problems that losing your insurance had on people who had lost their jobs. The Government only stepped in when Business ignored that problem. Sure, the Government made it a lot harder on Business than it would have been if they had developed the concept themselves. That's how the Government works. Business has no one to blame but them on that one.

My biggest problem with the Government's Healthcare Plan is that it ignores how the Supply of Healthcare is created. What is going to change on the Supply of Healthcare? Where will all of these new Doctors come? Do we think that all of our current Doctors are just sitting back and reading magazines and waiting for more patients to treat?

Or do we think that they will leave all of their **Rich** patients and rush out to supply the services for all of those people who have been going to the emergency rooms for their healthcare or just being sick? Will it be **Magic Medicine** and everybody is now cured just because it is **Fair**? I also think that continuing to make Healthcare Insurance a part of employee benefits is not the way to go. I think that just puts a middle man in the process.

I would like to see everybody pay for Healthcare Insurance directly. That way **self-interest** has a hand in controlling the cost. I also think that by giving people free Healthcare, you make insurance more expensive for everybody. I would like to see Healthcare provided to people who could not afford Healthcare done on a charitable basis. You know, let the **Fair Corporation** provide that service.

That way we have the demand for healthcare back with the people paying for that service. The Government is doing its part. The Government will increase the supply. Will it work? Yes, it will work if we don't start using some of those words that can mean whatever you want and if we all don't fall into the **Fair** trap. Yes, we can make it work.

Let's also not give up on Supply and Demand so quickly. Some economists are starting to notice that some Healthcare costs are not increasing as quickly as they have in the past. Seems all of the cuts in healthcare benefits in business are starting to have an effect. Just think what would happen to the cost of Healthcare if it came out of your pocket and wasn't just another benefit that the government or your employer provided. Would you watch that cost a lot more than what you do now? How would you respond to your doctor when he prescribed something that cost $100,000? Would you ask him more questions?

No, it is the Supply, Dummy!

"Wait a minute Richard; I don't trust that Supply and Demand thing that you have been talking about. What if we just came up with a Cheap Insurance Plan with High Deductibles and Large Co-Pays? It would not actually pay for any Healthcare and people would think that they really have something when they did not. You know something that wouldn't cost very much. Something that wouldn't cost our company anything at all. You know something that we could just Poor Boy and afford? "

Well, Mac, you have finally Woke Up! Don't you know that company or Governmental person that tried that would be run out of office? Even the people here in Louisiana are not that stupid.

Nobody would be that Stupid to come up with a Healthcare Plan like that! Would They?

9 OUR SOLUTION
SOCIAL SECURITY

Well, Clem, this is the one that I've really wanted to avoid. Yeah, you know what do we do about the **Big Lie** as in the **Big SS?** This is the tough one. I just wish it would go away, but you know unfortunately for you and me it's now about our time. Time to be depending on Social Security being there for you and me.

You see it was never there at all. Every dollar that I sent off to Washington for my Social Security is gone. I have looked into the magic box for my number and there is nothing in the box for me. Each year they spent it all. Now all that is left is hope that this new generation will be kind and take care of me.

Wait a minute! Didn't **FDR** create Social Security so people in their golden years wouldn't have to beg their young people to take care of them? You know, provide them with food, shelter and Healthcare. "What went wrong? I thought that was **My** money. My money was supposed to be just sitting there with the Government earning interest. Interest for me so I didn't have to go asking young people to support me when I couldn't work anymore and support myself."

"What happened to **My** money? Social Security was supposed to be there. How did it go so wrong? What's this talk about lowering Social

Security payments and Taxing Social Security payments?" You know including the value of your house to determine if you are **Rich.** What's it called "**Means Testing**," or is it just **Mean!**

What happened to my cost of living increases? You know, helping me cope with inflation. They're trying to lower my cost of living increases. How will I get by on that little dab of money? I can't pay my bills on that. Have they lost their minds? That's my money. I worked hard for that money. It's mine."

Does this come from some evil conservative politician? No, these are some of the words of my 77 year old mother who is finding out the hard way about Social Security. **The "Big Lie."**

For several years, all of us have been avoiding dealing with Social Security. We've sat by and watched a good program that could have helped a lot of people turn into a financial mess. What is the mess? The mess is that for all of the talk about the Deficit, without Social Security, the Deficit would be even larger. Yes, all of that money that individuals and employers have been paying the Government is gone. Right, gone and it is not there. It never was there in the first place.

You see, Bubba, Social Security has always been a pay-as-you-go system. All of the money that is paid in Social Security Taxes goes into the Federal Government with all of the other Revenue. When you read about the Deficit being $300 Billion, that includes all of the Money collected from Social Security. If we weren't paying Social Security taxes the $300 Billion Deficit would be closer to $400 Billion.

There is no separate fund for Social Security. It is all part of the moneys that are collected and spent each year by the Federal Government. Do you want to get real depressed? Did you know that?

Federal Insurance Contribution Act (FICA)

A combined tax rate of 7.65% (6.2% for old-age survivors, and disability insurance (**OASDI**) and 1.45% for hospital insurance (**Medicare**)) is imposed on both employer and employee. The **OASDI** rate (6.2%) applies to wages within the **OASDI** wage base, which is $55,500 for 1992 and $57,600 for 1993. The **Medicare** rate (1.45%) applies to wages within the **Medicare** wage base, which is $130,200 for 1992 and $135,000 for 1993. *U. S. Master Tax Guide, 76th edition 1993 Guide, 1992 Commerce Clearing House, Inc.*

"Gee, Richard, what does all of that mean? I thought you said that you weren't going to throw a lot of numbers and complicated things at us? Why, nobody I know can make heads or tails out of all of that."

Well, Bubba, that's part of the problem. We haven't been paying attention. What all of the above means is that you and I and the rest of us except government employees are giving the Federal Government over 15% of your money and mine just for Social Security? That's right on top of the regular income taxes that you and I have been paying. We are sending them 15% of our hard earned wages.

"Hold on, Richard, your figures don't add up. Why, I am only paying about 8% in Social Security Taxes how do you figure that I'm sending them 15%. Can't you add? What kind of Accountant are you?"

Well, Bubba, I'm that kind of Accountant that has had some time to think about all of this. You remember that Commercial a few years ago for "Die Hard Batteries"? Yeah, that one. It's funny how you get to feel about some things when you have had a little time alone to think about those things.

See, Bubba, your boss is doing what they call matching your contributions. That's right, whatever you send to the Federal Government in Social Security Taxes, and he sends the same amount. From his point of view he could be paying you that 8% that he is sending to good old Uncle Sam. Doesn't matter to him if it goes to you or to the government. It's still a cost of doing business.

Does it matter to you? Let's say that you started out your working career making about $13,000 a year. Fifteen percent of that would be about $2,000. Let's also say that you continued to put that $2,000 a year into a real safe investment that would pay you interest of 5%. You let this money earn interest and you kept making the same $2,000 contribution each year and the government left it alone and didn't charge you any taxes. What do you think you would have in that investment for your retirement after you had worked for 30 year.

You would have over $130,000. You would have even more if you got raises and your $13,000 in wages had increased. You would have paid in $60,000 and would now have $130,000, about 10 years of work. This is how a real investment works not what the government calls investment. Their idea is to do what is **Fair** and what will get them reelected. Keep looking for somebody else to take the money from and do the **Fair** thing. But when will it be your turn to look into the magical box and see if there is anything in there for you?

"Back up Richard, how does this tie into what you said about depending on young people to take care of me. What does all of that mean?"
It means that the Government is counting on getting the money that it gives you in Social Security payments when you retire and start drawing Social Security from people and businesses that will be paying taxes when it comes your time. Remember, Pay-as-you-go. You know that they will be **Fair** to you. Why, they will not have a problem with all of those other young people continuing to pay higher and higher taxes.

Remind you of those complicated money schemes that you have read about. What were they called? Something about Geometric Progression or something like that. You know, you have to keep finding somebody else to take their money just to give it to the ones that you promised you would help. Am I on the right track?

Yes, unfortunately for all of us you are on the right track. That's real close to how Social Security really works. Keep looking for more and more money to fund a promise that you cannot meet.

Still not sure that there is a major problem here? Go into your room and close all of the doors and windows. Take some time to really think about all of this. Your money that you paid all of those years is not there. Stop, before you go on and really see that. Your money is not there. Forget interest. Your money is not there! Also remember

Truth Number 1: The government does not

have any money of its own.

The government will have to take some money from somebody who has earned that money in order to pay the cost of social security.

Sure, a few years ago, they started using T-Bills and government notes to keep up with how much they had taken from Social Security. Look in up in the annual Federal Budget where they show facts about the National Debt. You will see a column on the National Debt table called Government Debt held by other Federal Agencies. Yeah, that is where it is. They have done a good job of keeping up with all of that debt.

The problem is that the money is just not there. Just an **IOU** from the Federal Government. What will the Federal Government have to do to pay that **IOU**? Why collect more taxes that's how they are going to pay for that **IOU**. What do you think? Do you think that they really have another source of magic money?

Now you are starting to see the whole picture. You are depending on somebody in the future to pay more and more taxes so that you can have some money to live. What do we know about everybody's **self-interest**? If you think there is a problem now on the Deficit and taxes, wait until that really big bomb finally goes off. What new ways will they come up with to increase taxes by using means testing? Will they include some value for you having children that could help you? Will they include this in your income subject to taxes?

What can we do? Is there a **Future Solution** for this mess with Social Security? Yes, Bubba, there is a **Future Solution** for this. This is a **man-made** Problem and men and women can fix this problem In order to fix Social Security we must look at all of our own self
interests. We have to separate this problem from the government. If we continue to let the government deal with our financial needs for retirement, we are doomed to failure. They will always try to answer the **Fair** questions. They will always act in their own **self-interest** not our **self-interest**.

It is in our **self-interest** that the Government sells Social Security to the Private Market Place. Yes, I said sell Social Security to Business. "Have you lost your mind, Richard? How could this possibly work?" What I am saying is that we will be in big trouble as long as we send our money to the Federal Government to invest for our retirement. What kind of business is the Federal Government in anyway? What does the Federal Government do with all of the money that they raise?

Right, they spend our money in order to get reelected. They try to make everybody happy. They also are not financial geniuses. Remember the House Bank and The House Post Office? "Yeah, you'd have thought that some of them could have learned how to balance their Check Books." Our **Future Solution** says, "Let's develop a real Security System for our retirement needs. Where will that security come from? It will come from the only place it could have come in the first place. It will come from **Us**. We are the only ones that can make a difference. We are the only persons that truly have our **self-interest** at heart. Each person has to be the one who does it."

You see, there is no other person or organization on this Earth that can give you something that you don't already have: talent, ability, ambition, smarts, desire and all of the other things that go into making someone good at what they do.

Is there any government that can give you Michael Jordon's ability to soar in the air and create the excitement that goes with him? Can any Government take away his skills and give them to you? No, we all have our own abilities, talents and desires. The best thing that we can do is to use our own abilities and talents. Remember that great movie a few years ago about Indiana Basketball. Yes, I'm talking about **Hoosiers.** In that movie a bunch of little short kids beat the best and most talented basketball teams in the State of Indiana.

What was it that the Coach in that Movie said before the big game when they were playing for the State title of Indiana? Yes, he said something about "don't think about the size of the other team or winning or losing. Just try as hard as you can. If you play hard and play with the ability the you have, you will be winners in my book."

That is what it all boils down to: our own abilities and talents. We are the ones that can make it work. Anybody else just doesn't have our own self-interest at heart.

"That's great talk about winning a Basketball game and all of that. But, how would it work? Show me! How will it work?"

The way it works is step by step. We have several parts of this problem that we have to fix. So, let's look at the solution in steps. The steps in this solution are people. All of our people have to be considered according to their ages and what their options are. By this, I mean there has to be a different step in the solution for People who are already retired and those people who are working now for their retirement.

You see we are going to sell Social Security to the Private Sector. We are going to Privatize Social Security. The main goal that we will have is to try to help everybody. Yes, everybody, not just the people that we think have not been treated **Fair** in the past. The solution only works if we are looking to create a system that provides for people's needs.

On second thought, this is another good place to go get another cold one and sit down and relax, but be patient it will work. Before the current Social Security System is sold to the Private Sector we would have to give some people some other options and choices.

That's right; we would want people to decide how their needs for Social Security were going to be met. We have to do this in order for the New Social Security System to have any chance of working.

Their choices would involve them either staying in the current system with a few changes or taking the money that they and their employer had paid into the system. This choice would be made available to all people who were within two years of retirement or had started drawing Social Security for less than two years.

You could either choose to have all the money that had been paid into Social Security (By you and your employer) or continue to receive your current Social Security Payments. If you chose to receive your current Social Security payments, they would be capped at that amount for the rest of your life. Either way **No More Social Security Taxes** on individuals or employers.

The government would continue to fund Social Security payments to individuals out of General Tax funds until all obligations to those individuals had been met. The election would be a one-time election made by all people. There would not be another opportunity for anyone to elect to be covered by Government Social Security. Retirement Security would be offered by the private Sector from the election date.

Now, Mikey, don't start turning blue, don't you remember the story of the eight short little Hoosiers who won the Indiana State basketball title? You know the story about trying to do the best you can and using your own abilities and working hard to be all you can be. Yes, that one. You see, we all have choices in life and we can only ask for the opportunity in life. We can't call "time out" and try to change the rules so that we win regardless of how the game is going. Our problem with Social Security has grown because; we didn't want to disappoint anybody when it came to their choices. The government had to get in the **Fair** business. It doesn't matter that it almost sent this country into bankruptcy. We kept delaying the cost of something that we could never have.

"Why those people can't get by with only that little dab of money. They need to have an increase in their Social Security Check, so they can get by? That little old lady who worked hard all of her life and struggled to put two kids through school deserves a break. She dropped out of College to help her widowed mother. She worked at low paying jobs all her life and never once thought about her and living in a fine house, having a new car, nice clothes or taking vacations. She was one of the poor folks and poor people couldn't afford those things."

You think that I'm being cruel Mikey? Well, I know that person. You see that is my mother, but she could be everybody's mother. I am her son and I love her very Much. I wish that I could be the one that helped her. I also know that the government can never hope to truly meet her needs.

You see, the government can't just think about my mother. The government is taking on the job that should be mine; the job of taking care of somebody that I love. No, The Government doesn't do it out of love. The Government has to do it Out of all of the wants and needs of all the taxpayers and voters. That is the Government's self interest in responding to voters, not in responding to love.

But my mother made her choices long ago.
She counted on the Government always being there to provide her with Social Security. The Government cannot run from that obligation. You see her choices were made with that promise in mind.

No, Bubba, the Government didn't promise to keep raising the amount that it would pay her each month in Social Security. We have to be careful here or we will fall back into the trap. If the government tried to keep up with my mother's needs it would bankrupt all of us. No, we can only do so much. I remember when mother first retired when she reached the age of 64.

Yeah, there was a lot change going on at her job. She worked for a little Utility company in a small rural town in Tennessee: Lexington, Tennessee. Lexington was the county seat of Henderson County had 5,000 people and it was where Mother was born and where she wanted to stay.

Mother worked at the **Lexington Electric System** in downtown **Lexington** for most of her working life. She was a Bookkeeper for them and just barely got by on the small wages that they paid her. She also worked at the local movie theater to bring in some extra money.

Mother also wanted me to tell all of you that **Lexington, Tennessee** was not a small town and she didn't think that the **Lexington Electric System** did her wrong by what they paid her.

"Why everybody in **Lexington** was always real good to me and I was real proud to have lived in **Lexington, Tennessee** and worked for that **Fine Electric System**. I also didn't think that the **Lexington Electric System** was so little and their wages that they paid me were not small. It could have been a lot worse. I was real happy to have that job. I just wish that I could be working now."

The change that was going on at mother's job involved computers. You know those things that make you change the way you do work. They also tend to frustrate a 64 year old woman who was used to doing things the same way as she had done them in the past. Well, mother decided to accept their offer of early retirement.
With her retirement, she could either take a guaranteed $490 a month for the rest of her life or take all of it in a lump sum of $65,000. That was her choice.

This was during the super high interest rate times when interest rates were around 16% and you could get a pretty safe annuity that would pay you 14% a year. For mother this meant that the interest on her lump sum would be $700. Not a hard choice, right?

Everything went great for mother while interest rates were that high. Mother took the $700 a month along with her social security and lived okay. It didn't concern her that during this time very few young people could buy a house or business could not get a bank loan because of the high interest. Her needs were being met.

Times change and now interest rates are down and young people do not have to pay interest of 16 % for a house loan. That doesn't change my mother's wants. She wants **HER $700** a month back. Why that would only be **Fair.**

But you see that is our choice. The only way that my mother can get more money from the Government is for somebody else to pay. Either, they pay with higher interest rates on things that they need to buy or we take more money away from them in taxes. Somebody has to pay.

In our **Future Solution** for Social Security that somebody is the **Fair Corporation**. Yes, if there is a human need that needs to be met, let's do it with a happy heart. Let's let people help that want to help. Remember the people whose **self-interest** is in helping people. I also want to help my mother. She's my **Mother**. All of you government types better keep away. That's my **Mother** you are messing with now.

What about the other people? The people that have not retired yet, what do we do about them? We will let them take the money that has been paid into the Social Security System and buy what they thought they were getting all along. Let them buy a true insurance policy for their retirement.

Yes, there are several institutions out in the market place that specialize in investments for people's retirement. The main thing the Government would do would be to regulate these companies similar to the **SEC**. Call it the **REC**.

Retirement Exchange Commission.

What I'm talking about is regulations and oversight so that people don't end up buying a "**Pig in a Poke**." I'm sorry Mikey, that's a phrase I heard of when I was working for Bubba. It means paying too much for something because you believed all of the marketing hype that went along with the sales pitch.

No, we want people understanding what the **REAL DEAL** is that they are buying. Let people understand the facts and choose their investments. Not some advertisement that comes on the Television with small print that you have to have a **VCR** and a microscope to read everything that is bad about their product. You know those commercials for leasing a car that you couldn't afford to buy with a regular bank loan.

Yeah, we need to make sure that this doesn't end up like our current Social Security. Give the people the true facts and let them make their own choices. They should have their own best interest at heart. It is their retirement.

What's the Cost? I knew you would ask that. You think that you have me trapped? Let us take the cost of people continuing to draw their Government Social Security checks. This cost would be paid by the Federal Government.

The money to pay those benefits would be generated by selling the assets that the government had that were a part of the Social Security

Administration. Remember we are getting out of this business. When Businesses close they sell assets that they will not need. The government will not need those assets if they are getting out of that business.

The cost for regulating the Retirement Exchange Commission or **REC** would be paid by a small use tax levied on all companies that offered Retirement Investments to the public.

Does that satisfy you? Oh, and if the assets of the Social Security Administration would not generate enough money to cover the cost of funding social security to the people who had elected to continue the old social security? That would sure tell us something, wouldn't it? Well, just wait until we start talking about The Deficit for a backup system. Either way we have to get the Government out of this business. The sooner the better.

Stop jumping up and down and waving your hands, I can see you Mikey. What do you want to say? What about the social security taxes that businesses are paying the government now? Oh, you mean the matching contributions that are going to the government. Those taxes. Well, this would work just like healthcare insurance. All business would have to increase their salaries and wages that they paid their workers for this reduction in their taxes. That money along with the rest of their salaries and wages would go to the employees.

Now, if any of the people who were still working were to decide to continue in the Government Social Security System, then they would pay 15% of all of their wages into the Government System. All of the Social Security Taxes that had been paid into the system in the past would remain with the Government.

The current rules regarding the payment of Social Security would remain in effect for those people and anybody that continued their government social security system. Payment would be frozen at current levels. What would they do with this money? They would get a choice. They could either elect to continue the government social security system as we talked about or they could use this money to buy a private retirement plan. Either way all of the money that had been going to the government would now go to the employee. Do you think that this would work?

It would work if the government acted as a referee and didn't try to be a daddy for all of us. What choices would you think that the people would want to make? Trust them and us. Get the government out of the deal. We would hope that there was enough money in the government assets that had been used for the old Social Security System to pay for either all of the money that would go to the people who elected
to have a private system or to continue with a Modified social security system. That would be nice and neat. We will not know the answer to that one until we try.

Either way that cost was going to come home to hit us in the face sooner or later. This way, we can start preparing for the future. Does anybody else think that something else will work? **Is there another magic money tree?**

"What would you do if people just took their money and wasted it and didn't invest the money for their retirement? You know some people would just take the money and spend it on having a good time."

Well, Mikey, I agree with you that some people would make bad choices. We will help them out a little bit. All of the money would have gone into a Retirement account. There would be a 50% federal tax withheld on all of this social security money that was sent to the people who wanted out of the government system. When they had invested their money in an approved investment fund then the other 50% would be sent to that fund.

What would happen to their 50% if they just wasted their other 50%? Then the remaining 50% would go to a Fair corporation that was set up to help people who didn't have any means to provide for themselves when they retired. Everybody would get to make their own choices. Do we save for our Future or do we depend on the Fair Corporation? Either way, the government would not take money away from one group of people and give to you if you had made a bad choice.

The choice will be up to you. What are you going to do?

10 Our Solution
Jobs and More Jobs

"Hey, Bubba isn't it just terrible about all those people up North losing their jobs. You know, what with all those automobile companies having to close plants and let people go. Isn't it just terrible? Why can't the Government do something about them people losing their jobs?"

"Well, it serves them right. If those lazy union bums hadn't got so greedy, they would still have a job. It's their own fault. Yeah, they need to get a real job. Why doesn't the government do something about all those foreign cars? Why don't they put the unions in their place? Yeah, the government needs to do something."

Is that the solution to our problems on jobs? Let the government do something? Does the Government sell products and services? No, the government was in the **Fair** business. It didn't sell products and services. The best thing that the government can do is to create a situation where it is in the best interest of business to hire people for real jobs, no, not make work temporary jobs, **Real jobs**.

Before we look at the job solution, we need to understand what is going on with people looking for jobs. Yeah, they are hurting. Forget that they may have done this or that. Forget that they are union or white collar workers. They are hurting and they cannot provide for their families.

Why is that important? Why do we care about lazy people not having a job? Because it is in our own **self-interest** for people to have jobs. Jobs that let them spend their money on products and service that other people work to provide.

"Wait a minute Richard, you're starting to sound like a Liberal, I thought that you were a businessman. Don't you know that supply and demand will take care of that problem? Just like you said, the Government can't really create any jobs."

Bubba, I'm not just talking about the Government, I'm talking about all of us. We need to start thinking about helping all of those people who don't have a decent paying job. And I mean really help those people and not just do something that makes them stop asking for our help?

"What do you mean Richard by that? I've tried to help some people but I am not going to help somebody who is too lazy to help themselves."

For all of you who have tried to get a job, does that sound familiar? Does that sound like the friend or relative of yours that doesn't even return your telephone calls now that he knows that you are looking for some help in finding a job? Yes, the **Disposal People** who were let go by their companies so that those companies could improve their profits and other people could keep their jobs. No, you wouldn't want to talk to them. Why, it would be too depressing to talk to them.

Think that is depressing, Bubba, think about all of the men with B.B.A.'s and M.B. A.'s that are staying home and being a housewife while their wife works to try to support the family. Yeah, you know all of those men who have the cleanest looking cars and houses because of all of the time that they have to keep them nice and clean.

Think about the wife that starts to avoid eye contact with her husband because of his job prospects. Think about all of the friends and relatives of those talented people who are out of work and how they don't even mention those people. It's Just like those people have gone on a long trip. Out of sight and out of mind. It's just too depressing to think about that.

"But, Richard, I am just one person. I am not the government or the head of a large company. I don't have anything to do with hiring people. It's not my fault that some people don't have jobs. What does this have to do with me. I do what I can to help people."

Let me give you a big tip Bubba. If somebody ever asks you to help them find a job don't do any of the following:

1. Tell them to call___. You heard that they may be hiring
2. Call them up and tell them about the Ad for a job that you saw in the Sunday Paper.
3. Tell them that you will help and then tell your Secretary not to ever put them through when they call.
4. Tell them that you are going to leave the decision up to one of your Employees on who they hire for the job that you have open and then tell that friend of yours to send you a copy of their resume.
5. Tell them how great that you are doing at your job.
6. Tell them that they ought to take anything to provide for their family.
7. Tell them that there are a lot of job problems going on out there; just like the doctor who says that there is a lot of that going around when he doesn't know how to help you.
8. Tell them about all of the things that you would do if it were you.

The problem is that it isn't you. It is **Them**. They are really hurting. Don't just rationalize in your mind that they are probably lazy and you don't help lazy people who don't help themselves. When you do that you are just trying to give yourself a reason not to help them. But you never know when it may be your turn to stay at home and become the best house and car cleaner on your block. Do you want to be *Home Alone?*

There is a generation of overachievers who now stay at home. They do the laundry, wash the dishes, clean the house and try not to get fat. They used to command armies of other workers and achieve great victories in the Business World. Now they are arguing with Sears on getting their Lawnmowers fixed. Where did it all go so wrong? Why did it have to end like this?

Why has this country lost all of its wealth and become so poor? The country didn't lose all of its wealth. We messed it all up because we didn't remember our history lessons. This is not the end either. It could be the start of a new day if we can remember how we got here in the first place.

A brief history lesson will be covered here. Have you ever heard of **Adam Smith**? Well, it seems something like over three hundred years ago, he wrote a book called, *The Wealth of A Nation*. Now, you need to understand, that during the time of Adam Smith, most of the people thought that Wealth was determined by how much Gold or Silver that you had. He who had the Gold made the rules. Adam Smith wrote that this measure was wrong. Gold was just another commodity. It had value only based upon people's needs for that commodity. The real Wealth of a nation was in the value of the goods and services that a Nation generated.

Goods and Services created Value, and most Importantly, Jobs.

People have to have jobs and our country has to produce goods and services that people want both in this country and outside our country. There is a mutual relationship between business and workers. Both need the other in order to survive. But, what's been happening in this country since the start of the 1980's? No, Mikey, not the part about the

Republicans looking out for the **Rich** or Pat's point about Billy trying to penalize the Businessmen and raise the taxes on the Middle Class.

I'm not talking about the issue of **Fairness**. What has dramatically changed? Yes, a lot of people have lost their jobs. What's the number? I don't know. It keeps changing, but there are a lot of people out there who don't have a job. People doing this and people doing that. People who can't afford to buy that new house and people who can't afford to buy that new car.

What's it like to be without a job? How does it feel? What do you do?

"Why don't they do something? Are all of those people lazy or what? Why, if I lost my job, I'd pump gas to provide for my family. I'd do something. I would not just sit around.

"Wait a minute, Richard, that guy is right about pumping gas to provide for his family. Don't you know that people should be willing to take anything in order to provide for their family? Some of those things that you have on the list are just a lot of complaining from somebody who really doesn't want to work for a living. If it was me, I would be out there each day. You know knocking on doors and asking people for a job. Why, I would ask to see: **The Vice President of the Company** and show him how I was willing to do anything. I would be willing to start at the bottom and work my way up. That's what I would do if it was me."

Okay, Bubba, let's pretend that you are me for a minute. Let's say that you do all of the right things that you are suggesting. You get your resume fixed up all nice and neat. You list all of the accomplishments that you have achieved during the last twenty years. You list all of your education and honors. You somehow by magic get through to that Vice President. You somehow talk him into letting you come and talk to him. How does that meeting with that Vice President go?

You tell him about how you are willing to start at the bottom and you are not afraid of hard work. You tell him about how you are willing to dedicate yourself to making him look good for hiring you. Just about then you notice that the whole time that you have been talking to him, he has not looked up from your resume. He sees all of the important jobs that you have had. He sees all of the valuable contributions that you have made to other companies. Then he speaks.

"It's kind of ruff out there isn't it? Had any good prospects lately?" Then by Magic you are able to read his mind. "Why am I talking to this loser? Even if he could do all of these things, why would I want to bring in somebody who could maybe replace me someday? I don't need somebody else that could take my job. Why am I wasting my time? Who is this guy fooling? Why would I want to hire somebody that had all of that experience? Heck, he has even had a bigger job than me. Why is somebody who had been a Vice President talking to me? Sure, I know what he said, but I know that he really wants his old job back. I am wasting my time talking to him."

See, Bubba, times have changed. We are not all a bunch of people without education and skills. Times have really changed. But some things never change. **Supply and Demand** still are working. There is an oversupply of experienced and educated people. Those are the people that got to be part of the downsizing and companies getting lean and mean. They are some of the people who are now saying home and trying to find a job.

"But, Richard, if that is today's business climate, why wouldn't they be willing to go to work for any job that puts bread on the table."

Well, Bubba, some of the jobs that you are suggesting might put bread on the table, but they would also pull the meat out of the skillet. You see times really have changed. You forgot a major point. Some of those jobs that you are talking about involve moving to another area of the county. What do you do about your wife's job? How do you replace that income? And how do you get around the conversation with the Vice President that we talked to before?

Have you been on any of those types of interviews lately? Do you know what it is like to interview for a job when there is a shortage of jobs and an oversupply of people with your type of skills? Here let me take you on the road to finding a new job.

You have read all of the books on how to create a winning resume. You have all of the latest in word processing equipment. You even have a laser printer to make everything look so impressive. You even have a spell checker and a grammar Checker on your computer. You have a **Power Resume**. You get up every Sunday morning and look through the local Newspaper and open the want ads first.

You read them three times to make sure that you haven't missed any jobs that advertised for your skills and education. You finally locate some jobs that are similar to jobs that you did over ten years ago. You cut them out very carefully and paste them on to a piece of paper that you will keep to remind you of the job when they call.

You start writing and updating the letter that you use to send out to ask for an interview on all of these jobs. You carefully use your computer to check the spelling and grammar in your letter. You use your computer to print another copy of your power resume. You neatly sign our letter and put it and your resume in the envelope. Then you wait for the mailman to come and pick up your letters.

The next day you even get a few calls. Calls from some of your friends that want to tell you the good news. Yes, they want to make sure that you have seen the Sunday newspaper. Did you see the one about this job? The phone call is short and to the point. They have done their part.

What about the time when the phone does ring and it is a Hiring Manager. What happens then? Yes, they ask you a lot of questions and somehow that question always comes up quick. "How much money are you asking for? What have you been making in your last job?" The game has started. What will you say? How do you keep them still interested and not cheap sell yourself?

But this time you do get called in for that interview. What happen first? Yes, you get to fill out an application. You are willing to take anything and people who are willing to take anything have to do a lot of things that they don't like doing. Forty- five minutes after you have filled out the application you get to talk to somebody. They ask you some more questions.

You try to look important and talk like you can do anything. You remember all of the books and articles about how to interview and show employers that you are a winner. You also remember to always ask for the job. You end your interview with a Statement that lets the employer know that you want the job and that you are a winner. You ask what the next steps are in the process. Here the real game starts. It may be a week or it may be a month before you know. It may even be two months before you know.

Will you get a telephone call or will a piece of paper appear in your mailbox, the same mailbox that you used to first start the game with sending off that letter asking for a job. You want that phone to ring. You want to hear them offer you that job. You don't want another piece of paper in that mail box.

But what does that person do who doesn't have a job. What can he do? What are his options? What happened in the Eighties that changed all of our jobs? Accountants showed some companies how to save money by eliminating jobs. That's what happened. When some companies hit a rough time making their profit goals, they fired people. Yeah, a lot of companies cut the fat. Have you ever seen a fat machine or building? No, when most companies cut the fat, they mean flesh and blood. People lost their jobs.

"But, Richard, **Business** has to cut back in hard times. You know, reduce unnecessary expenses in order to survive. Why, if they didn't reduce their overhead, they would lose their jobs. Don't you remember what happened to the Chief Executive Officer of General Motors and International Business Machines? Yeah, they went too slowly in cutting their work force and they ended up losing their jobs. What are you, anyway, a **Socialist**?"

No, I am not a **Socialist**. I am a **Realist**. Do you know what happened when Companies fired their employees? They fired their **Customers**! **Customers** that couldn't afford to buy their old company's products and services. Every company that reduced their **"Excess"** work force assumed that they could go on making products and services for people to buy.

Why, they were just cutting out unneeded expenses. They forgot supply and demand. Why, their employees were only overhead. All their employees did was cost money--money that was needed to pay dividends and Good salaries to all of the top people making the decisions on how and who to fire. "Yeah, we have to do our job and save the company." Translation: We have to fire them so we can keep our jobs.

There was a major problem with this concept of cutting out the fat. **Not just one company fired their employees, a whole lot of them did**. The accountants had made a point. That was the accepted logic on how to fight back. If your Revenues were not going up as fast as you needed, then cut your overhead. You **Fire People**. But no one looked at the overall picture. Where do all these people go? What do they do?

Well, those people quit buying products and services. Their incomes went down and some went away. Everybody felt it in this country. Even the Federal, State and local governments felt it. It's real hard to increase your Revenues when people don't have jobs to buy those items or pay the taxes.

What's being done to help these people? The government has talked about Jobs Programs. What kind of jobs are those? You know rebuilding our infrastructure: roads, parks, libraries and government works. Will that work? What's being done in the Private Sector? Yeah, more cut backs. They're getting lean and mean.

Really getting **Mean**.What about the individual? What is he doing? What's it like to be out of a job. Not just a job, but to be out of **His Job**. Isn't there any kind of help out there for people looking for a job? Why can't someone do something? Well, Bubba, we have forgotten how to care. Yes, we have tried to shut our eyes and hope that it would all go away. You know hope that it stops with him, not **US**.

I worked for one of those companies that made products for the Oil Industry in the early Eighties. We got caught in a real bad situation. The whole industry had messed up and had manufactured more products than was needed at that time. We were in big trouble. Our Revenues were going down and our expenses were going up.

What did we do? We fired employees. Heck, we weren't firing

181

customers, we were cutting overhead. And besides, if we only fired them we could keep **Our Jobs**.

How bad did it get? Have you ever had to fire yourself? Well, I did. It got so bad, that my boss would not even talk to me in the morning. He didn't want to tell me the bad news--that my job was going to be eliminated in order to cut expenses. He didn't like to do that. So, being a good soldier, I bought the issue up myself.

"You know, Paul, things aren't looking any better."

"Yes, Richard things are real bad," Paul said. "Times really are tough, why we even had to let that real cute girl in Personnel go. What's the World coming to?"

"Well, boss, I think you need to think about my job. You and I both know that it is not needed with everything else going on in the company."

"Richard, I sure am glad that you feel like that, I was going to wait and tell you after we came back from Christmas. I didn't want to spoil your holidays. You have a month of severance pay coming. Next Friday is your last day with us."

How did the next week go? Some people came by and said how sorry they were and a lot of people avoided eye contact. Then there was the going away lunch. Companies that fire people always buy them lunches before they are let go. Kind of reminds you of the last meal that they give to the condemned man before he leaves for good.

Is the last lunch meeting with your co- workers for you? No, it is for them, so they Can say good-bye and be thankful that it is you that are going away and not them. See, the problem has been solved. "This will not happen to me. He was part of the problem. My job is safe. So sorry about Dick."

What does good old Dick do? He goes home and tells his wife about finally being free of that dumb old company. He relaxes for a few days and reads a lot about How to find a job. He finds out how to create a winning resume and a winning attitude. He reads about how to market his talents and abilities. He reads about how to find the

"Hidden Job Market."

He sends out hundreds and thousands of letters that are developed for him to market his talents and how he can help some other company. He learns how to use the telephone as a tool of his new job. What is his new job? It's looking for **"Another Job"**.

He learns about people who don't return his phone calls. He learns about friends, relatives and former co-workers. Still, the phone does not ring. He learns about what's really going on. We have forgotten some of the simple lessons that we all learned when we were children. People act in their own **self-interest**. There has to be something in it for all of us. How can somebody help you get a job when they are worried about losing **their job**? Where is the incentive? Where is the benefit? What's in it for me?

We have forgotten that we are people who depend on other people. We have forgotten how to care. No, not just for people that we like. That's easy. Care for all people. Especially, the ones that we may not agree with how they live their lives.

Do you remember what happened in World War II? Yeah, when we all beat the Original villain, Hitler. You remember him. He was the first real mean leader to invade another country and then refuse to leave.

He also said that it was only **Fair** and that the German people had a natural birth right to take what was only theirs. Yeah, we sure beat him. We sure showed him. Did you ever think about his biggest mistake? No, not in trying to fight both Russia and England at the same time. I mean his mistake on how he treated his Jewish people.

Hitler blamed all of Germany's problems on the Jews and set out to rid Germany of them. To him, Jews were responsible for all of Germany's problems. If he could just eliminate the Jews, everything would be great for the real German People. He did such a good job of this that a lot of Jewish people living in Germany left Germany before Hitler really got mean.

A group of Jewish scientists named Albert Einstein and others left

183

Germany. Just think about what would have happened with Germany if Hitler had not attacked the German Jews?

What would Hitler have done with an Atomic Bomb? Yeah, he was one of the first ones to try to attack other people and to lay all of the blame on somebody else. Scary isn't it? Blaming somebody else for a problem that you have is not a solution. It never has been and never will. In the situation of jobs, the solution comes in dealing with supply and demand and everybody's **self-interest**.

If we want to see more jobs created, then we have to make it the **self-interest** of business to create those jobs. No, not just jobs that are here today and gone Tomorrow. **Real jobs**. Jobs that will give people the ability to afford to buy more stuff.

Let's make it more profitable for a business to hire people than to fire people. Sound's simple doesn't it? It is that simple but how would we do that? Remember that new tax that we are going to create and charge all companies that advertise their products? Yeah, That One. Well, we are going to use that money to reward businesses that hire people. We also are going to make it harder for them to fire people, but let us look at the positive side first.

As part of the Federal Government's new job of providing for our se curity, we would expect it to help create jobs. The Federal Government would establish a Permanent job credit for all businesses that hired new employees.

Every time that a business hired a new employee it would receive a check from the Federal Government for 8% of the first year's salary that they had paid to the new employee.

The full cost of the employee would still be tax deductible for the business. The credit program for hiring new employees would be similar to programs in the past have been tried to encourage investment by business. This time the goal would be to encourage business to hire people. Now that's a real investment.

Rules for this program would be real simple. Each quarter, businesses would submit a form that gave the government information concerning all the new employees that had been hired by the company. The company would submit the following information:

1. Employee name
2. Salary and wages paid to that employee by month
3. Date each employee was hired
4. Social security number. See, there was some good use for that number.
5. Year to date stubs and Federal tax withholding.

There would not be any limit on the amount of salary or wages paid to the employee that would qualify for this credit. Why? **Simple Dummy**. We are more interested in creating more high paying jobs so that people can buy more stuff and when you make more stuff you create more jobs.

Don't worry about somebody else making out. We will all make out. Remember what people do with all of their money? Yes, they either spend it or save it. Either way we still make out. The goal is to help create more jobs not in making it **Fair**.

How would we pay for all of this? Remember the 5 % tax on all advertising. Yes, it is now time to talk about that. The money that was generated by that tax would be used 100% to fund the Jobs Credit. Business that created demand for their products would have to help in generating jobs for people to purchase those products.

Help Them Get More Stuff. We would also have a special rule for The Long Distance Companies and "The Home Shopping Network." Yes, for them the tax would be a flat $10,000,000. No, I am only kidding and I know I told you that before. I won't try to talk about what I think is **Fair,** but I just had to say that again, it sure does sound good.

So, who cares if a company does a small amount of advertising but hires a lot of high paying employees? We are looking to create jobs not in judging people. We also don't care if a Business gets a check for $1,000,000 in this program. All that means is that they have created jobs that pay some of our people $12,500,000. Isn't that what we want? More people with jobs buying more stuff. Stuff that we all work at making and stuff that we all would like to have.

If that's the good news, what is the bad news? What's the down side? The downside is what we would have to do with unemployment compensation. You know the long lines that go nowhere. Yes, that program. You see, we have been going about this issue all wrong. We have a program called Unemployment Compensation that doesn't do anything but cost us a lot of Money.

The money that the government gives to people who are out of work never comes close to meeting their needs and the government doesn't know how to Create jobs for them. The amount of taxes that business pay will never raise the kind of money that is needed to help people who are out of work.

What is the solution? Let's get the government out of this business. Let's not let the Business that fired employees off the hook so easily. Let them pay for firing that employee. Rather than charging business an Unemployment tax that doesn't work, let's let business pay for all of the damage done to a person when he loses his or her job. Now, that is really radical! Making a business pay for the cost of firing employees that don't have a job to buy the products and services that the business sells.

That's just too much. No, that was what the government was trying to do with their Unemployment Program. It just didn't work. This will work. What I am talking about is like a good old fashioned Pension Plan. You remember them. We had them back in the Fifties before business started running **Lean and Mean**.

Yes, pension plans for employees that rewarded them for staying with a company for their whole working life. Our pension plan would not cost a company a red cent. Yes, I said not a dime. Companies would not have to put any money aside to fund this pension and if we could hold down all of the **Accountants**, business would not have to reduce their current earnings for the possibility that they would have to spend this money.

No, the Accountants would not get to make **Accruals**. Those little things drive Businessmen crazy anyway. Especially, Retail people in management who just know that the accountants have lost the money that they worked so hard to make. Forget that their revenues have been going down forever. It was the **Accountants** and their evil **Accruals** that done them in.

You see, the only time that a business would have to pay this cost would be when they fired people. You fire somebody and you have to continue to pay all of their salaries and benefits until they get another job. You also have to pay for any additional training that they may need to get another job.

Wouldn't this be kind of tough on a business? No, in a way it would help them. Remember that business's employees are somebody's customers. It would increase business. People would have the stability of knowing that they could make spending decisions. You know go out and buy more stuff. **Stuff** that created jobs. **Jobs for Us and for Them**.

Wouldn't this cause problems with employees that had you know have done wrong by the company-- employees that had been fired for cause. This wouldn't apply to them would it? Yes, it would apply even to people who had been fired for cause. The only exception to this would be people who had been convicted of committing a felony and had been sent to the island.

If and when they came back from the island, they would be starting over again. As long as they didn't break any more laws they would be covered by this new worker's security system. Mess up and get convicted by a court of law and you go to the island and start over again. We would just take the judging away from business and give it to the courts.

Can it be that simple? Create a benefit for hiring more people and create a penalty for firing people? Yes, it is that simple. Look for what would be in the self Interest of business and all of us. You also have to forget about looking for the bad Guy. We are not interested in the past. We are looking for solutions to the **Future**. Forget who you thought was wrong and what they did in the past. We have to look toward the future. The President also needs to forget about making all of the Democrats and people with an axle to grind or some other special interest happy.

The President needs to lead the charge on creating more jobs, not just jobs working for the Government or somebody's pet project. (Not low or high paying jobs but all jobs.) Wasn't that what he said was so important in the last Election? Didn't he talk about how Jobs were the most important thing on everybody's mind?

Jobs are the Economy, Stupid.

Do you remember reading in your history books about what some of the Presidents in the past have done when there were problems between Labor Unions and Business Corporations? Have you ever heard about the President telling the Unions and Business to "Cool off" and go back to the Negotiating table. Do you remember what President Ronald Reagan did with the Air Controller's Union? "Yeah, he sure told them." Maybe it's time for the President to stop all of the Businesses from firing their employees and putting more and more people out of work.

"What about small companies, Richard. Why if we did all of what you have suggested, small business would not hire anybody. They wouldn't want to end up with lifetime employees. What would they do if they couldn't meet their payroll? Sounds like you are just creating another welfare state."

No, Bubba, we are looking at how to avoid a really big welfare state. We are also looking at how to avoid overcrowding on the island. We are trying to create jobs. Now, for your point about small business, yes there would be an exception for Companies or individuals that hired less than ten people. If you hired just nine people you would not have to provide your employees with this security.

You would also have to really tell them that this was not available to them and they would get to make the choice on going to work for you. If they went to work for you and you fired them in the future then their only source of help would be the Fair Corporation. It would be up to them. They could decide. The government would not have any other programs. If they wanted to take the risk it would be up to them and the **Fair Corporation**.

"What about companies and individuals that went bankrupt and left their employees without anything. How would those employees get paid and retrained? Got you now. You think you are so smart. What would happen to them?"

Well, Bubba, a few things would change. For starters we would change our Bankruptcy laws. The first order of who gets what in Bankruptcy would now be the employees. Forget the government, lawyers and secured creditors. Any assets of the people who owned the business, except for widely traded corporations, would go to the employees. And by that I mean that your old mother who owned a few shares of this company would not have to fork over her money. Closely held corporations and corporate officers of these companies would.

They would also win a trip to the island. That is right. If you broke your promise to your employees you would get to spend your time on the island. Here you could have the time to think about why it went so wrong.

"But Richard, all that would do would be to keep inefficient companies from becoming more competitive. Business has to be able to cut back in hard times. Why, they would go out of business if they had to keep spending their money for labor when their Revenues went down."

Well, Mikey, sounds like you have never been in a War. Anybody who has been at war knows that when the enemy shells your boat, the first thing that you do is put out the fire. There will be time later to find out who to shoot back at after you have saved the boat. This is a war. Especially for all of those men who are learning how to keep house and not get fat. We also need to think back to World War II. Remember what happened when all of the troops came back from fighting that **Great War**.

What happened to our Economy when the troops came back? Our economy took off like a Rocket. People were buying houses, cars, clothes and whatever you could throw in front of them. Why did they do that? For one thing, people had gone a long time without buying

189

some new things.

How does that relate to now? Well, it doesn't sound as if you are out of work. If you are in that situation, you know what I mean. You know about all of those things that you have postponed or not spent your money for. You have forgotten about new cars, new homes, new clothes, new Televisions and other consumer goods. You have forgotten about vacations and a lot of things that you used to think were requirements for a good life.

Just ask yourself one question. If those people who are hurting now were to believe that their job situations were solved, would they want to go out and spend some money? Would it create a lot of consumer spending? Could it really help all that much? Think about them for a minute. Could we possibly see a repeat of what happened when all of our military people came back from World War II?

You remember when our economy exploded after demand for goods and services had not been satisfied for so long due to the Great Depression and fighting a major war?

You see candidate Clinton was right. Jobs are the most important things that count in this country. Forget trying to do anything else unless we do that first. Forget trying to help some poor country where we see children going without food. Nobody has any means to help their fellowman if they don't have jobs to generate income.

Creating more jobs should be the prime objective for everybody. Not just the government, but each and every one of us. When your neighbor is working you live in a good neighborhood. When your neighbor is out of work and worrying about keeping his house and feeding his family then you need to start worrying about your house and family. It is in all of our best **self-interest** to help our Neighbor find a job.

"Wait a minute, Richard, I thought of something else. What would you do if companies cut back on the amount of advertising that they did? How would you come up with all of the money that you needed to fund the jobs tax credit? What would you do then?"

You think that you have me don't you, Mikey. When will you ever learn? Why, there would be another level to go to just like in education. The force continues. We will win this war. We will create jobs for our people. What do you want to do, have a government that doesn't have any money of its own to just print the money? No, if companies stopped or slowed down their advertising then we would use their revenue base.

We would communicate with them. And if all else failed we would hire some of those old Football coaches to communicate with them. The force would increase.

If you still don't think that creating jobs is all that important, go have a little talk with your eight year old daughter. Go into her room and listen to her tape recording of that song that won an Oscar a few years ago. Yes, listen to the theme Song of the movie from Walt Disney, *Aladdin*. Stay in her room for a while and listen to the words and music of "*A Whole New World*".

As you listen to those words, tell her that nothing can be done to help all of those people who are out of work. Tell her that what you and her teacher have been teaching her about building a better Future is not possible. Tell her that it is just too hard. Look into her eyes and tell her. "There you go talking about songs and cartoons. You are starting to make stuff up again--just like you did when you worked for me.

What does a silly song for children have to do with some lazy person looking for a job?"

Well, Bubba, a lot. Don't you know that music has always been used to inspire us to greatness and to overcome problems? Why do you think that the military always uses music and can you ever think of a successful movie that did not have good music? No, you can learn a lot from music. Didn't you know that one of the smartest men who ever lived used a lot of music? His book in the Bible is even called *The Song of Solomon*.

"Okay, you win on that one, but you are living in the past on why companies are letting people go. Business has to modernize and stay ahead of the competition. Business is competing with other countries that have a lower cost of labor than we do in this county. Business has to lower their costs in order to compete with those other lower cost countries."

Is that the reason that you are thinking about spending over three hundred thousand dollars on machines that will replace pharmacist in your pharmacies. I thought all of your stores were in this country. Have you made a deal with somebody to buy up all of the pharmacies in Mexico?

What does the cost of foreign labor have to do with what you pay pharmacist in this Country. Isn't that just an excuse to lay the blame on somebody else. What about all of those kind words that you used to use to tell everybody how your company really knew the value of a pharmacist. Have you forgotten those words?

"But Richard, we have to lower our costs somehow, the government is cutting back on the amount of money that they will pay us for the drugs that we sell to Medicare and Medicaid customers. Why, they are only going to pay us our true costs and give us just a dollar to fill the script. We can't make any money that way with what we have to pay Pharmacists.

We have to change over to using machines and reducing the labor in our products. It may not be the Christian thing to do, but somebody has to make the hard choices. That's what we get paid to do in management--make the hard choices."

Bubba is right. Business is reacting to what is happening in the market for goods and services. Other countries that do not have our level of laws and political concepts are beating us on price. Here in domestic operation, we are trying to cut the price of Healthcare. Both of those concepts involve reducing what business pays to their employees. What can we do? Is this the result of discovering computers and does this mean that machines are going to take over the world?

Is it hopeless? What can be done to increase and save jobs? What can we do? The starting point has to be the knowledge that above everything else, jobs are the most important things to our people. People have to have a means of supporting themselves. None of our goodhearted ideas are possible if people don't have the means to support themselves first.

People will not support your idea if they cannot support themselves. Now with that knowledge that jobs come first, we must act. This cannot just be a noble concept that the people at Harvard and Yale talk about during lunch. We and the government must act. What we have been talking about will work if we want it to work. First we must have a vision of that future.

Do we want to see machines taking our place in that future or do we want to be in that future

"Is that all it will take to provide jobs for the people who want to work? Isn't there something else that we can do?

Yes, Mikey, there is something else that we can do, but you will have to wait a little while. It's getting about time to talk about the deficit and I know that you can't wait for that one. Just hold on till we talk about trade, **NAFTA** and other trade issues. You are in for a big surprise if you are only patient. We are talking about our **Future.**

Do we want that vision of a Future? Then we have to create more jobs for our people. All of them. Do we want more people waiting for that phone to ring or do we want more people working and buying more stuff? Forget Fair and is it a Republican or Democratic solution. Let's help people buy more stuff. It is in our own self-interest.

11 OUR SOLUTION
THE DEFICIT

The **Deficit** is one of the biggest and hardest problems facing us and our future. What is it? Could it be? **One Trillion, Two Trillion or Three Trillion dollars!**

Whatever your answer is it would be wrong. It is that and more. Worse of all it still is going up. It is growing like a Cancer in the body of our fiscal health--a Cancer that takes more and more of the resources than we have in this country.

As **of July 1, 1993**, the total Public Debt outstanding was **$4,249,493,000,000** or **$4.249 Trillion Dollars**. As of this date, Congress also had given the authorization for the National Debt to go as high as **$4.370 Trillion Dollars**. They will probably continue to vote for larger and larger Debt levels.

Is that a big number or what? Is this just a problem of the wicked Eighties or have we always had such a huge deficit?

TRENDS IN FEDERAL DEBT HELD BY THE PUBLIC
(Source President Clinton's 1994 Budget 1st submission)
(Dollar amounts in Billions)

	Debt Held By The Public Current Dollars	Debt held as a % of GDP	by the public as a % of Credit Market Debt	Interest on Debt as a % of total Outlays
1950	219.0	82.4	55.3	11.4
1955	226.6	58.9	43.3	7.6
1960	236.8	46.9	33.7	8.5
1965	260.8	38.9	27.0	8.1
1970	283.2	28.7	20.8	7.9
1975	394.7	26.1	18.4	7.5
1980	709.3	26.8	18.5	10.6
1981	784.2	26.5	18.6	12.1
1982	919.2	29.4	20.0	13.6
1983	1,131.0	34.1	22.1	13.8
1984	1,300.0	35.2	22.4	15.7
1985	1,499.4	37.8	22.8	16.2
1986	1,736.2	41.2	23.1	16.1
1987	1,888.1	42.4	22.7	16.0
1988	2,050.3	42.6	22.6	16.2
1989	2,189.3	42.3	22.2	16.5
1990	2,410.4	44.1	22.7	16.2
1991	2.687.9	47.7	24.3	16.2
1992	2,998.6	51.1	25.8	15.5
1993 estimate	3,303.8	53.5	....	14.5
1994 estimate	3,574.4	54.9	....	14.8
1995 estimate	3,826.9	55.8	....	15.1
1996 estimate	4,052.8	56.3	....	15.6
1997 estimate	4,293.7	56.9	....	15.8
1998 estimate	4,575.7	58.1	....	15.8

.

Gee, those are some really big numbers. No wonder people look back so fondly on the fifties. Back then our National Debt was only 219 Billion Dollars.

"I've heard that the **Deficit** for 1992 was over 290 Billion Dollars. Where does all of the money come from and go?"

THE FEDERAL GOVERNMENT DOLLAR
FISCAL YEAR 1994 ESTIMATE
(Source President Clinton's First Submission)

WHERE IT COMES FROM		WHERE IT GOES	
INDIVIDUAL INCOME TAXES	37%	DIRECT BENEFIT PAYMENTS	
SOCIAL SECURITY	31%	FOR INDIVIDUALS	46%
BORROWING	17%	NATIONALDEFENSE	18%
CORP INCOME TAXES	8%	EDUCATION	14%
OTHER	4%	NET INTEREST	14%
EXCISE TAXES	3%	OTHERFEDERALOPS	6%
		DEPOSITINSURANCE	2%
TOTAL	100%		100%

"Hold on, you mean to tell me that if we did away with almost all of our National Defense that we would still have a **Budget Deficit**? What's that line for Direct Benefit Payment For Individuals? Don't tell me that over 46% of my tax dollars goes to other people?

That's not **Fair**! Where is mine? Maybe that's what they mean about **Entitlement Programs**, especially, if money is coming from the **Rich** and going to the **Poor**. Yeah, I bet that kind of action would be hard to stop."

"Wait a minute Richard, what about the fiscal year 1995 Budget. You are just playing fast and loose with the facts. That is old history. What about the new Budget?"

Okay Mikey, for this one time I will show you what Fiscal 1995 looks like in President Clinton's first submission to Congress. After this we go back to the facts and figures that I bought to this little meeting. Heck, we could spend our entire Time taking about the changing numbers like they do in Washington.
The important thing is what the big picture really shows us. Have you forgotten that are you are in a deep forest? Okay. Here goes.

THE FEDERAL GOVERNMENT DOLLAR
FISCAL YEAR 1995
ESTIMATE
(Source Office of Management and Budget)

WHERE IT COMES FROM		WHERE IT GOES	
INDIVIDUAL INCOME TAXES	39%	DIRECT BENEFIT PAMENTS	
SOCIAL SECURITY	32%	FOR INDIVIDUALS	48%
BORROWING	11%	NATIONALDEFENSE	18%
CORP INCOME TAXES	9%	NET INTEREST	15%
OTHER	4%	STATE AND	
		LOCAL GRANTS	14%
EXCISE TAXES	5%	OTHER FEDERAL OPS	5%
TOTAL	100%		100%

Now on the left side the government has increased the amount of taxes from individuals (2%), social insurance receipts (1%), corporate income taxes (1%) and Excise taxes (2%). The borrowing as a percentage of incoming money has decreased by 6%.

Look on the right side. The government has increased direct benefit payments to individuals (2%), increased net interest expense (1%). They have decreased other Federal ops (1%) and National Defense and Education and other state and local grants have stayed the same. They sure know how to keep the money going to individuals don't they. Sure it is nice to see the borrowing percentage on the left side drop, but when will they make the deficit go away for good?

Will those direct benefit payments to individuals make that hard to do? It sure will make it hard. When will they make the deficit go away? When will They tell me the truth? Has there ever been one Politician that tried to solve this Great financial problem?

No, they have told us that it wasn't too bad. You know, it was only a small portion of our Gross Domestic Product (**GDP**). They have told us that we needed to get all the **Rich** People to pay their **Fair** Share. You know the line about "we can't balance the budget on the backs of

American working Men and Women." Are they still looking to tax the Mexican workers?

Democrats have said that it was the fault of the Republicans. The Republicans have said it was the fault of the Democrats. Both have developed programs that were supposed to reduce the **Deficit**? The **Deficit** still grows and grows and needs more and more of our money now just to pay the interest on that really big debt.

"Didn't President Clinton and all of the Democrats in Congress pass a Budget Reduction Bill to lower the **Deficit**?"

 "No, Bubba, that just reduced the amount of the increase in the **Deficit**."

"I'm confused, Richard, you're not telling me that the **Deficit** is going to keep going up are you? That can't be true? All of those boys in Congress and President Clinton would not mislead me? How can that be?"

Well, Bubba, according to President Clinton's own figures that he used when he developed his deficit reduction program, the **Deficit** will still grow from over $3 Trillion dollars in 1993 to over $4 Trillion dollars by the end of 1997. With all of this talk about reducing the **Deficit,** the **Deficit** will still grow by almost a Trillion more dollars during this time.

Does this seem a little odd? A **Deficit** reduction program that increased the **Deficit**? Why did the Deficit get so large? How can it be really reduced? There is only one way. We have to start paying off the **Deficit** and not spending any more of the money that we do not have.

We have to stop the play on words and all that talk about **Fairness**. Now is the time for real action. We don't have any more time for that shot who game. Have you ever heard any politician say that? No, that's something that is just too hard. You know it would wreck our economy and throw a lot of people out of Work. Well, what do you think is happening now? We have that and a lot more. We don't have a **Future** to look forward to seeing for us or our children.

We have spent the **Future** trying to solve problems that were not solvable like trying to be **Fair** and changing the past.

Can this be turned around? How can we afford to pay off the **Deficit**? "Why, we can't even raise the taxes for the programs that we already have? How can we get people to pay any more taxes? That wouldn't work. Have you lost your mind?"

No, but there is a way to pay off the National Debt. The first step is to get the Federal Government out of the **Fair** Business and make the government pay their bills like any other business. If we used the other "**Future Solutions**" for how government should act and let the market place deal with those other issues then the Government could operate on a balanced budget.

A balanced budget, you know, where The Government only spends what they receive in taxes. No more saying "Never mind, the people wouldn't pay this tax for this benefit, so we will just borrow the money. Leave that to somebody else to pay the freight. We've got to give that benefit to the voters."

In our new **Future**, everybody pays for what they get. Remember pay-as-you-go. There are no free lunches. There also are no bad guys just citizens. No, we won't play like **Robin Hood** and Rob from the **Rich** and give to the **Poor**. That's how you end up with all **Poor** people. So the Government is now under control, but what about that **Deficit** isn't it still there and growing like a cancer?

Yes, it is and it's time for some major surgery. We are going to operate on the **Deficit**. We are going to cut it up into little pieces and make it go away. We have gotten the patient off the cigarettes. Now we are going to cut out the Cancer.

What tools can we possibly use to pay off the **Deficit**? What does the government have that could be used to pay off the **Deficit**? The Government has **Assets**. The Federal Government owns a lot of **Assets**. When a company is selling out of a major business to another company then it sells those assets in the business that it is selling and no longer operating. Our Federal Government would do the same thing. We are going to:

Sell the Grand Canyon.

Okay, get up off of the floor. I didn't say pass the jelly. Some people are just too sensitive. Lighten up and be more accepting of what other people have to say.

Got you didn't I? "That would be horrible. Why, we wouldn't have anything to leave our children. You also couldn't trust business to preserve our national treasures. Why, there is no telling what they would do with the Grand Canyon or the rest of our country's treasures. Some real estate tycoon is liable to build condos and ruin that beautiful natural wonder. We can't do that!"

But, the point is that we have already done that. That's what happens when you keep running up bills and not paying them. What other solutions do you have? Do you want to assess a special tax for every man, woman and child in this country. Would that work? Not really.

To retire the national debt of $4.4 Trillion dollars we would have to assess 200 million Americans $22,000 in extra taxes. And I mean everybody, not just the people who **we think** could **afford** to pay it. Doesn't sound too realistic does it?

"Now, Richard what would it cost us to pay that off over time? You know something like a mortgage. Say, maybe over 30 years. What would that cost?" How does almost $2,000 a year for 30 years strike you and the rest of the 200 million Americans? That is what $22,000 costs to finance over 30 years. Do you want to start the ball rolling?

Do you think that everybody would agree to pay that?" What about just "A walk away" from our debt like in Bankruptcy?

Do you want to tell the people who hold the government debt that we're not going to pay our debts? A lot of retired people who depend on that income and money for their retirement needs. No, that would just create more **Poor** people for the **Fair Corporations**. Is there any other solution that might work? Forget a solution that sounds good.

Will it work? No, our only realistic solution is to pay off the **Deficit** by selling the assets that the Government owns. This country is supposed to be owned by people, not by the governments. The Government is not supposed to own the country. We are all supposed to have an opportunity to own things here. Let's make the government sell their assets to pay off the **Deficit**.

Now, what are we talking about. Just any old asset or what? No, we are talking about all the lands, parks, buildings, equipment that's not generating enough money to cover the cost of that asset and a decent return on that investment. Yes, I am saying that the Government has to look at those assets and how they are used.

According to the U. S. General Services *Administration's Summary Report of Real Property Owned by the United States Throughout the World as of September 30, 1989,* the Federal Government has over 32,000 installations worldwide. These installations are situated on 662,411,625 acres of land with 454,745 buildings occupying over 2,834 million square feet. The government paid over $1.72 billion for this property. I bet it is worth a whole lot more than that to a business that knows how to make an investment pay for itself.

No, it is not all used by the military. The Defense department only accounts for 3.9% of the total land owned by the Federal Government under the authority of the Defense Department in the United States and Foreign Countries. The Interior department is the biggest Land owner in the Federal Government and owns 432.4 million acres of Land or 65.3% of the total Land owned by the Federal Government. The Agricultural department owns over 201 million acres of Land and over 30% of the total Federal Land. Whew, that's a lot of land. I wonder how it breaks down by agency.

Table 2.4 Principal Land Controlling Agencies
By Major Geographical Areas Total in Millions

Agencies	U.S.	Outlying Areas U.S.	Foreign Countries	Total	% of Total.
Interior	432.4	0.2	(1)	432.6	65.3
Agriculture	201.9	(1)	(1)	201.9	30.5
Defense	26.0	(1)	(1)	26.0	3.9
All other agencies (26)	2.1	(1)	(1)	2.2	0.4
Total, all agencies	662.4	0.3	(1)	662.7	100.0

(1) Negligible

Table 3.1 Federal Real Property   By Major Reporting Agency

Agency	Land Acres (in millions)	Square Feet (in millions)	Total Cost (in millions	% of Total
Defense	26.0	1,935.9	$79,864	48.6
Interior	432.4	87.3	17,095	10.4
Energy	0.1	106.8	10,822	6.6
Agriculture	201.9	32.9	9,073	5.5
Tenn. Valley Authority	1.0	3.6	8,750	5.3
U.S. Postal Services	(1)	137.4	8,009	4.9
Veterans Affairs	(1)	122.8	7,351	4.5
General Services Admin.	(1)	231.9	6,248	3.8
National Aeronautics and Space Admin.	0.3	43.1	5,086	3.1
Transportation	0.1	33.1	1,765	1.1
Other Agencies (17	0.6	71.4	10,347	6.2
Total all agencies	662.4	2,806.2	$164,410	100%

(1) Less than 0.1 million

Let's take the Park Service whose figures are included in the Interior Agency for a minute. Does the Government charge a sufficient fee to the public for using all of those parks? Does it generate enough money to pay for all of the upkeep of those parks? No, that would not be **Fair**.

That is why we have to pay extra taxes, so people can afford to go see the parks. That is also what got us into this trouble in the first place--doing things that we could not afford and pushing the cost off into the future.

Back to the Grand Canyon for a minute. The government would put the Grand Canyon up for bid to any business in the private sector that wanted to purchase the Grand Canyon. The highest bidder would get to buy the Grand Canyon or any other asset that the Government was selling.

Wait a minute, Mikey, you have been quiet for a long time. Slow down and I'll answer all of your questions. Let's take the first question about preserving this asset for our children.

You see, I have a big surprise for you. Any business or individual that bought the Grand Canyon or Land in Alaska would not just go out and rape the land. That would not be in their **self-interest**. Why would they destroy a valuable asset like that? No, that would not be very smart.

What did you say, Bubba, "We couldn't do that with all of the Environmental Laws and the **EPA.**" Well, just ask yourself, "Who wrote those laws? Men or **God**?" If those **EPA** laws were written by men, then men can change those laws. It all boils down to two things. **Time and Money**. How do we want to spend both of them? Do we want to spend all of our money on having the cleanest and most environmental safe country where nobody has a job or do we look at this issue like anything else that requires our time and money?

We also don't want to put a lot of restrictions on the businesses that buy those Government Assets. We can't continue to let the Government be in the **Fair** business.

We have to let the use of those assets be a function of their value and the Market for those assets. No, any serious business that bought a major government asset would want to see that asset used for as long and as profitable as possible. It would be in their own **self-interest** to maintain and grow that asset. Why would they want to destroy the Grand Canyon? Why, they might even figure out how to improve the service so they could get more people to visit that asset.

Why would they do that? **To Make More Money.**

How would they pay for that asset? Are you talking about another Government War Surplus program? You know like in the early days of the Resolution Trust Corporation (**RTC**). You remember when the **RTC** had all of those assets that the failed Savings and Loans (**S & L's**) left the **RTC** when the **RTC** bailed them out and the **RTC** tried to give away assets in failed **S & L's**. Seems as if all that did was make a lot of people, with money, rich. How would they pay for the assets that were to be sold?

They would assume parts of the National Debt. We would get them to take over paying off the National Debt. Now you really need to sit down. Yes, we would sell some of our Government Assets and get the people and companies that bought those Assets to take over Paying the interest and principal payments on the National Debt. Just like selling a house with an assumable Mortgage. How would it work? Let's take the park system for a starter. The government could put the park system up for auction according to the Geographic area of the country. The Grand Canyon would be in the Southwestern region and would be part of other Federal Parks in that area of the country.

Let's assume for the purpose of analysis (That's an old Accounting Term that we use to try and make Mikey be quiet while we are talking) that the Southwestern parks were valued by the market place at $10 billion and that was the highest bid. The company that had purchased those assets from the Federal Government would assume part of the Federal Government's debt of $10 Billion. Okay so far?

Now, we are going to look at this debt a little differently than the politicians have been handling the national debt in the past. We are going to develop a way to pay it off over time. Yes, we are going to treat it very much as if it was a Veteran's Home Loan. The national debt that is assumed with the sale of Government assets would be paid off and retired over a 30 year period.

"But, wait a minute, Richard, not all of the National Debt is long term. Some of that debt is in short term financing of less than a year. What would we do about that?"

That, Clem, is a lot more complicated, but I promise if you stick with me, we will have a real good solution. Now, that's not like "The check is in the mail or "Trust me" but there will be a solution. Let's just look at the long term financing, first.

We have sold a portion of the Park Service for $10 Billion, right. Are you with me so far? Assume for a minute that the interest currently being paid by the Federal Government is about 8%. The new debt on this Park Service would be 9% and would be fully guaranteed by the Federal Government.

The extra 1% would be charged by the Federal government to cover administrative costs of the program. Interest and Principal Payments would be paid each month to the Federal Government in advance.

New debt instruments would be drawn up by the Federal Government showing the people and companies that held the old debt what their new investments would pay to them. Payment schedules would be established that disclosed principle and interest to be paid to the holders of this new debt over the 30 year payment period.

The Federal Government would then send payments for both interest and principal to the holders of this new debt each month. The government would have been paid by the people who had bought the government asset in the previous month. In the example of our $10 Billion Park Debt, this would mean that whoever bought those Park assets would have to pay about $73 Million a month or over $880 Million a year for 30 years just in principle and interest. Is this Government asset generating that kind of money after all other expenses now? What do you think?

No, they are not, because if they were then we wouldn't have run up all of this Debt. Are we just talking about the park service? No, the Grand Canyon is just one example. The real money would come from the lands, buildings equipment and other assets that the Federal Government owns.

Hold, on Mikey, yes I am talking about mineral rights and oil and timber leases. I am also talking about military bases that we no longer need to fight yesterday's war. Pieces of this country's wealth that we don't want the Government to own and are mortgaged already by all that debt.

You remember all of that talk about converting our unneeded military structures (**Assets**) into high tech manufacturing. That's what I am talking about here. Let's come up with a way that can move this along. Yes, let's make it easy for the market place to convert those unneeded military assets over to peace time uses. This would be a real Peace dividend. Selling unneeded military bases and other government assets would work similar to the example of Parks. The assets would be sold to the highest bidder and involve the same financing.

The only stipulation to this bidding for all of the Government Assets would be that all bidders would have to put up a refundable deposit with their bid. They would also have to prepay 3 months' interest and principal payments on the debt. We want serious bidders here not tire kickers. The winning bidder would then be free to utilize that asset as long as they were paying the interest and principal payments. If they stopped paying their payments to the federal government then the Government could foreclose on those assets like any other property. The same would be true if they were not paying any of their other expenses. The Government would retain a lien on these assets and make sure that the assets were maintained in good market condition.

Yes, I am ready, now, to talk about the short term debt that the federal government has. There is a lot of that out there. What Industry uses those short term government debts? Right, the Banking Industry and other investment institutions.

Well, grab on to your chair, it's really going to get bumpy here. We are going to Federalize the Banking Industry.

Are you okay, Pat? You look as if somebody just spit in your Green Beer. Yes, we are going to Federalize or Nationalize all of the Banks in this country. Why, would we want to do that anyway? Because, since the Great Depression we have let our Banks operate as no other business in this country has operated. The Federal Government has been there to bail out Banks when they mess up and lose money.

The Government through the Federal Deposit Insurance Corporation (**FDIC**) has guaranteed all of the money in banks in this country. The Federal Government is in the National Bank business already. The only difference now versus our **Future Solution** is that the Banks get to keep all the profits. The only thing that the government gets to keep is to pick up the tab when banks fail. Now that's a great deal. Yeah, a great deal for the owners of the bank.

What kind of deal is that? For the purpose of Analysis (Be quiet Mikey), assume that a Savings and Loan Institute (**S &L**) has to have equity or capital equal to around 5% of their assets at any given time. That means that Savings and Loans can make loans equal to around 20 times the amount of money that they have placed at risk in the **S & L**. Now that is great leverage on your money.

In our example the people that owned an **S & L** could put up a million dollars of their money and make $20 million in loans that they would receive $2 million in interest income at an interest rate of 10%. They could also do some other things. They could pay themselves a salary of $1 million dollars a year. Let's say that they did this for ten years, paid themselves $10 million in salaries and slowly made bad loans. What would they have?

They would have received $10 million dollars during this time plus cash and dividends that they had been able to funnel to themselves. They also probably would be bankrupt. They would have funneled a lot of cash out of the bank. Yes, they had put up $ 1 million in capital and paid themselves over $ 2 million in Cash plus dividends. They also could let the Federal Government take over the Failed **S & L** when they became Bankrupt.

Did all of the **S & L**'s end up this way? No, but it was a great deal for the people who figured out how the system worked. Great for them, but not great for all of us. In our **Future Solution**, the Federal Government would purchase Banks and Savings and Loan Institutes with new Federal Mortgages similar to the new Mortgages that would be created to retire old government debt.

The purchase price for those Banks and Savings and Loan Institutes would be the amount of Certified Capital that each institution had on their books at a specific purchase date. Payments on this new government debt would be over some reasonable period of time. Payments would also be adjusted if the audited capital was less than the amount of Capital on the Banks or **S&L**'s books.

Adjustments would also be made for any bad loans that Banks or Financial Institutions had not already written off against their Capital. All financial institutions covered by **FDIC** insurance would be covered by this. All other financial institutions that did not have **FDIC** insurance would not be covered.

Now, back to the short term Federal Government financing that still would exist. If the Federal Government is going to become a National Bank, then that financing would still be needed. Call it a new version of money market certificates or pass book interest. The new Government Bank would use these funds to make loans to people, just as Banks operate now. The only difference would be that the Government would get to make a profit that could be used to fund some of the needs that we might have such as an emergency flood or any other national disaster that we had not foreseen. Does all of this mean that the people who work down at the Unemployment Commission and the Internal Revenue Service would be working at all of the new Government Banks? No, what I am talking about is much closer to the example of The Tennessee Valley Authority (TVA). The TVA is a Federal Agency but it operates like a private business that has products and services to sell to its customers.

No, we want really good professional bankers working for the New National Banks. The only Difference will be in how the banks are owned. If your **self-interest** is in being the best banker that you can be, there will be a great and exciting opportunity for you in the New Government Banks.

Why would anyone even suggest that the Federal Government get into owning banks? How does this fit in with the other solutions of getting the Federal Government out of our lives? Is it only the profit that you don't like going to all those greedy Bankers?" No, Bankers are not any greedier than anybody else. They just have had such a great deal for too long. A deal that has to change. Really change.

You see, think back to **The Great Experiment of FDR**. We had to do something to get people trusting in Banks again. People were afraid of trusting banks with safe guarding their money. Banks were failing right and left and people couldn't get hold of their money in the Banks to pay their bills when they really needed their money. Creditors were forcing more and more people into tight spots. Something had to be done to restore the confidence in the Banking System.

FDR's solution was to have the Federal Government guarantee the people's money that they had put in the Banks. That way people could be secure in knowing that The money would always be there. As time went by, the government kept increasing the amount of this guarantee until it was over $100,000. Now we are talking real money.

The solution that **FDR** came up with was only the beginning. At some point, the Government would have been unable to afford to give this guarantee. Banks would not have been able to afford the **FDIC** insurance premiums that would have supported this insurance.

The Federal Government also didn't use the money that Banks paid in premiums like normal insurance works. You know, invest the premium money so that it increases to where you have the money to pay off the big claim that you insured in the first place.

You know like in Social Security: don't invest the money so it is there to pay Claims, just pay out all that you have coming in and let somebody else worry about the **Future**. No, the Federal Government even used the **Fair** Principle in regulating Banks and Saving and Loan Institutes. The Government was afraid that if they charged sufficient insurance premiums to cover the projected cost for **FDIC** insurance, then, Banks would either go out of business or this would force up interest rates to the Public, so they put off that cost to the Future.

That Future is now and it is called the cost of funding the Savings and Loans mess under the Resolution Trust Corporation (**RTC**). Just as in the old commercial we have a choice to "Either pay me a little now or pay me a lot later." Our political leaders have always chosen to let somebody else pay a lot later. Our new Federal Banks would be organized as an agency of the Federal Government but would look similar to a regular Business Corporation. This National Bank would have a board of directors elected by the people of the United States. They would serve one six year term and each state would have two directors.

Now, hold on, Mikey, and all of the rest of you representative government experts. I know that this approach gives more weight to small states but what we want here is that all of the states are represented and that we keep it a small group. We don't want to have another **Congress** on our hands. We want some smart decision Makers overseeing the operations of this bank. We also would do away with the Fed and that system.

If you keep using the **Fed** as the Banking Referee you eventually end we something that is just too big to **Fail.** The board of directors of this new Government Agency would meet just like a private corporation annually and at other times as needed. They would be paid very much the same way that private corporations pay outside directors for the use of their time and effort.

The National Bank would be organized along State and local boundaries. Each State would be considered a major division of the National Bank and state, counties and cities would be considered to be regions as needed. The local banks, Regions and Divisions would be staffed as needed to meet the needs of those areas. The employees of each bank would be all operational in nature with staff persons as needed to be employed at the Regional, State and National levels.

What was that you were hollering about, Mikey? "How would the Pension Plans companies invest their money that people had given them for their retirement needs? There wouldn't be a lot of federal debt or T Bills for them to invest their money in?" Well, Mikey that wouldn't be so bad would it? The Good news would be the no more debt that takes over $22,000 for each American to pay off. Could you use An extra $22,000? To answer your question, there would still be investments that could be made in American Business that produce jobs.

Companies would still need capital to fund their growth and the creation of new jobs. On a practical matter, Pension Funds could still invest some of their cash short term in short term debt that the National Bank would issue. Right, short term debt that the National Bank would use for making loans, just as the local Banks do now.

What does all of this mean? This means that we have to be realistic about **Our Solutions**. Just as **FDR** concluded, it is vitally important, for all of us to have a reliable Banking system that people and business can count on being there. In the past, we tried to let business operate this Banking system with the Federal Government standing by with some regulation and always there to safeguard the depositor's money.

That system didn't work because the government didn't operate like a true Insurance company. The government didn't charge high enough premiums to the Banks that were insured under the **FDIC**. The government also didn't invest those premiums so that money would be there to pay for the problems that were going to occur in the Banks and **S&L's**. Just like all previous government programs, they spent the money. Any problems in the Banking system had to be funded by new spending and money that wasn't there and the Deficit kept growing and growing. **Our Future Solution** for the Deficit is simple and realistic.

211

1. Get the Government out of the Fair Business.
2. Reduce the size of the Federal Government.
3. Reduce the number of laws and the Government's Ability to create more laws.
4. Sell Government assets to pay off the existing Deficit.
5. Force the Federal Government to operate on A-Pay-As-you-go system.
6. Nationalize the Banking System and operate Banking As any other Business.

This last concept is most important. We don't want the new Government Banking System to operate as other government agencies have in the past. We want this system to operate as a money making business. We want it to have a very good business plan and not need any help from the taxpayers. We want it to be self-sufficient and attract people who want to be in the business of being Bankers.

Will all of this work? Yes, it will if we truly want it to work. It will not work if we want something else. If we want to fool ourselves and say that the government is different and the government can keep spending more and more money that it doesn't have. If we finally realize the government doesn't have any money. The government only **Has money that it takes from all of us**.

All right, Mikey, what is it that you want to say? What do you mean, what would we do if the assets that were to be sold to the public to retire the national debt were less than the Four or Five Trillion dollars that we needed to come up with to pay off that debt?

Good question. Think about what you have just said.

The government does not have the means to pay off all of that debt. Wouldn't we have gotten to this point sooner or later? How long would we have put off that day of final action?

Well, I still have some faith in the words of Adam Smith. You remember him and *The Wealth of a Nation*. No, I believe that there is enough value in all of the Government assets to pay off that debt. Guess what the other alternative is? Do you remember how much it would cost for everybody in this country to pay off that debt? Yes,

$2,000.00 a person for the next 30 years.

No, I think that we can come up with enough value in the Government assets to use that approach. We will also remember not to try to pass the buck and get the government to mortgage our Futures again.

What about waiting for a **Hero**? "Yes, we don't really have to make major changes. Someday, **white knight or a really bright maybe even a really clean black knight** will come along and he will have all of the answers and fix this problem. Yes, we can wait." That is what we have been doing all of this time. Waiting for a Hero that would make it all go away.

"What's happened to all of the **Great Men**? When will there be another great leader? You know, another Great Man who can solve all of our problems." Well, we have had those men and guess what? Most of them have thrown the "**Stupid Switch.**"

"But Richard, the American People will not be that stupid. They would not listen to some one that just told them what they wanted to hear. No one would follow a President that just talked about "**Hope and Change**", without any real plan to help us grow as a Country. Why that would probability make the Deficit grow to something unheard of. Our **Deficit** is only around **$3 Trillion dollars now in** 1993.

Nobody thinks that it will ever get out of control. Do you think that it will explode to what? $5 Trillion or $10 Trillion?

You are dreaming if you think that the people would every let a Real Leader put us in that kind of debt. There would have to be some Great Depression for us to give up our values for that."

No, All of you it can and it could be much worse. 2013? Trillions and Trillions of National Debt and Growing.

12 OUR SOLUTION
STOP THROWING
THE STUPID SWITCH

"Richard, what in the world is the **Stupid Switch**? Is that some far out financial theory?" No, Bubba, that is some good old common sense that you develop when you have a chance to look at the world from a fresh perspective.

You see, Bubba, we keep forgetting that there are still two types of problems in this world: man made problems and problems that we can only explain as Problems that God has to deal with. I bet you thought that I was just going to let that slide and not even try to talk about that. Well, you are wrong, Bubba, if we let that slide, then we are going to repeat a lot of the mistakes of the past. You know, try to throw some money at that problem and hope that it will go away.

Do we want to go through the pain and effort to reduce the budget deficit and get the government out of playing god, only to be waiting for somebody else to come along and tell us that it was not our fault? Somebody who will tell us that it was somebody else that caused all of the problems. Somebody that will be quick to lay all of the blame on somebody that we don't understand. No, we don't want to turn on that **Stupid Switch** ever again for that.

Hold on, Clem, I know that doesn't fully explain the **Stupid Switch**. Give me a minute. This is real hard to talk about and you have to be very careful when you start talking about **God**. Kind of like when you were a kid and you started to think about how you got here and where you were going. You know the time that you let your mind think about your place in the universe.

Well, since the beginning of time, men and women have asked

themselves the question of why they were here and is there a **God**? To a lot of us, that question was answered by **Jesus Christ**. Yes, to me, there is a **God** and He is real and He is my **Savior**. Does that mean that there is no other way? Yes, for me there is only one **God** and **His Solution** comes through **Jesus Christ**. But **God** is real and alive in this world and He is at work. Some of our problems will never be fixed by men. The conflict that has existed between the Arabs and the Jews will never be solved by any of us. That is a problem that only **God** can resolve. The whole problem started over 3,000 years ago and the solution is in his hands not in ours.

You know, it seems that every human being has a special switch in our body. We never see that switch. It can't be seen on an **X RAY** or an **MRI**, but it is there. A person could live a long time and never know it was there. Let that person think that **God** doesn't exist and try to start solving some of the **God** problems and whoops there goes the **Stupid Switch,** and what a mess it makes.

The stupid switch reminds me of a man who had a son who was considered to be very dumb. His father had tried everything that he knew to help his son learn how to think. Nothing seemed to work and finally his father gave up. He gave his son a walking cane with the instructions to walk with this cane until the son found someone else who the son thought was dumber than himself.

When the father was about to die, his son visited him on his death bed. The son still had the cane that his father had given him years ago. The son asked the father if he was prepared to die and if he knew where he was going. The father told him that was still a mystery to him and he had never thought much about that. The son took his cane and gave it to his sick father and said, "Here you will need this where you are going."

Yes, there is a **Stupid Switch** in all of us. That switch is there to be turned on when we think that we are all alone. That switch is there to remind us that there are some things that we cannot solve, regardless of how smart and talented we think that we are. Have we ever seen the Stupid Switch being turned on in any of our government leaders? Yes, throughout History, there have been people who thought that they could solve God problems or thought that they were **God**.

Remember good old **LBJ**? **Yeah, President Johnson**. He thought that we could do something that had never been achieved in all of recorded history. He declared war on poverty. If we only listened to him, we could have eliminated poverty for good. We would not have any more people who were poor.

That was almost 50 years ago and the Federal Government is still trying to eliminate poverty.   Has the government been successful? No, after spending Billions and Billions of dollars we still have **Poor** people and we probably will always have **Poor** people.

You see the government has turned on the **Stupid Switch** and they are trying to pretend that they are **God**. You know, if we only spend enough money we can change people. We can change people's values and abilities and eliminate poverty forever.

You want to know a secret? There is only one guaranteed way to eliminate all of the **Poor** people. Take away everything from everybody and then everybody will be in the same boat. That was what they tried to do in Russia and Eastern Europe, but they finally got smart and realized that trying to tear down the **Rich** people did not benefit the majority of the people.

All that did was make more **Poor** people and helped a lot of government people make a good living and live in fine houses. No, our **Stupid Switch** has been wide open for a long time. It sounded good to have a war on poverty and to have the government provide Welfare for people who were **Poor**. Did that enable them to stop being **Poor**? No government or any person can snap their fingers and change people like that. That is in the province of **God**. You have to want to succeed and have a burning desire to provide for yourself.

Now hold on, Mikey. Don't start hitting me over the head with a bunch of **Fairness** talk. You haven't had to walk two miles to school and get by on one pair of shoes a year. You haven't had to drink powered milk that was mixed with a little bit of real milk to try to fool you when you were a kid or wear clothes until they rotted from washing in cheap soap.

"Now, Richard, I told you not to talk like that. Why, you will make everybody think that we were all just a bunch of poor white trash. You know that you always got a real nice pair of shoes from Mr. Frizzlard's and I bought the best pair of pants that they would let me charge at Mr. Hancock's Dry Goods store. You never went for wanting the essential things. Why, I even sacrificed so you could have a new sport coat and pants and be part of the little people beauty contest. Now, you tell that Mikey fellow the truth."

Okay mom, maybe, it was only 1.895 miles to walk to school and the Buster Brown's with greap soles were okay. Mom did forget about Dad mixing up the real milk and the powered milk that he bought once a month at the Navy Exchange when he loaded up on Lucky Strikes cigarettes.

And you were right, Mom, you didn't use cheap soap and the pants and the shirts were okay. You did forget about dad not letting us get our hair cut in a flat top like every other kid. No, for us it was a **GI Special**. He saved two bits that way. And mom was right about her sacrificing for me to enter that cute little person beauty contest. I sure wish that I hadn't come in second to that **Hart** fellow.

I got back at him though when I pushed him in the goldfish pond at my cousin's birthday party. No, what pulls a kid out of poverty or not having a lot is a burning desire in that kid to be successful and good family values.

God and your mother give that to you. Your mother may even pass on her pride and competitive spirit without you or her ever knowing that pride and competitiveness may be the secret of your success. No government can ever give that to you regardless of the money that it spends. When the government says that it is going to eliminate poverty it is spreading: **The Big Lie**. A lie that sounds so good. A lie that will only cost us more and more. A good example of this is what the government trics to do with the concept of the **Earned Income Credit**.

You see if you are married and have kids but you only make a certain level of income the Federal Government says that is not **Fair** and gives you some extra money. It's just not **Fair** that anybody that is working for a living is living in poverty. What's wrong with this? Shouldn't everybody that works for a living not be in poverty?

Well, you are asking the wrong question. What is the value that all of us establish for this work? That is what determines what we all receive for our labor. It may not seem **Fair** or right that Doctors make more money than people who sweep the floors but we are the ones that have set that value. We are the ones that send our money to whomever or whatever companies employ that person. We establish value for the skills, training, effort and talents that are required to sweep our floors.

"Wait a minute, Richard; you are not one of the **Brothers**. You haven't had it so rough. You are a college boy. You had it easy. You never had to bend and break you back sweeping and cleaning floors like I have."

What do you mean, I haven't ever swept floors. Have you ever worked part time at Sears on the Midnight shift? When do you think they clean all of those floors and carpets? Yes, they hire some low skilled people to do that work. They hire some people who don't make enough money in their day jobs to come into the store and do that work. It pays minimum wages and is real boring. It can also make some people determined to educate themselves and find a better paying job.

Does that kind of work make everybody so mad and determined to find a way to train themselves for a better way of making a living?

No, that is part of our problem. That is in each person's own hands.
I remember when I was going to college on the GI bill. Even though I was getting a pretty good check from the government to go to school, I still needed more money for some of the other things that I just knew I needed. Yes, I wanted some **Fooling Around Money**. Money that went for the things that twenty-three year old students have to have. For those kinds of things I had to work.

I found a job in a Factory at night that manufactured parts for automotive brakes. It was real hard work. Each day after college from 3:30 PM till 12:00 AM, I worked in that factory. Five nights a week and sometimes on Saturday and sometime a little over time. It was rough! Do you know how I made it through each day?

Anytime that I started to feel sorry for myself and all of this hard work that I was doing, I thought about my major goal. I thought about someday graduating from college and becoming a Lawyer. I was going to graduate from college and leave all of that hard factory work behind. I had **A Plan**. I was going to make something of my life. The future belonged to me. I had **A Plan**.

What about all of the other people who worked at that plant? How did some of them feel? How did the people who weren't going to college and were working in that factory feel? Did they have a plan? What made them get up in the middle of the afternoon and go to that dirty and grimy factory where each day and each hour were the same? Pick up a piece of metal and put it in a machine.

Wait while the machine went through its process. Take out the finished brake drum and put it in the stack of finished products. Pick up another piece of metal and start all over again. Do it over and over until the first bell sounded for the first break. Every hour and day more and more of the same.

One day, I asked somebody that was about my own age who worked at a machine next to me. "How do you do this? What is your plan? Why are you working here?" Do you know what his plan was? He said, "This is what I do for a living. I come here and I work. This is my job. **There is no plan**. I don't dream about tomorrow. It will be the same. I do this to live. This is how I pay the bills. All of this is just a job. **I work and they pay me money**. I work and they pay me. No dreams. No hopes. **Just work and Pay.**"

Did he think about the value of his efforts and work? Did he think about how it was valued by the market place? Did he think about how valuable the brake drums were that he was making? No, he thought about work and they pay me. Work and pay. Did he understand that people got paid in the value of their effort to produce that product or service? No, somebody else could think about that.

Somebody else could establish that value. To him it was only work and pay.

Work and pay. That was all that he thought about until that last bell sounded for the end of this day. He left the valuing up to somebody else. Kind of makes you mad doesn't it? All of us are the ones that cause **Poor** people to have to work for wages that won't keep them out of poverty.

Yes, that is what I said. We are the ones that determine what wages are paid for all of the work and effort that produces our goods and services and there is nothing that we can do about that. There is no evil person controlling all of our goods and services. Everything has value and that value is represented by prices on goods and services.

We will always place some value on the works of others. That is only human nature. Right now in our society, we will pay more money to somebody for a nice car than we will pay somebody to come and clean our house. We have valued the Labor of producing a car higher than the labor to clean our homes.

What the government has done is to try to take away money from successful people and give that money to people that don't have the skills that command a high wage. They have even convinced a lot of us that will work. The problem is that there is not enough money in the world to eliminate this problem. It is a **God** problem. What can we do?

Is there no hope for us? What can be done with the problem of poverty? Is everything hopeless? Do we just hope that the problem will go away? We have ours and let them get theirs. Think of yourself first. Forget them. No, that is not the way. That's the way back to the dark places. There are ways to try to help people who are not as fortunate as we are. You can find some of these places where leaders are looking toward the future.

Some of the leaders in Memphis, Tennessee are even looking for solutions to these problems.

One of the major problems that we have now in Memphis, Tennessee is how to provide affordable housing for **Poor** people. This city has struggled with this problem for years. Several different Mayors and other elected officials have tried to develop programs that would make housing more affordable for the people in Memphis, Tennessee.

What is making this problem so difficult for the government of Memphis to solve is that there are a lot of **Poor** people in Memphis as you can see from the table that was published in the *Memphis Commercial Appeal.*

Affordable Housing in Memphis

Income Range* (Less Than)	Percent of population	Rent Affordability/month** (less than)	Mortgage affordability/***
$ 5,000	11.7	$ 125	$ 145
$10,000	11.5	$ 250	$ 292
$12,500	6.0	$ 312	$ 365
$15,000	4.7	$ 374	$ 437
$17,500	5.7	$ 437	$ 510
$20,000	4.9	$ 499	$ 583
$22,500	5.2	$ 562	$ 656
$25,000	4.3	$ 624	$ 729
$27,500	4.7	$ 687	$ 802
$30,000	3.5	$ 749	$ 875
$32,500	4.6	$ 812	$ 948
$35,000	3.0	$ 874	$1,020
$37,500	3.3	$ 937	$1,094
$40,000	2.6	$ 999	$1,167
$42,500	2.9	$1,062	$1,239
$45,000	2.0	$1,124	$1,312
$47,500	2.0	$1,187	$1,394
$50,000	1.6	$1,250	$1.458
$50,000 & above	15.6	$1,250+	$1,458+

*   1990 U.S. Census
**   Assumes 30% of income spent on rent/utilities.
***   Assumes 35% of income spent on mortgage and other home costs.
Source: Division of Housing and Community Development, Memphis, Tennessee.

According to this article that was published during this time, one out of every five households earns less than $10,000 a year and can only afford to spend $250 a month or less on rent or $292 a month or less on a mortgage, according to statistics compiled by the city's Division of Housing and Community Development.

The median income among blacks in Memphis is $16,946; among whites, $35,054. A couple of other things jump out at me. Only 15.6 % of the households in Memphis, Tennessee earn $50,000 or more a year. You know $50,000 a year sounds like a lot of money, but I don't think that those people have lots of money just lying around that we could use to give to the people earning less than $10,000 a year. You also don't have to be a Certified Public Accountant to figure out that over half of the households in Memphis, Tennessee make less than $22,500 a year. That raises another important question.

Memphis, Tennessee was trying to get a National Football League franchise at the present time. How can all of those people earning less than $22,500 a year afford to go to a professional football game when tickets will probably cost over $20.00 a piece? Would that be **Fair**?

Well, it may not have been **Fair** to the owners of all of the other National Football League teams because Memphis didn't get a franchise. A lot of people sure talked a lot about it not being **Fair**. Could the owners of all those other Football teams have seen this same information about the income levels in Memphis? Why, that would definitely not have been **Fair**!

To be **Fair** the current Mayor at that time, Mr. W. W. Herenton and the city government in Memphis, Tennessee realizes that our problem is not too many **Rich** People but Too many **Poor** people. They have resisted the negative urge to create programs that tried to tax and penalize people who had some money. One reason is that There is a shortage of those kinds of folks. The other problem is that those kinds of folks can always move somewhere else.

No, the government leaders of the city of Memphis, Tennessee are always trying their best to attract more high paying business to the city. We had a very bright and Talented Mayor who was our Superintendent of Education for several years. He knew that the major part of the solution is to make Memphis more attractive to business that will employ high paying workers.

The city's Director of Housing and Community Development, Robert Lipscomb went on to say in the same article in the *Commercial Appeal*, "it doesn't take a financial genius to figure out that we don't have enough money to do all that needs to be done. I can have all kinds of programs, but you've got to have money to do them. Our problem is not housing, it is economic development. Our problem is that we've got to get people decent paying jobs to be able to afford decent housing."

Sounds like a very smart man doesn't he? He has seen **The Future** and **The Future** lies in encouraging people to become more productive and earn more. The future does not lie in taking from somebody else. It lies in helping people to be the best that they can be.

The Mayor of Memphis, Tennessee, W. W. Herenton, has also outlined several initiatives to reduce the cost of building and rehabilitating affordable homes in the city according to the *Commercial Appeal*. "The proposals, which include reductions or a waiver of development fees, could save a builder up to $2,000 on the construction of a new home," **The Mayor** said in this same article.

What all of this means is that the Mayor and the leadership of Memphis, Tennessee are turning off the **Stupid Switch** and are looking for a **Future Solution**? They are trying to help people without trying to take away from somebody else. That is a big difference. They could have gone to the press with a lot of talk about how greedy all the developers were being in not selling houses for less money. They could have even talked about it not being **Fair**.

No, they didn't do that because they knew that was not the problem. With Mayor Herenton's background in education, he knew that negative reinforcement was not as effective as coming up with programs that would appeal to the developer's own **self-interest**. He asked the important question. What could he do to make it easier for developers to build more affordable housing in Memphis, Tennessee? **Other governments could learn from that approach.**

Our first step as people who want to improve our lives and the lives of others is to realize that we are only human. We are not **God**. There are limits to what we can do with other people. We can have all of the great Education and Training in the world and we will still have people that will fail in life.

We will still have people who will not go to school and will not live their lives according to our values. We can always give them a chance to change and an opportunity to succeed or to fail but the choice is always theirs. We must also have charity and compassion.

All of the government programs have not had a lot of compassion. They may have started out that way but as the government's program failed to achieve its objectives and grew more and more expensive it got nasty. It got so nasty that the government has resorted to class warfare. Yes, there is a war going on in our country. It is a war between the **Haves and the Have Nots**.

Because the government started this war on poverty it had no choice but to play the **Haves against the Have Nots. It was called being Fair.**

Remember how the Russian Revolution started? Yes, class warfare between the working man and the **Capitalist**. Same song that we are hearing now in this country.

It is not **Fair** that the **Rich** people get all of the breaks. The government has to do something for the **Poor** people. How can we turn this **Stupid Switch** off and truly help our fellowmen and women that need our help? We can get the government out of our lives and truly start to love our fellowmen and women again. We can start thinking about somebody other than ourselves. It is in our own **self-interest** to help our fellowmen and women. Part of our problem has been that we felt that is was good for a cold government to do our job.

"Why that was why we paid all of those taxes in the first place? Why do we have to be bothered with that? That's the **government's** job. It's not **My** job." Well, it doesn't work that way. The government cannot Love and Love is the most important gift that another human being can give to another human being. It's one of the things that set us apart from all of the other animals. People may have different talents and dreams but we are all connected together as human beings.

No, we need to turn the **Stupid Switch** off and forget about the government trying to help people deal with poverty. For that we need **God's** help. We also need to start helping people on a one on one basis again. You know that guy next to you--**Him**. Don't just say it's not **my** problem. "The government has programs for people like him." Help that person. It is in your own best **self-interest**. The government's way will also cost you a lot more money.

No, when that old friend out of your past calls you and he asks for your help in finding a job, don't just write him off as another loser. Listen to what he is telling you and try to help him. He is asking for your help. He is not just asking you to come up with a lot of logical reasons for why he shouldn't be out of work.

He is asking for your help. Don't just call him up when you see a job in the Want Ads and tell him about that job. It may make you think that you have done something to help him, but you were just trying to make yourself feel that you had done something. You know, give yourself a good warm feeling inside. Help **Him** not you. It's really in your own **self-interest**.

You see if we really want to help the **Poor** people and people that we want to help, it must start with each of us. The key is **Love**. Yes, we have to start with ourselves and work from our own situation. We can't just turn it over to the government. When we do that, as hard as they try, somebody will end up throwing that good old **Stupid Switch**.

For all of the money that the Federal, State and Local Governments have spent on Black issues, there are still a lot of bad feelings in this country. The government tried by acts of law to change situations without changing how people think, feel and act. No government can ever do a good job of that in the long term.

No, that comes from their family and how people develop from children into adults.

Think for a minute about how a person feels who is out of work and cannot provide for his family. Yes, he is willing to look at anything that will shift the blame from him to somebody else. It can be that everybody else has all the right connections. It can be that they are younger than him. It can be that they know somebody that he doesn't know. It can be that they are part of a minority that the government shows preference for over him. It can be a lot of things that all take some of the guilt away from him.

How does this person react to the events going on around him? He blames all of the problems that he sees on this group. Yes, that is what is wrong with this country, all of those lazy Greedy Chief Executive Officers (**CEO's**) of those Companies that are paying them over a Million Dollars a year. Why that just isn't **Fair**! He also probably spends a lot of time talking about how bad **CEO's** are with his family. Yes, and Clem Jr., slowly develops these same thoughts about **CEO's**. Yeah, Clem Jr. learned to hate **CEO's** early. How does all of this relate to Race Relations? A lot. You see, you cannot improve one group of people's lives by taking away from somebody else. Negatives don't work. The key is to try to help the people who need our help and not try to hurt the other people who are more successful than the other people that we want to help.

In warfare, we learned this valuable lesson in the Great World War. No, not Desert Storm, I'm talking about World War I and World War II. After the end of World War I all of the winning nations tried to make Germany pay for all of the damage that Germany had done to them. You know, to the Victors go the spoils.

What happened? Yes, life was real tough in Germany living up to the terms of Surrender of Germany in World War I. Hitler came along and convinced the German people that it was not their fault. He even blamed the loss of World War I on the incompetent German Leaders and the Jews.

Yes, it was especially the fault of the Jews and Hitler would make them pay. Not only did the Jews pay, but the German people and the rest of the world had to fight another World War that took millions of lives. Are we making the same mistake that they made when we blame the **Rich** people for all of our troubles? Will we run off or kill all of the **Rich** people as Hitler did with the Jewish people?

Now, did the winning governments of World War II learn anything from this? Yes, the terms of surrender for Germany after World War II were a little different. Heck, we even had a Marshall Plan to help Germany and the rest of Europe rebuild their countries. Some people even say that we did too good of a job of helping them. You know they sure make a real good car now.

The main point is the results. It has been over 50 years and the world is basically at peace. No world wars are going on because of the last world war. Are we still trying to change what happened here in America over 150 years ago by penalizing some other group of people? Are we still trying to make it up to people who were in Slavery?

Well, there is no human way on this Earth that we can go back in time and right the terrible wrongs of slavery. What happened with slavery was a disgrace to every human being. No person should ever be a slave to another. We are all human beings. The best that we can all do is to live our lives with Love, love that recognizes that we are all connected together as human beings. We share a common bond. We are all people and Love is our solution on an individual basis.

Love that shouldn't blame our individual problems on another group of people that share some common culture that we may not understand. I know from experience that blaming groups of people for what happens to you does not work. For years, I placed a lot of my anger and frustrations on people who lived in Louisiana.

Yes, I am talking about **Cajuns**. You see I took a job working for a company in Louisiana and things did not work out. They did not work out because I did not do a real good job of thinking through what I was getting into.

I didn't consider that the people that I was going to work for would have different values from me. I don't mean that my values were good and theirs were bad, I just mean that they were different. I had always done what I thought was excellent work and everybody that I had worked for in the past had agreed and had paid me very well. They had also gone out of their way to make sure that I knew that they appreciated my work. That changed when I went to work in Louisiana.

My boss was a lot different from anybody that I had ever worked for in my past. From day one, I knew that I had made a big mistake. As they say in the Car Business, "Promises were made but were not kept." The biggest promise that was broken between them and me concerned moving my family from Houston, Texas to Baton Rouge, Louisiana.

Do you remember what happened in Houston, Texas in the mid-eighties? Well, the market for Real Estate and especially houses went south. Yeah, south like in Antarctica.

Really bad news. Well, I accepted the job of Chief Financial Officer for this little Pharmacy Company with the promise that they would take care of me and my house back in Houston, Texas. "Trust Us. We'll help you out. Our corporate procedures don't allow us to buy your house back in Houston, Texas, but we will make sure that you don't suffer on moving from Houston to Baton Rouge. We will take care of you." Sounds a lot like the promises politicians always make, doesn't it?

After I had moved my family to Baton Rouge, Louisiana and my house in Houston, Texas was still not sold, I found out about that "Trust Us" promise. My boss finally told me, "That if I was so concerned about my house in Houston, Texas, I could move back to Houston, Texas. A deal was a deal and he couldn't buy my house. Why, I should be grateful to have a job."

I also found out about those corporate procedures. They didn't exist. There were no procedures that said that. They didn't want to buy my house back in Houston, Texas, because that was what they had done on one of the guys that had my job before. He had moved to Tacoma, Washington and they had bought his house as part of their relocation procedures. The reason that they didn't want to do it in my situation was that they lost a lot of money on the deal.

Seems like they tried to sell the house themselves and avoid a lot of expenses. You know as Carl and Mac would say, "Poor Boy it because we couldn't afford to do it like the Big Boys could. We couldn't even afford to put real computers in all of our stores."

We definitely couldn't afford to have a real Internet or Web Page that worked. Yeah, they even sold the house to somebody and financed the sale themselves. They were going to avoid using a **Bank** or other mortgage company and save some more money.

A funny thing happened with this approach. They forgot to record their lien on the house and the person who had bought the house went out and got another mortgage. He also couldn't afford to pay both notes and finally left them holding the bag. It got real expensive trying to cut out the middle man.

So, I accepted a job where I trusted somebody to be **Fair**. That's when I first started to understand that word can mean several different things to different people. I expected one thing and they expected another. Either way I was left with a House that I couldn't sell back in Houston and I was living in Baton Rouge.

That was just the beginning of a real bad relationship. My boss was one of those old fashioned types of bosses. Yeah, he never heard about the positive approach. He didn't believe in complimenting or praising people when they did a good job.

"Why if I told someone how good a job they were doing, they would expect a big raise."

He also made it real clear that our stores came first. Accounting people were just a bunch of clerks in suits. They don't do anything important.

"Why we could lose our whole Accounting Department and that would not be half as bad as losing one store out of 150."

Ed was also a **"Bear Chaser."** By that I mean that he spent most of his time looking for new companies to buy. He would come up with some new deals that He wanted me to analyze for him all the time. He would turn a deal over to me just like his vision of bear hunting. You know, one guy has the job of finding the bear and bringing the bear back to the bear skinner.

Good old Ed would come running into my office with this new deal and throw it down with the comment, "Here you got this one, and I'm going to **Get another bear**." Yes, Ed loved to go bear hunting for new deals. He didn't really care about the other parts of running a company. He also was real cheap and didn't pay his people real well unless they were part of getting another deal that he wanted.

Finally after trying to live with Ed and seeing that was not going to

229

work, I decided to leave him and his company. Because I had always been a good solider, I couldn't put all of the blame on Ed. No, instead, I blamed **Cajuns** and told everybody that I couldn't live in a state that was that backward. Yes, I blamed a whole group of people for my problems with Ed.

What was really bad was that Ed was not even a **Cajun**. No, Ed was from Texas. He was cheap and not as understanding as I had expected. But I continued to blame **Cajuns** for my problems for years. You see, it couldn't just be that I had a problem with one person. No, there had to be a whole group of people that I could blame.

That was me pulling my **Stupid Switch**. Yes, it was stupid for me to place all of my frustration on **Cajuns**, when my problems were with Ed. It was easier and at the time, it sure made me feel good. Yeah, I came up with all kinds of stories to tell about the dumb lazy **Cajuns** that had driven me away from their miserable state.

If I had been a smarter person, I would have learned more about Ed and what his needs really were. I would have spent most of my efforts in trying to meet his needs instead of thinking about my situation or my house in Houston, Texas. Just maybe, if I had taken that approach, I would have gotten to see a different side of Ed.

Maybe he would have been afraid that I would leave if something positive for me didn't happen on my house in Houston, Texas. I never will know because I finally gave up and left.

Is that what we are doing as people in this country? Are we throwing the **Stupid Switch** and putting the blame on some groups of people because of something that happened to us in the past that didn't have anything to do with those people now or in the present?

"We only make a little dab of money but doctors make over $100,000. Why that is **Not Fair**.

Why do they get all of the money and we get so little money? We work in a factory running a punch press and make only $6.00 an hour and that's not enough to provide for a family. The Plant Manger makes over $70,000 a year. Why, that's **Not Fair**."

Do we think about the training that we passed up for whatever reason and the training and education that the Plant Manager went through to get his job?

Yes, it may have been more important for us to drop out of school and buy that new car or to get married and start having kids. No, we made our own decisions about our jobs. Nobody made us stop school and go down that path. Unlike that childhood Board game of "Life", what we did for a living was not determined by spinning the wheel. We got to make the choice on that one.

When I left Ed and Louisiana, I got to do something that I had always wanted to do. I got a chance to try to help people get a better education. I taught accounting courses at State Tech in Memphis, Tennessee at night. Now, State Tech is supposed to be a 2 year school for people who have not gone to college. Most of the courses that are taught there are technical in nature. Like in car repairs, restaurant management and other technical skills. They do offer some computer courses and some business related courses.

I was employed part time to teach college level accounting courses at night. Most of the people attending State Tech work full time at another job and attend State Tech either at night or during the day. To me this was an excellent way for me to help people learn skills that could help them improve their standard of living and provide for their family.

I had worked my way through school and this just made sense to me. Why, I would be inspiring people to help themselves by pulling themselves up by their bootstraps. Boy was I wrong! What, I didn't realize was that they were not me and they had different points of view. Some of them were looking for an easy way out. They were not interested in learning new skills. They were looking for another piece of paper to get them some more money. With all sorts of government aid money, they could even go to school with very little of their own financial commitment.

The majority of students that went to State Tech had problems in high school. They had barely made it out of high school and they thought that State Tech was just a continuation of that method. State Tech also didn't require you to make a certain score on the **ACT** or **SAT**.

Heck, you could even attend State Tech if you hadn't graduated from High School. There were also "developmental" courses (which sounds much more dignified than "remedial") that they could take if they had failed these subjects in high school. Come on in, just pay your money and get that piece of paper.

Well, I looked at it a little differently than that. I had spent my career supervising people who felt as if they could make more money and have a better job if only they had a better education. This was my opportunity to help them.

Boy was I in for a few surprises. Nothing had changed. I still listened to people complain about all the **Rich** people and how everything was not **Fair**. It was not **Fair**, that I expected them to learn the material or to spend time working on their homework. Why, they had jobs and families to raise.

No, I was not being **Fair** to them. I was supposed to be there to help them. Help them get a piece of paper that would give them a raise. It didn't matter about improving their skills and knowledge, just improve their paycheck and the people who worked at State Tech could also buy more stuff. Teach them how to think for themselves?

Why, that was just too hard and was not **Fair**. You see, that was stupid of me. Some of those kids that my wife had struggled with all of the years that she had taught in high school were now in my class at State Tech. They didn't want to learn anything hard then and now they were spending their money and some of them were spending Government grant money they sure didn't want to have to work hard. Why, that was my job to teach them?

"Wait another minute, Richard. Can't you even hear what they were saying? It was your job to teach them. What do you think that a teacher is supposed to be? Do you think that it is just being a cheer leader? Did you just think that they could Learn all the material on their own. What do you think that they were paying you for anyway? You were there to teach them. That was your job. Why, you were there to understand their needs--to make allowances for them--to care--to give them individual attention--to have them learn.

You know make a **Magic Moment** occur where they all understand and learn." We both had pulled that stupid switch. I didn't understand that nothing had changed with them. The same people who had struggled through public schools were now struggling at State Tech. We were not on the same page. They wanted a pill that could make everything better, so they could buy even more stuff. They didn't see that the problem and solution were in their own hands. You weren't there when some kids who didn't read their assignments and didn't ask any questions in class made those bad grades.

You didn't hear them tell you how their last teacher had made allowances for them. You didn't hear them tell you that when they got only three questions right and made a 20 on an exam that you should have given them at least a **D**. Why that would have been **Fair.** That was what had happened in the past. Wasn't that what all of the advertisement for this school was all about? Caring teachers who listened to students.

That was the way that they thought it should be. As a country we are still throwing that **Stupid Switch**. We will not let ourselves realize that people have to make their own decisions and we cannot take away from successful people and give that to unsuccessful people. We have to realize that some will fail. Regardless of all of our great intentions and government programs and money that we spend, we will still have people that fail in life.

Part of our problem has been that we could not face this fact. People will for whatever reason decides to live their lives in a way that is different from other people.

They will sometimes make bad decisions and mess up. There is no government on the face of the Earth that can prevent failure. The best thing that government can do is to provide the opportunity for people to make good decisions. If we continue to ask the government to try to make things **Fair,** we will only end up with the government throwing that good old Stupid Switch.

You still don't believe me? Well, say good-bye to **Number "50"**. Yeah, as in a company having 50 people that work for them. You see the Federal Government passed the "**Family Leave**" bill mandating that companies give their employees the right to take off time from a company for family needs such as the birth of a child. That was real **Fair** and the government gave them that right. The government also included a clause in the law that this law did not apply to companies that employed less than 50 people.

This would not be **Fair** to companies that didn't have enough people to do the work of the people taking off from their jobs. Well, say good-bye to number **50** in small companies. You can be sure that small companies that have close to **50** employees will not add that number **50**. If they do then they have to give this benefit to all of their other employees. They also have to protect this job for the person who took off from work, regardless of what that does to their business. **Say good-bye to Number 50.**

"Wait a minute Richard, There you go again. I still don't think you know what you are talking about. You probably think that the people are **Stupid**. That is just another example of the **Evil Rich People** limiting the good stuff to the **Rich People and not sharing with the Real People.**"

No, Bubba, that is just the way some Rich Liberals and other Guilty Rich People try to deflect any criticism away from them and on to somebody else. Like pointing out a small spot in your eye when you cannot even see the forest for the trees. Someday The Government might even try that **Old Number 50 Trick** to try to change this country even more. To change the country to what they think this country should be. A country that looks like: **Europe with Kings and Queens**.

A Government that tells you what your Rights are and tries to make everything **Fair.** No, the government is giving into our perceptions of what we think is our problems. We think that the problem has to be with somebody else. It can't be with us.

Just remember you cannot have **Kings and Queens** without having a lot of **Serfs. Serfs** that work the land and give everything to the **Kings and Queens** that will treat them **Fair**. If they think that they are worthy. And of like one of the stories that I read in my daily devotional guide, **The Upper Room.** "Several years ago I served as a

234

police officer. One afternoon we received a call to respond to a drowning in a small lake that we knew was only about five feet deep.

We assumed that the victim was a child or teenager. We were shocked to find that a man over six feet tall had fallen out of a boat and drowned in five feet of water. I imagined him thrashing and fighting the water until he was completely exhausted and all hope of being saved was at last abandoned. How sad it is that if only he had been able to stand up, he could have saved himself.

Often when the storms and crises of living assail us, we look for answers all around us but ignore our own God-given resources and strengths. Many times the answers and solutions we seek are with us. We look for difficult or complex solutions, when what is needed is quite simple and within our grasp.

The storms in our lives come from many places, and they seem to last forever. But we can trust that when the storms of life are raging, **God** will help us to stand." Eugene Blair, The Upper Room. Have we forgotten how to stand up? Can part of our solution come from first realizing that the solution has to come from within us? Is there a special place that we can go, talk with **God** and get this power?

13 IN YOUR ROOM

That magical place does exist where we can solve all of our most difficult problems. That place is our own room, where we can all go in time of great problems and troubles: **Our Own Soul**. How can you get there? Pick out a room in your house or wherever you live. Close all of the windows and doors. Turn out all of the lights and turn off the Television and any other noises. Now you are alone in your room.

Think about just you. Are you alone now? Close your eyes and be truly alone. Now is the time to be honest with yourself. You are in your room and you are ready to think about everything that you have heard during our conversations. It is now time for you to ask yourself a few serious questions.

Are you really satisfied with what has happened to you in your life up to now? Do you really think that anyone in this world has your own best **self-interest** more at heart than you do? Is there anybody in this world that thinks about you more than you do? If you are real lucky you may have your mother, your father, your brothers or your sisters, your husband, your wife or your kids. But after them do you really know anybody that is more interested in your well-being and success than you? Now be really honest, remember you are in your own room and you cannot fool yourself.

No, everybody is their own best cheer leader and supporter. It's called Self-preservation. Do you still not believe me? Did you know what **Jesus Christ** did when he walked on this Earth? Yes, he walked with people just like you and me. He walked and talked with everybody and he didn't associate just with **Poor** people or **Rich** people. He tried to help us **All**.

Do you know what he said when he met somebody for the first time that was really bad off and needed a lot of help? Yes, he asked them what they wanted **Him** to do for them. He dealt on a personal level.

He helped people as individuals. He worked one on one. He didn't try to start a revolution against the government or to create a lot of new social programs. No, he just asked that we love **God** and **One**

Another and follow **His** examples. St. Paul went on to write in Corinthians Chapter 13.

1.   **Though I speak with tongues of men and of angels, and have not charity I am become as sounding brass, or a tinkling cymbal.**

2.   **And though, I have the gift of prophecy, and understand all mysteries, and all knowledge; and though I have all faith, so that I could remove mountains, and have not charity, I am nothing.**

3.   **And though I bestow all my goods to feed the poor, and though I give my body to be burned, and have not charity, it profiteth me nothing.**

4.   **Charity suffereth long, and is kind; charity envieth not; charity vaunted not itself, is not puffed up,**

5.   **Doth not behave itself undeemly, seeketh not her own, is not easily provoked, thinketh no evil;**

6.   **Rejoiceth not in iniquity, but rejoiceth in the truth;**

7.   **Beareth all things, believeth all things, hopeth all things, endureth all things.**

8.   **Charity never faileth: but whether there be prophecies, they shall fail; whether there be tongues, they shall cease; whether there be knowledge, it shall vanish away.**

9.   **For we know in part, and we prophesy in part.**

10.   **But when that which is perfect is come, then that which is in part shall be done away.**

11.   **When I was a child, I spake as a child, I understood as a child, I thought as a child: but when I became a man, I put away childish things.**

12.   **For now we see through a glass. darkly: but then face to face: now I know in part; but then shall I know even as also *I am know.***

13.   **And now abideth faith, hope, charity, these three; but the greatest of these is charity.**

Our solutions for the future have to call upon our **Love** for our fellow man. We can no longer just depend on some distant government to do **Our Job**. Our job is to **Love** our fellow men and women.

Yes, I said it is our job to love our fellow man. Sounds hard and it is hard to love someone who may not look and act like us. But what are our other choices? To let the government take more and more of our money and try to take the place of what we can each do for ourselves and others. No, we are the main ones that have our **self-interest** at heart. Our solution has to start with us. We have to want to see those **Future Solutions**. We have to want to be part of the American Dream.No government can give that to us. A person has to want that deep down inside of **himself or herself**.

I remember when I was a kid and sitting in church and hearing the minister give one of those good old fashioned Baptist sermons about Fire and Brimstone. The trouble was that we were Methodist, but sometimes the minister got carried away and thought he was Oral Roberts and had a big church loan to retire.

Well, this time the minister was really cooking and giving it to everybody that had two nickels to rub together. He was talking about everything that day. He talked about every sin that was in the Bible and some that hadn't even been thought of at that time. A lot of people started to say **AMEN** until they realized that they were in a **Methodist Church** and they just nodded their heads instead.

What did my dad say about the sermon? Yes, he was real impressed with what the minister had to say. Why, "he sure told all of them a thing or two." My dad Missed the point, the minister was Talking to him and all of us. Sometimes, like my dad, we think that the bad tasting medicine is for everybody else but us. No, it is for all of us.

Yes, the Future starts with each of us. There are not a lot of Mikeys out there for them to try it first. We are the ones that have to change. Our first change has to come from a long hard look at ourselves and how we want to live our lives. Do we want to continue to be governed as a child or are we now grownups who want to live our own lives? Do we really think that the Government is the answer to all of our problems, that it always has our best interests at heart? A government that can take money away from somebody else and give it to us. Do we really believe that?

Now, that you are in your room think about your past experiences dealing with the government. If all of your experiences have been positive ones with the government, then change is not for you. But if your experiences are a lot like mine then you are looking for a **Future Solution**.

Think back to how government has dealt with you in the past. Remember the time that you took your daughter to enroll in the 3rd grade. How there were a lot of Long lines and people sitting behind tables with that bored and tired look on their faces. Remember how they talked to you and treated you that day. Remember how they asked you to fill out two identical cards of information on your daughter.

Remember, how when you protested that this was something they could copy for themselves, they told you they were too busy and they were just doing what the office told them to do. Yes and how dare you bother them? Well, our government can act like that because we gave them the control. We give them our tax dollars and they created the laws that tell us how to act with them. Very seldom do you see a government worker treating people like customers. Why should they? The government is a monopoly and it has control.

Is that the way that you want to live your life? Do you really want the government to take your money and control your life? Do you really believe that the Government has your best interest at heart? No, the government is made up of people that have jobs that run on procedures and rules. You are just a civilian and can't quite possibly know what they have to go through.

All you can do is cause more work for them. The law is already on the books and the taxes have to come in. That is the law and they have control. But it doesn't have to be like that at all. Remember the

Constitution and the ### *Declaration of Independence*?

This government is supposed to be for **All** of us. We are the ones who hold the power: **Us**. We are the ones that are supposed to be in control. This issue is not a case of electing Democrats, Republicans, Liberals or Conservatives. For too long we have tried that approach. You know, just like a Football or Basketball game. Our side against their side. We could really change everything once we got our team into the game.

Has that worked? What do you think? No, that has not worked out real well. Now that you are in your room, think back to what has happened over the last 30 years. During this time we have had seven Presidents. Four Presidents have been Republicans and three Presidents have been Democrats. True, the House of Representatives has been under the control of the Democrats for over thirty years but Representatives are more closely attuned to specific groups of voters.

Our national government leaders that have governed us for the last thirty years are not the cause of the problems. Our problems are caused by what we expect Government to do for us and our own system. We are still thinking as a child and expecting the government to take care of us. We have to grow up and stand on our own two feet.

"Hold on here! Don't tell me that you are trying to tell us that Billie and Hillary are not the cause of all of our troubles. Don't you remember when Ronnie was in charge? Everything was all right until Billie and Hillary messed everything up for all of the productive people. You know the ones that aren't too lazy to try to make something out of themselves."

Now, I know that didn't come from Mikey or Bubba. Could that have come from Pat? You sure have been silent for a long time. Did you just catch up with the rest of us? Don't you know that Clem and I figured out your game? Yes, the game those politicians try to play. Avoid issues of **Black and White** and deal in the gray areas. Don't make anybody mad at you. Make the voters think that you are on their side. Do you want proof?

Think about the **Abortion** issue. Few politicians are taking concrete positions on this issue. Some may try to sound like they are on your side, but be careful and really listen to what they say. They may use words like **Choice** and **Life**, but they will not come out in public and say that **Abortion** is bad and they will never support **Abortion** under any circumstances.

No, what they are doing is leaving some room for them to operate in and get enough votes to be reelected. They are lawyers. They are brokers. Kind of reminds you of a Real Estate Broker. You remember those people who tell you with pride, that they represent you. Yes, they will take your money that comes from selling your house or buying your new house. They are brokers. They make money whether you win or you lose. That is what a broker is. They make their living off of the action. They don't risk their money. They represent you. Our government leaders are a lot like those Real Estate brokers. Especially when they come up with laws for all of us. Laws that they create that don't apply to them.

No, the current system will continue to disappoint us more and more. We also cannot continue to blame our leaders when they fail. That's right, Pat, let's give Bill and Hillary a break. Get off of what they might have done years ago when they both had real good hair. Give them a break. They are no better or worse than the rest of the other politicians that we have now or will have in the future if we continue our current system.

Bill and Hillary need to get off trying to act like the proper little government leaders. Forget talking about all of the greed that was in existence in the Eighties. Some of those people are now getting checks back from the government because of hard times and the government's earned income credit. What are you going to do for all of them--show them how to make money on commodities? No, enough is enough.

Forget trying to blame political leaders. The problem is in the system not the people.

Other government leaders and politicians have failed in the past and will fail in the future if we try to continue our current system. There is not enough money and wealth in the whole world to pay for what we have asked our leaders to give to us. Our only solution is to shrink that government and put the power to make decisions concerning everyone's life back in their own hands.

This solution does not come from complex analysis that only Ph.D.'s can understand. No, these solutions come to all of us when we are alone with our own thoughts and in **Our Own Room**. Our solutions cannot be tied just too how we Have acted in the past. We are interested in the future.

A future that is there for everyone to have a chance. Not a guarantee but a chance to succeed or to fail.

No, government never was our answer. Over two thousand years ago, Isaiah the prophet of **God wrote:**

> **15. Behold, the nations are as a drop of a bucket, and are counted as the small dust of the balance:**
> **Behold, he taketh up the isles as a very little thing.**
> **17. All nations before him are as nothing; and they are counted to him less than nothing, and vanity.**
> **23. That bringeth the princes to nothing; he maketh the judges of the earth as vanity.**
> **24. Yea, they shall not be planted; yea, they shall not be sown; yea, their stock shall not take root in the earth: and he shall also blow upon them, and they shall wither, and the whirlwind shall take them Away as stubble.**
> **25. To whom then will ye liken me, or shall I be equal? Saith the Holy One.**
> **26. Lift up your eyes on high, and behold who hath cre ated these things, that bringeth out their host by num ber: he calleth them all by names by the greatness of his might, for that he is strong in power; not one faileth.**
> **28. Hast thou not known? hast thou not heard, that the everlasting God, the Lord, the Creator of the ends of the earth, fainteth not, neither is weary? There is no search ing of his understanding.**
> **29. He giveth power to the faint; and to them that have no might increaseth strength.**
> **30. Even the youths shall faint and be weary, and young men shall utterly fail:**
> **31. But they that wait upon the Lord shall renew their strength: they shall mount up with wings as eagles; they shall run and not be weary; and they shall walk, and not faint. Isaiah 40, 15-31.**

Yes, our **Future Solution** comes to all of us when we turn back to **God** and to **His Solution Jesus Christ**. That is **our solution** and our only way. For too long we have fooled ourselves into believing that man and government was our solution. We forgot and turned our backs on our past just as the Jews did when they finally were out of Egypt. "Why we are Americans and we can do anything.

We don't need anybody but ourselves. We beat Hitler in World War II and we can do anything." We were wrong. We are just human beings created by God. We have forgotten. He showed us the way to our **Future** and we forgot.

"Now hold on a minute Richard, are you trying to say that we all need to go back to **Church** and send them all of our money and let the **Churches** fix the problems? I just knew that this was going to be another sermon and somewhere you were going to try to get me to join your **Church** and give them my money."

No, Jim Bob, this is not about joining any church or sending in your money. This is about going to **Your Room** and being honest with yourself. Who do you really think that **Jesus Christ** was? Was he really the **Son of God** or was he the biggest Liar that ever lived? There are no other choices.

Either he is a Liar or he is the **Son of God**. If he is the **Son of God**, don't you think that we should listen to what he said about loving **God** and our fellow man?

"But what is the catch? Every time that I go to church now, all that the preachers talk about needs more and more money. Money for new education classes. Money for more church buildings. Money for this and that. They are even starting to sound like that little blond haired woman who comes on Television and tells me how I could feed some children in Africa.

Why doesn't she just go on a diet and send them the money that she was spending on feeding her face."

"I don't trust any of those people. They don't care about those starving kids or what going on with me. They don't care if my family ever gets fed. How can they know what **God** wants me to do? Why, I have heard about how they waste my money and why do they always try to help the people in some faraway place?

Why can't they help some of the people here who are out of work? Do those people asking me for my money and going to that big church ever help those people who are begging for work and food here in this country?"

Now, calm down, Jim Bob, you are falling into another trap. You are trying to equate the people who you see going to some church with God. You are wrong. All of us are sinners and need **God**. We are no different than you Or anybody else. We all need **God's** help. You also need to remember that even Jesus had problems with the **Church** when he came here the first time. Don't you remember that it was church people and church leaders that demanded that the Romans kill **Jesus**?

They did this even when they were given the opportunity to let **Jesus** go free. They wanted the Romans to let a common criminal go free instead. They heard him speak about love and saw his many miracles and still they turned away from him. You need to be real careful not to confuse what you see the earthly church doing with what Jesus taught us to do. There is a big difference.

Jesus taught us to **Love**. Some of the churches are just asking for your money to pay their bills? When you are in **Your Room** think about that and where you are really going. Now this is strictly my own personal view, but I think that we will all go to Heaven when we leave this Earth.

There's only one **Big Problem** though. I think that if you haven't learned to love your fellow man then Heaven will be your own Hell. I just don't think that anybody that doesn't learn to love his fellow man will really enjoy being around that much **Love**.

No, our solution comes from turning back to **God** and remembering that everybody is our brother. Yes, the **Rich** and the **Poor**, blacks, whites, yellows and all colors. **God** created man in **His** own image. Not just you and me but all people. We have to remember that and learn again how to love our fellow man.

This is not a commercial for any Religion or Church. This is a voice deep inside of each of us that reminds us that we are not alone. A voice that comes to each of us when we are alone and in **Our Room**. A voice that reminds us to Love one another. Not love that is a law that we all pay taxes to the government and then they decide who is needy. We cannot delegate that to some powerful government to decide what is **Fair** and what is wrong that is for **Us** to do. If we change our minds about helping our fellowman and start with ourselves then we have **a Future**.

If we continue to let somebody else does that then we will always be disappointed. The **Future** is ours. Do we want a **Future**? It all comes down to what do you really believe? Are we truly alone in our room or is there someone greater than ourselves who has the **Future Solutions**? What do you think?

Yes, we can shrink the government down to a manageable size. Yes, we can pay off our National Debt. Yes, we can make increases in the supply of Healthcare. Yes, we can develop ways for people to provide for their retirement needs. Yes, we can improve the Quality of our Education Systems. Yes, we can create more jobs. We can do all of these things and still miss the main point. **Love** has to come first into our hearts.

Love for all of our brothers and sisters. That can start with each of us. We don't need to wait for someone else to start. We can start with the person next to us right now. Now, what about the government? Where is the beginning to a new government? Where does the change start? How do we start to change our government? Just open that old History book of yours. We can look in that old History book and read all about how we start some of this change in our Government. Where is it? Oh yeah,

The United States Constitution. Article V.
The Congress, whenever two-thirds of both Houses shall deem it necessary, shall propose Amendments to this Constitution, or, on the Application of the Legislatures of two-thirds of the several States, shall call a Convention for proposing Amendments, which, in either Case, shall be valid to all Intents and Purposes, as part of this Constitution, when ratified by the Legislatures of three-fourths of the several States, or by Convention in three-fourths thereof, as the one or the other Mode of Ratification may be proposed by the Congress; Provided that no Amendment which may be made prior to the Year One thousand eight hundred and eight shall in any Manner affect the first and fourth Clauses in the Ninth Section of the first Articles; and that no State, without its Consent, shall be deprived of its equal Suffrage in the Senate.

There for all of you technocrats that is how we do the easy part. We amend the Constitution of The United States. Yes, in order to shrink our Government we have to amend our Constitution.

The starting point in changing and shrinking our Government has to start with changing our Constitution. Our Constitution has grown and changed over the years until it reflexes our present views of **Rights and Fairness.** Any change in our Government that did not start with the **Constitution** would be doomed to a failure of court challenges.

"Well, that sounds real hard Richard, how do we do that?" We start first with ourselves and ask ourselves a few questions. Are we satisfied with our current system of government or do we think that there is a better way? Do we agree with what we have been talking about in *Future Solution* and do we really see how this will be in our own best **self-interest**?

If we are ready for that *Future Solution* then we start demanding that our political leaders give us that **Future**. We demand that the people running for political office share our vision for the **Future.** We give our support only to the people who are dedicated to that Future. A **Future** that belongs to all of us, not just to the Government.

"But what will we do if the politicians don't see it our way?" Then Bubba, we have to be those leaders. Yes, we have to be our own

leaders and that means that we have to start getting more involved and maybe even run for National Office. It is in our best **self-interest**. "But what about the Democrats and the Republicans, you know that they would never go for that. What would we do?"

Maybe Bubba, it's about time for another political party. You know the **Future Party**. All that we need is for enough people to really want to have that **Future**.

All we would need is another **Hero.** "Where have you gone, John Wayne?" We need you now. Have you ever asked yourself that Question? "Where have all of the **Heroes** gone? There just aren't any more **Heroes** like there were back in the good old days." Do you know why there are not a lot of **Heroes** running around now? You remember our ancestors that got on those boats and came over here to start this country--those **Heroes** that struggled in this wild country and started it all for us-Those Heroes that fought and died in The American Revolution so we would all have a country.

Say do you remember those Heroes that volunteered to fight and give their lives so that we could have the opportunity to live our lives? Do you remember Davey Crockett? Yes, that Tennessean that volunteered to go to Texas and help Texans fight for their independence at The Alamo. That **Hero** that gave his life in what we would call a **"Hopeless Cause"**. Where have they all gone and why do we not have anybody like that now?

Why have we had such a shortage of Presidents who were **Heroes** since we lost John F. Kennedy? You remember President John F. Kennedy. What was it that he said? **"Ask not what your country can do for you, but what can you do for your country."** He also talked about going to the Moon: **"We chose to go there not because it is easy but because it is hard."**

Do you think that those great Heroes waited to see if somebody else would take their places? Were they waiting for somebody else to be that Hero? Would they have been **Heroes** if they were thinking about **Fairness** and **Rights**? No, as John Wayne would have said, "I saw my duty and I did it." Heroes don't wait for anybody else to do what they see as their duty.

What have our Presidents done since John F. Kennedy that made them look and act as Heroes? Let's see when we had the Great Communicator what did he do to inspire all of us? Yes, he got us to sacrifice and gave us a tax cut. What did the New Democrat do to inspire all of us?

He talked about **Fairness** and wink-wink we all knew that he was going to take the money away from them and not us.

No, that is not what **Heroes** do. That is what Santa Claus and the Local Golf Pro do to make people like them until all of the money runs out. We are kind of stuck in place on Heroes. We are still waiting for somebody else to take the first step. You know -- try the bad medicine first and see if it is all right for us. Nobody wants to step up to the line.

We are waiting. You know it is only **Fair.** If we want a **Future** that has to change and the change has to start with each of us.

"Wait a minute, Richard; I just know that there has to be some kind of conspiracy here. You remember all of that talk about a group of **Rich** and **Intellectual** people forming some kind of organization to control the world. What were they called? Something like "Skulls and Bones" or the "Trilateral Commission." Didn't George Bush and Nelson Rockerfellow belong to the Commission? That has to be our problem. Yeah, all of those people are controlling everything. It's their fault."

No, Jim Bob, it's not their fault. Remember what Hitler tried to pull on the German people. Remember how he told **The Big Lie** and placed all of the blame on the Jews. That's what we are doing when we want to believe that our problems don't start with ourselves and go looking for somebody else to blame. There will always be somebody waiting to give us a villain so we don't have to look at ourselves. We can't listen to those people who see a conspiracy everywhere.

You know those people--the ones who still think that the landing on the moon was rigged but they believe that Professional Wrestling is for Real.

"Hold on there, Richard, you can't get off that easy with making that little funny. What about all of the conspiracy that goes on in the Memphis City Public School System.

You didn't even mention the problems that we have had with our school system and how the mangers of the school system are wasting our tax money."

"Bubba was right about you. You just hit the high points and forget a lot of the important details. I sure am glad that Bubba asked me to sit in on this meeting when he had to go check on his Bingo operations. You're just glossing over the top of the issues. What about all of the money that they are wasting in the Public Schools. Don't you remember the conversation that I had with that good for nothing Superintendent a few years back?"

249

"Why, the nerve of that man, trying to tell me that we spend too little money on educating our kids in Memphis. I sure set him straight on that one. Why, I told him that a $300 million dollar school budget was plenty to spend on educating our kids each year. Why, they are just wasting our money down there at the school board. One of these days, somebody like good old Ross will get in power and set all of them straight.

They have plenty of our money now. They just need to learn how to spend all of it more wisely. You know do the right thing and cut out all of the wasteful programs. They don't need any more of our money. Wasn't that what you were saying before on the Deficit?"

Gee, Jim Bob, you sure can tell that you have been around Bubba for some time. You are starting to sound like him. You haven't done your math on what you said to the Superintend of Education. Let's look at the numbers again and think about what they really mean. For a minute let's assume that we are taking about an annual school budget of around $300 million dollars. It could be a little more or it could be a little less than $300 million. For now sit over in the corner with Mikey and follow this logic. Are you with me? No, you don't have to say **Amen**. Just be quiet and follow along with the numbers and the numbers will have a lot to say.

Now, with this $300 million dollar annual school budget we are going to fund the operation of around 150 schools in Memphis, Tennessee. This works out to around $2,000,000 per each school per year.

Sure, Mikey, I know that some schools are larger than others and not every school would get $2,000,000 a year. Some of the schools would get over twice that amount with some schools getting quite a bit less per year. But for now let's follow the $2,000,000 per school per year number.

What does this also mean when we start talking about the spending per student? Let's see assuming that there are over 150,000 students in the Memphis School System, then that would work out to only $2,000 dollars per student per year. Doesn't $2,000.00 a year also mean that we are spending just a little over $150.00 a month attempting to educate our kids?

Isn't that what some people are spending on day care? I bet that there is not a lot of waste in that figure. Sounds like we may be getting about our money's worth with that money. Sure, we may not like seeing the current Superintendent of Education get a high salary. We might even want to see one of our people get that money, but we would still miss the main point.

"Well, we are waiting -- what is the main point? Me and Mike and Bubba have held our breath for long enough. What is the main point of all of this?"

The main point is that Memphis, Tennessee has always been a poor city and still is. There is a shortage of high paying jobs in Memphis to Fund Education and our **Other Needs**. We will continue to have this conversation in Memphis until we can educate and train our people for better paying jobs. That is the villain in this city. It is too many **Poor People**. It is not some Mayor or Superintendent of Education that has wasted all of our Money.

"There you go again. It sounds like you are not coming up with specific solutions to our problems. I like Jim Bob's theory on the conspiracy better than your theory. You don't know. Heck, there are a lot of things going on here. Things are really getting complicated and hard. Who knows where all of our money goes?"

No, it's not really that hard. We make it hard when we don't want to face some of the difficult facts of live. In Memphis, Tennessee, we don't want to face the fact that we are a poor little River Town with an under educated work force. You hear some of the Economic teachers and politicians calling this a **Service Oriented** work force.

They talk about how this keeps Memphis from experiencing some of the ups and downs of other labor markets. What they really mean is that we don't have a lot of high paying manufacturing or high tech jobs here. We are service labor like in working at *Wendy's* and **McDonald's**. Don't you remember that median household income among blacks in Memphis was $16,946 and $35,054 among whites?

Don't you see that the money was not there in the first place? You're starting to sound like that Retail friend of mine who just knew that the accountants had lost all of the money that he made. Well, in Memphis, **The Money is not Here**. Nobody lost the money or wasted it. The money was never here in the first place.

Think about the $35,000 that the median white households have and the $16,900 that the black households have and tell me where all of the money came from in the first place. It is not there to waste. That is the hard part and the main point of **Our Solution**. We have to turn away from looking for others to blame. We have to learn to look inside of ourselves first before we go looking for someone else to drop the blame on each time.

We also can't keep waiting for some solution to occur in the Future. We can be like that six foot man who drowned in five feet of water or we can stop thrashing about and finally just stand up.

It is Our Future. **Do we want to stand up?**

14 SAYING GOOD-BYE
TO BUBBA

"Richard some of your solutions are just too hard. Why nobody would ever go for all of those things. Take Healthcare for an example. Don't you known that other countries have a better system of Healthcare than we do? Why, up in Canada, they have a real good system. I'm hearing all the time about their National Healthcare System and all of the good things that the Canadian government does for their people."

"Yeah, they got control of their Healthcare costs and the government has a real good Government Healthcare Program."

Well, Bubba, I have some real bad surprises for you. Did you read the *Wall Street Journal* recently? According to the *Wall Street Journal*, Canada is having some real tough problems with their National Healthcare System.

"What about all of the other countries that have National Healthcare? I bet that England and Italy have a real **Fair** system! I've heard that over there that they do a much better job of making sure that all of their people get affordable Healthcare. What about them?"

Sorry to disappoint you, Bubba, but according to this same article those countries are struggling too. Here look at these numbers:

**Comparative Deficits
(Percentage of GNP)**

Italy	11.1%
Canada	6.6%
Britain	6.6%
United States	4.8%
Germany	3.2%
France	2.8%
Japan	-1.3% *

*Budget Surplus. Source: OECD and Department of Finance

Yeah, that's right; Japan doesn't have a Deficit problem. The Japanese have something that we have forgotten how to do. They have a surplus. You know what a surplus is. A surplus is when you spend less money than you have coming in and you end up with some leftover.

The article went on talking about how the Canadians have continued to borrow against their **Future**. Seems as if they are spending over 32 percent of their taxes just in servicing their debt. They are also cutting back on their spending too. They are especially cutting back on the level of National Healthcare. The article went on to give examples of how Healthcare staff and benefits were being reduced.

"But what's that got to do with us. We are Americans we won't make the same mistakes that those people made up in Canada."

But will we? Canada thought that they had it all. A country with "so many natural resources and so few people" that they could have it all. Why, people didn't have to work hard and earn it. That was old fashioned. The government could make it **Fair.**

What happened? People started to spend more time not working and depending on the Canadian Government for their living. Just listen to what the *Wall Street Journal* went on to say:

"Years earlier, Canada had borrowed heavily to invest in railroads, pipelines and other basic projects, but in the past 20 years or so the borrowings have been Financing other kinds of spending. The federal government sent a monthly check to every mother, even if the family was rich. Public subsidies kept college tuition low; at Montreal's prestigious McGill University; it is still under $1,500 a year.

Unemployment insurance is so generous that in some parts of the country it has become a way of life: three months of work and nine months on the dole. In the little province of Prince Edward Island, the New Democratic Party lays off its leader for three months each year so he can collect federal unemployment benefits and save the party about $3,100."

Now, you see why I bought this up Bubba? Canada is at the end of the line. They have run out of solutions. Do we want to follow them into the sea? The article also went on to say:

"It is impossible to tell precisely at which point national debt-servicing burdens are so high that investors' confidence evaporates," Economists at Royal Bank of Canada wrote in a report last spring. But "there is such a point," they warned, and "if that point is reached, it will come without too much warning."

Do we think that we will be warned? We also are going to hear a lot of talk about increasing the minimum wage. Why will we hear a lot about this? "Why it is not **Fair** that people work so hard and make so little. Why they can't live on that?" But that is not the important question. The important question is why did they not get the skills to better provide for themselves?

Remember our conversation on Jobs? Where will the money come from to pay those increased minimum wages? Are we as consumers willing to pay more for our products and services so those people can get a higher minimum wage? Will we pay more for American Goods than Foreign goods that don't have our high minimum wages?

Where will the money come from? Who is going to step up and give them that money? How much of your money will you give them? That's where it will all come from. **From You**. If we increase the minimum wage higher than what the Free Market Place will pay for that labor then we all will pay more. We may even pay for that minimum wage by losing more jobs to other Countries that don't have a minimum wage law.

Hold on Bubba, I know all about that article in the Wall Street Journal: The Working Poor: Minimum Wage Jobs Give Many Only a Miserable, Week-to-Week Existence.

Sure, I read the part about the guy who works in a hockey stick factory in Newport, Vermont and makes $4.25 an hour. I read about all of the problems that he had in providing his family with a decent standard of living. Anybody that is human has to want to cry when you read about somebody that has to live each day in those kinds of conditions.

Yes, I remember the part of the article that said, "Soon afterward, the Deyos, seeking work in higher-wage Massachusetts, sold all they owned to go there. But they ran out of money before finding jobs. Two years later, they are still making Payments on the used, now-tattered furniture they bought on their return north. Plagued by painful rotted teeth, Mr. Deny waited two years until he was laid off and eligible for Medicaid before having a few pulled.

Yes, his condition is horrible and we all need to help him but raising the minimum wage will not help him. Don't you remember the government doesn't have any money of its own? All of the money that the government has comes from somebody else. Where does the Money comes from to pay the increased minimum wages? That money comes from companies that employ those workers.

How do they get their money? They get their money from selling the goods and services that those minimum wage workers produce through their labor. If we raise the minimum wage then companies that employ minimum wage workers have three choices:

1. Raise the cost of the products that they sell to the public.
2. Pay the increased cost of minimum wage labor and make less Money.
3. Find ways to reduce their use of minimum wage labor.

But what would you do if it were your choice to make? "But what can we do? That was a real sad story about all of those **Working Poor** and the living conditions that they have to look forward to each and every day of their lives. We just have to do something. Don't you feel bad about how they are living their lives?"

Yes, Bubba, I really do. We wouldn't be having this conversation if I didn't care. Did I ever tell you about an old friend of mine named Billie? No, not that Billie. This Billie was a Yankee from Chicago.

On second though, I wonder if he ever knew Hillary. Naught, she wasn't his type. Well, Billie has been probably the best friend that I ever had. We used to get into some real knock down and drag out fights on our different beliefs. Heck, we even almost had a good old fist fight on the way to O'Hare airport once.

One of our biggest disagreements was on how businessmen should conduct their affairs of business. When I was just starting my business career, I used to think that Businessmen should conduct their business a little differently than what Billie thought. Billie's answer always was that **Congress** could never **Legislate** morality. According to him that was a value judgment that the government had no right forcing on somebody else. Billie was all for leaving the issue of morality up to each person.

Well, Billie was right. This is how the **Fair** issue has gotten so warped and blown out of content. How can the government that doesn't have any money of its own get all of us to do something that we will not do out of our own love for our fellowman? What do you mean, Bubba, that if we don't have the government helping people then it is charity and charity is a bad word? Don't you remember what we read that **The Lord** said about charity?

And though I bestow all my goods to feed the poor, and though I give my body to be burned, and have not charity, it profiteth me nothing. And now abideth faith, hope, charity, these three; but the greatest of these is charity. Corinthians Chapter 13 verses 3 and 13.

No, charity is not a bad thing. It's part of **Our Solution**. We have to learn how to care about people and to help our fellow man. We cannot keep looking to the government who has no money except what it takes from all of us. One other thing about being **Fair**. Did you know that **Jesus** covered this in **His Book?** Yes, **Jesus** was being questioned by several other men and his disciples about how they should live their live

No, our solution on low wages does not come from getting the government to take money from somebody and give to somebody else. Trying to make everything **Fair. Jesus Christ** in the story of the workers didn't try to please people who wanted to judge his actions for their own political reasons. No, **He** was only interested in offering to help all of us.

Our solution comes from ourselves. All of us should want to have love and charity for our fellowman. Do you remember that conversation that I would like the President of the United States to have with all of us? You remember that conversation that you have never seen on Television.

You remember how rather than spending money that the government doesn't have the President reaches in his own pocket and puts up some of his own money to help somebody who is hurting. Well, I am ready to start this conversation with me. I believe so strongly in this **Solution** that I will put up my own money. I am willing to start a **Fair Corporation** that will provide food, clothing, shelter and healthcare to **The Poor** People like the **Working Poor** in the *Wall Street Journal* **article**.

You can also be a part of this. You see I will donate 10% of whatever I receive from all of these conversations to that fund. Call it the birth of the **Fair Corporation.**

That also relates to something else that everybody was concerned and talking about: **NAFTA.** You know the North American Free Trade Agreement. Our agreement and treaty with Canada and Mexico to have free trade among the three countries. What do you think will happen to those minimum wage jobs? That's right; they will go south to Mexico because Mexico doesn't have our Minimum wage standards.

Companies will look real hard at relocating their plants to those low wage areas of Mexico. Ross must have been right! That big sucking sound was all of our jobs going down to Mexico. Are we just going to lose all of those American jobs?

No, that big sucking sound that you heard was another political demigod sucking you and your brain into believing that he had the two minute answer to a generation problem. Those jobs are already lost. Ross or the **NAFTA** treaty will not give them back to us. It will give us a chance to sell some other goods and services that take more educated and trained labor. If we want to compete in the **Future**, our solutions are to educate and train our people for those higher paying jobs.

Our solution is not to try to hold on to jobs we want somebody else to pay more than the Free Market will pay unless we are willing to look at how the game of International Trade is being played right now. Are you willing to stop calling the Mexicans, Japanese, Germans and Chinese names and look at some hard realities? Are you willing to look at the rules in a knife fight?

I take by your silence that you are open to the subject. There are no rules in a knife fight are there? That's what we have been doing in this country since the end of World War II. We have been trying to act on a higher plain of human action that what exists in the world at present. We cannot see that World War II didn't end. We just swapped the weapons in the current war. The War of trade.

"What do you mean about the rules in a knife fight? What does that have to do with trade? Are you just making stuff up again?"

No, Bubba, do you remember the movie, *Butch Cassidy and The Sundance Kid.* Well, about in the middle of the movie, one of Butch's Men decided to challenge him for leadership of their Gang.

He said that there had been several changes since Butch and Sundance had been away and the rest of the men had elected him Leader of the Gang. That's when Butch, said that before they started to fight, they would have to discuss the rules for the knife fight. Do you know what happened next? The other gang member who had challenged Butch stopped what he was doing and looked kind of funny at Butch and said, "There are no rules in a knife fight.

That's the time when Butch hauled off and kicked the supposed gang leader in the balls. Butch then said, "You are right there are no rules to a knife fight. Anybody else want to be the leader of the gang?" Everybody just sat around in silence and that was the end of the fight. That's kind of what's happened to us on trade. We are more interested in the rules than in winning the war of trade.

"Okay, Butch, are you suggesting that we kick Japan in the Balls. What would you do about us losing all of those manufacturing jobs? What about all of those clothes that we keep buying from the Chinese where they pay their people only about 30 cents an hour and we have to compete with them? What would you do? Make our people work for only 30 cents an hour! You know that they couldn't live on that. What would you do?"

What I would do would be to discuss the rules for a knife fight. I would look at the rules that everybody are going by in the war of trade.

"Hold on Richard, we already had a General Agreement on Trade and Tariffs. Isn't that going to make a big difference in our ability to sell to other countries? Didn't that fix the problem?"

No, that didn't fix the problem of how to provide for our people who don't get all of the training that they need to compete for high skilled jobs. Regardless of all of our plans, there will always be people who need some type of job. The government can't produce those jobs.

Those jobs have to be there for people who don't qualify for the higher skilled jobs. "Don't keep beating around the bushes. What would you do?"

I would start using Tariffs to protect our jobs just like the other countries do now. Somebody go get a Doctor for Pat and Mikey.

They look like somebody was talking about their mother or stole their Sunday chicken dinner. Yes, we need to rethink how we could use tariffs to protect low skilled manufacturing jobs in this country before it is too late. You see we are just like that gang leader in **Butch Cassidy and The Sundance Kid**.

We are not concentrating on the battle and we are letting the other side talk us to death. We are more interested in defending an ideal than in winning the battle. We are not paying attention to the bigger picture. We are losing jobs and we are somewhat rationalizing that we have become too rich for those types of jobs. We are like the Romans who became too good to fight their own battles. High Tech will save all of us.

We have forgotten to look at how the rest of the world is competing with us. Do they all have markets for our goods and services that are truly open to us without tariffs? Are we all on an open and level playing field? Most importantly does the rest of our competitors have our same laws concerning the environment, the safety of the work place, child labor laws, workman's compensation and most important minimum wages?

Just ask yourself some questions the next time that you pick up that 10 dollar shirt at Wal-Mart. Did the person who made this shirt:

1. Start working to make shirts before they turned ten years old?
2. Work only eight hour days with breaks for lunch and rest?
3. Make the minimum wage like we have in this country?
4. Have workman's compensation and Healthcare?
5. Have a clean and safe place to work?
6. Work in a country that had clean air and water laws?
7. Have political leaders that looked out for them?

No, you won't see any of that when you compare that 10 dollar shirt with an American shirt that may cost three times that to produce here. You may not even find an American made shirt when you go to the store. You sure won't find any American made Television sets there. All of the Television sets are now made overseas where the Labor is cheap and they don't have our laws that add more cost to the cost of producing that product.

"So what would you do, Richard, make all of the other countries pass minimum wage laws and other laws like ours that add cost to our products. Or would you do away with the clean air act and minimum wage laws?"

No, I may disagree with some of those laws, but I would let those laws stand on their own merits. If we ever decide as a country that those laws are not in our **best self-interest**, I would go with the rest of the people who want to change them based on the merits of each law. I would use tariffs to even out the rules of completion among all of our so called trading partners.

If it was all up to me, I would come up with a set of tariffs for each country that had different national laws that gave them an advantage between us in competing for the sale of goods and service. For example if a country such as Mexico didn't have child labor laws, minimum wages, clean air and some of the other laws that we have I would place a tariff on those projected goods that Mexican wanted to sell in this country.

Let's say we are talking about shirts that are made in Mexico using labor that cost only 30 cents an hour and none of our labor or environmental laws. This cost of the shirt with the lower cost of production due to different national laws would be adjusted with tariffs.

If the production cost of the shirt that had been selling in Wal- Mart for only ten dollars was three dollars and a similar shirt made in America cost 20 dollars to produce here in America an adjustment would be made to reflex the differences in each county's laws. In this case a tariff of 17 dollars would be applied to the shirt produced in Mexico.

"Wait a minute Richard, most of the shirts that are imported into the United States come from the orient and not Mexico. Why did you use that country? Don't you like Mexicans or what? How do you know that the difference between the laws of Mexico and American would result in a Tariff of 17 dollars? Did you just make that up?"

No, Mikey, I didn't just make that up and I used the example of Mexico because of all of the hype that we heard when **NAFTA** was so hot. The name of the country doesn't matter so much as what is happening. We are losing those jobs and nobody is doing anything to get them back.

Any tariffs that would be charged would have their goal to even the playing field and get those jobs back in America. Make no mistake about what the major goal would be. The Goal would be to keep those jobs in America. Forget all of the logic for why and what we would say to our trading partners. This is a knife fight and the goal of a knife fight is to win the knife fight not in coming up with the best rules for how you fight.

"But Richard, haven't you forgot about your History lesson. For all of your talk about loving History, you have forgotten what Adam Smith said in

The Wealth of Nations.

You have forgotten what happened in the **Great Depression**. Don't you remember that some people think the Great Depression was caused by Tariffs? What do you say about that?"

No, Mikey, I haven't forgotten about what Adam Smith said. It is still true that

"The Wealth of a Nation is Valued in the Goods and Services that it Produces."

When Adam Smith wrote that over 200 hundred years ago, you didn't have some trading partners using different rules. It was as close to even as you could get except for the Indians that sold New York City for only 24 dollars' worth of beads. Maybe they were trying to figure out the rules to a knife fight.

Now, get your hand down, I remember what you said about the Great Depression. The key phrase here is "Some People thought that it was **One** of the causes of the Great Depression. You had a lot things going wrong at the same time.

They had over heated Stock prices in relation to stock value; you had farms failing due to the long shortage of rainfall. No one thing caused the Great Depression. Have you forgotten how to be brave? Have all of us become like the Romans and now are afraid to fight for our jobs. We need those jobs for our people.

Oh, okay you still have a question about what we would do next if the other trading partners just came up with other tariffs for our products. Well, just think for a minute. If we are having such a big trading deficit with the rest of the world, what does that mean? That means that they are selling more here than we are selling there. Forget everything else. They have more to lose than we do.

We also have the largest consumer market in the world. It is not to late to try to hang on to those markets for jobs. If the other trading partners don't like the rules then they can move their production facilities here to produce those goods that they want to sell to us. Remember our talk about education. Regardless of the next problem the force continues. We will keep those jobs here. What do you think that the Japanese were doing with their Tariffs on farm products?

That's right. They were protecting their jobs for their people. Forget everything else that they say. Everything else is just talking about rules in a knife fight. They are doing this and all the Treaties that we have signed will not change that.

What would we do about the **General Agreement on Tariffs and Trade (GATT)** treaty that we have already signed? We would change it. If you want to sell in the largest consumer market in the world you have to agree to our rules. Would there be problems? Sure, we are making a major change in our direction as a country. We are stopping the talking about the rules for a knife fight and concentrating on winning the war. If they want to trade with us they have to follow our rules. No more selling New York City for beads worth 24 dollars. See, Bubba, we are back to our starting point. What are **we** going to do to help ourselves? What is in our own best self-interest?

"Hold on Richard, you have chickened out of explaining something to us. Is this conversation about Politics or Religion? What's the main point of all of this? Don't just leave us hanging. Should we try to elect some real good Republicans or Democrats or should we all throw in with Ross? What's the answer?"

Well, excuse me, Bubba, you were always real good in pointing out any little mistakes that I made even when you were busy picking your nose. It all comes down to losing **Mike**. You remember hearing about Michael Jordon retiring? "Now, Richard, you have really lost it now. What's the retirement of some basketball player got to do with all of the important issues that we have been talking about for so long?"
A lot Bubba. Do you remember what Kelvin Hale; the former All Star Basketball player of the Boston Celtics had to say about the question of what would happen to professional basketball after losing their star player? Kelvin said, "In a few years, people will be asking, 'Michael Who'?" He knew that as time goes by we tend to forget.

Now Bubba, you don't have to remind me that Michael came out of retirement and looked great. That is only temporary. Someday he will retire for good and then there won't be any more Michael.

There is somebody that we have forgotten who will really come back and he will come back forever. We have forgotten about him. We forgot the best of all. You see we have forgotten a lot. We have forgotten that over 2,000 years ago, **God** walked on this Earth and brought us **His Solution**. **God** knew that we were hurting and he answered our cries for **His** help. It has been more than a few years and a lot of people are asking **Jesus** who?

Yes, we had the **Future Solution** given to all of us for **Free**. **The Solution** that was learning to **Love** our Fellowmen as ourselves. That is the good part. The center to all of our other **Future Solutions** is learning to **Love**.

Has it been so long that we have forgotten? Are all of our churches so worried about making their budgets and coming up with enough money to pay the bills that they have forgotten too?

No, **The Real Future Solution** is about what **Jesus Christ** said when he came here to help all of us. He was the answer to all of our hopes and dreams. **His Way** has to be the starting point for any plan of action to solve our major problems. A plan that doesn't call on you to send in your money to some church or Television program. You don't have to join a new organization or church that has beautiful buildings. All you have to do to start that journey to **His Future Solution** is to read his Book: the **Bible**.

All that you need to know about **His Future** and how to learn to love your fellow man and **God** is in there. **He** is the starting point for your journey to the **Future.**

Now, Bubba, there is no conflict between **Love** and the other solutions for Jobs, Government, Healthcare, Deficit, Education and the other issues. Remember there are two different types of problems--man made problems and problems in God's world.

We first have to learn to **Love** our fellowman and then the other solutions can be possible. There is also a major difference between all of the great men that have ever lived and **Jesus Christ**. **Jesus Christ** is coming back. Yes, **God** loved all of us so much that he came on this earth to be our friend. Yes, he will come back someday. And when he comes back, it will make Michael scoring over fifty points when Chicago played the New York Knicks look like child's play. He will come back as **Lord of All.**

What do you think that he will ask you when he comes back? Will **He** ask you what your position was on abortion or who you voted for in the last great election?

Will he ask you how much that you paid in taxes or were you for the War? Well, he told all of us what he would ask all of us. It is in His book the Bible., He wants us to be like **Him** and give our love to our fellowmen. He wants us to care and to be friends with the people that need our help. He doesn't want us to send some help. He wants us to carry that help to them. That's what he did for us. He came **Himself** to give us **His Solution** and **His Friendship and Love.**

There is no conflict. There is only opportunity to turn back to our **God** and **His Solutions** and to get our government out of trying to solve these problems. There is opportunity for all of us to learn to love our fellowmen. There is an opportunity to put government back in its limited role in all our lives and to put **God** back where he belongs.

Are you still with me Bubba? Are you still awake? Come back soon and have a nice day, Bubba.

I took your advice and finally quit smoking. Did you ever stop picking your nose? What are you doing now? You are not going to pull that old elevator trick on me again, are you?

Now, Bubba, look what you have done now. I told you what would happen if you kept drinking all of that beer and eating those peanuts. I told you that you would End up leaving some elephant chips. Don't leave me here with that mess. You don't seriously think that I'm going to clean that entire mess up do you?

Now, what are you looking at? It was him. Come back here Bubba. Don't leave me like that.

Bubba!

15. DO YOU REALLY
WANT A FUTURE?

Do you remember my telling you about that good friend of mine that was such a Great car salesman. His name was **Rocket Rick** and even though I have an **M.B.A.** degree, I learned more about business from that car man than all of my college courses. Well, Rick used to start off his sales meetings with a simple question.

Rick would ask all of his salesmen, "Do you really want to be **Rich**?" If they were really interested in learning how to become Rich and Successful, then Rocket Rick was there to show them how they could change their lives. Heck, Rick even took a guy who the year before was working in a *McDonald's* frying French fries and showed him how to make a hundred thousand dollars the next year. That's right a hundred thousand like in **$100,000.00**.

"Why in the world have you started talking about a car salesman? Don't you know that people trust them about as far as they can throw them? You can never trust them at all. They are just out to take your money. You can't trust car salesmen."

Yeah, Pat, they are about as trustworthy as Politicians, aren't they. Well, who are you are talking about when you keep saying that some government tax will hurt the small businessman? Car people are small business! They are some of the business that is creating jobs and Rick was one of the superstars of the car people.

How good was Rick?   Well, when he started selling Subaru's the dealership that he worked for had a big problem. Yeah, he sold so many of those little cars that they didn't know how to pay him. How many did good old Rick sell? Oh, about 60 of those little Japanese beauties in one month. Do you know how hard it is to sell that many Jap cars especially in Texas? Go ask Bubba how many of those things he saw when he was in Texas. No, what Rick did was a Record. What kind of a Record? Oh, a Record like in they give you a big **NUMBER 1 TIE PIN**

So that you never forget and people are always coming up to you and asking you, "What is that on your tie?" No, Rick had proved many times that he knew how to sell. He also proved that he could train other people how to sell cars. When I met Rick he was the General Manager of a Porsche Dealership in Houston, Texas. Rick had continued to be successful and was making a real good living training other people and running a very successful dealership.

What was Rick's secret? How could Rick take people with little education and no previous experience in selling and teach them how to be top performing sales people? Rick had discovered the secret that all successful people have always understood. You have to want to succeed. The desire to succeed has to be inside of you--nobody else can put it there--not the Government--not your parents--not even Ronnie or Bill can make someone want to succeed and change their lives if it's not inside of them. You have to want that yourself.

I also need to tell you something else about Rick. You see as successful as Rick was for that Porsche dealership, he still got fired. Yes, Rick is like a lot of people who have found that just being successful and talented is not enough. There are other things going on in our workplace. Some of those other things involve numbers.

What kind of numbers? Bad numbers. You see, we are firing people to save our jobs. Do you remember when we talked about what happened in the Oil business back in the eighties? Well, we are starting to see a lot of that now. And Pat don't start telling me that companies have to cut out unnecessary expenses when their revenues are going down. Sometimes it has nothing to do with what you call becoming more efficient. Sometimes it just involves numbers. "I own or run a company that is losing money and I am going to sacrifice your job and your number so that I can save my hide."

What's that got to do with a car man named Rick? Plenty. Rick was the general sales manager for a Porsche dealership that had been making big money selling what is called **"High Dollar European Cars."**

Rick was mostly paid on a percentage of the Gross Profit of the dealership. What is the Gross Profit of a dealership?

The Gross Profit of an auto dealership is just the difference between the revenue and the cost of the revenue that is produced by selling cars. Rick was paid a percentage of this Gross Profit. And how much money had Rick made on this commission basis. Oh, I think that Rick only made $140,000 the year before he was fired for not producing enough sales and gross profits. To earn this Rick and his salesman had to produce over $1,400,000 in Gross Profit.

How did the dealership communicate their appreciation for what Rick had done? They fired him. Or, as they typed it on his notice that went to the Unemployment commission,

"He was terminated for lack of production."

How did Rick respond when he was terminated? "Wait a minute, what do you mean lack of production, I was producing enough sales? Why, I am paid on the commission basis and my checks have been going up every month that I have been here. What's going on here?" What was going one there was the new game. A game that is called cut them before we get cut.

Cut them even if we are cutting valuable people who may produce more than the people who are doing the cutting. It is all a numbers game. Cut their number before our number comes up.

Was this the end of the story for good old Rick? No, Rick found another job running another large Texas city dealership. This time Rick was selling Mazda's in a dealership that had never sold over 50 cars in a single month. Well, to Rick that was a golden opportunity. You see Rick was used to selling at least 150 cars a month and he just knew that here was a place for him to really succeed.

What went wrong? Remember that Retail People don't like Accountants and Accruals. Well, this is why Retail People don't like those little Accruals. Rick sure enough, did his thing and his first month the dealership had the best sales month that this little Mazda dealership had ever had. Rick set records for both the number of cars sold and the dollar value of Gross Profit.

What did Rick end up with as a check for his effort? Rick got a check for $2,500.00 that month. Now, you have to remember that this was when Ronnie was still President and the government hadn't raised the tax rate to make everything **Fair**. Rick was shocked.

Well, Rick started digging and found a whole bunch of accruals had been planted   in his gross margin. Those accruals had reduced his Gross Profit that he had generated down from $125,000.00 to about $25,000.00. To Rick's surprise, he found out that he was working for two accountants who had come up with accruals that resulted in $100,000.00 more expenses for the month. With Rick getting 10% of the Gross Profit he went from a $12,500.00 month to a $2,500.00 month. Rick was not a happy camper or a happy car man.

What did the two accountants that owned the dealership have to say when Rick confronted them with these facts? "We are sorry that you didn't have a good month. We can't pay you for what you haven't done"

What did Rick do? Did Rick tell the government on them? Did Rick tell everybody about how they weren't treating him right or being fair? No, Rick just decided to go open his own small dealership and stop trusting people to be **Fair**. He knew that he had talent and he had faith in himself. Rick wanted that future of being successful. So, to paraphrase my friend Rick, "Do you really want a Future?

Do you want to succeed in life? Are you ready to be a winner? Do you want to stand up? Are you Ready to change? A change that you want and not some change that somebody else has in mind for you according to their own values." Why is it so important to have this desire to have a better future? Remember our one and only rule?

Everybody Acts in Their Own Best Self-Interest.

Yes, that rule. Well, if you don't have the desire to change your life for the better, who will want you to change just for you? Who will be more concerned about you and your future? Guess who is learning this just like they call them now down in Tunica Mississippi, that new capital of Gambling in the South. That's right just like in a dice game "**Making the point the Hard Way**". Yes, President Bill Clinton is learning about **self-interest** the hard way. **Future Presidents** will also.

Do you remember when Hillary and Bill attacked all of the Evil Drug Companies for being so selfish and greedy? President Clinton was even going to cut out the $3 Billion dollar tax break that Drug companies got for having plants in Puerto Rico. We are still waiting and the law is still on the books that allow Drug companies to get this tax break based on the amount of profits that they earn rather than the number of jobs that are created in Puerto Rico.

How could this happen? Did the President lose his mind or did he inhale? No, what happened was that the Drug companies got a lot of the labor people in Puerto Rico convinced that if the tax breaks for them were changed in any way, it would mean the loss of jobs in Puerto Rico. A lot of lobbying money was thrown around, and before too long, enough support was generated for the Drug Companies' tax credit that has basically remained as it was before Hillary told all of us that it was so bad.

I wonder how successful the President will be in getting people to change their ways and really make a sacrifice for the good of our children.

Can there be any possible way that we can ever change for the better? How can we ever have that **Future** and what does **God** have to do with all of this? Do we just give up and let **Him** take care of the problem?

No, that is what we have been doing all along with the government. We just changed **God's** name and gave all of our hope and faith to the government instead of **God**. **God** is still very much alive and is still here. We just can't have what I call Selective Religion.

You know, put all of the blame on **God** and keep doing what you want to do regardless. It's like the scene from an old Western Movie, where all of the settlers are fixing to get massacred by about a million Indians. You remember the scene, where the local preacher, played by somebody who looks like Gabby Hays, stands up and says, "Thank you, Father, for the blessings that you are about to bestow on all of us."

Well, there are a lot of people who think like that .when something doesn't work out for them, they are all ready to turn it over to **God**. You know take themselves off of the Hook so that they don't have to think about how to solve their problems.

I used to work with a real smart Italian guy name Carl. Carl thought that solving problems was what Management was all about.

He couldn't understand why some of his managers would get so upset about having to deal with problems each day.

Carl looked at having to deal with problems and coming up with solutions as just a part of his job. Heck, if he came in and there were not any problems waiting for him, he started to worry. He knew that probably meant that Bubba was going to come into his office and mess up his day for sure. That's what we are trying to do in this country right now. We are trying to have it all and to fit all of it in neatly with what we want to accept as solutions.

We are not really interested in the hard work and effort that would be required to really change things for the better. One night, my wife who is a public school teacher, told me that we were going to watch a news special on one of the local Television channels. She had heard a station Promotion for this special and we just had to see how they had come up with Solutions to the problems in the Public Schools in Memphis, Tennessee.

As we sat and watched the special, we kept waiting to see some of the problems that my wife and other teachers had experienced teaching kids in public schools in Memphis, Tennessee.

We kept waiting for the special to show kids shooting other kids at school. We kept waiting for the special to show kids buying and using drugs at school. We kept waiting for the special to show kids hollering and fighting in class. We kept waiting for the special to show kids hitting and stabbing teachers at school.

We never saw any of that. We did see the Black Superintendent of Education talking about how hard and long **She** was working. We did see and hear one of the Black school Board members tell everyone that the problem was that the white schools were getting all of the money and the black schools were not getting their **Fair Share**. She said this even though; the Memphis School System is over **80%** black and has been for some years.

We even saw and heard one of the local Television News men (Who used to be a Television Weatherman) tell everybody that the solution to the problems in our schools was that we should make them important

273

and that they needed more money. Gee, I wonder if he read Karl Marx. You remember that Karl Marx said that Religion had become the opium (Drugs) of the masses. Could Television and government now be taking the place of Religion in Karl's model?

Either way, that Television special was not about what was wrong in the public schools in Memphis, Tennessee. That special was about making money for the Television station and they hoped that we didn't compare the special to that scene from the Movie *Broadcast News*.

You remember when the **William Hurt** character shed a tear and the camera man missed it. Remember how he told the camera man to give him a minute and he would cry for the camera. No, the local Television station didn't dig real deep on what was wrong with our schools. If they had looked hard at the problems it wouldn't have been real interesting and probably too hard to do. So, they took the easy way out and just showed us a few pictures of a cute little black kid who needed our help in order to be able to afford to go to college. And everybody said Amen.

Cut to the Superintendent of education walking to her car and fade to commercial. We have a wrap.

Unfortunately, there are a lot of problems that we are attempting to deal with very much like our local Television station dealt with Memphis's education problems.

Sometimes it's just too hard to deal with. You know living in a modern world has made everything so difficult. Everybody is working so hard and not making any progress on anything. Yes, life was a lot simpler back when our parents were starting out.

Does this sound as if we are back to the beginning of our conversation? Didn't we talk about the Fifty's and all of that in the beginning? Are we just going around in a circle? That's what we have forgotten. We have forgotten about our beginning. This country was created for everybody to have a chance to live their life as they saw fit, not for everything to be **Fair** and everybody to have it all.

We can make all of the changes in our Government, Social Security, The Deficit, Healthcare, Jobs and Charity and Love for our Fellowman and we can still fail if we are not interested in being part of the solution.

That's right, we have to want it and be part of that change. It can't just apply to some of the people who can't help themselves; the changes have to apply to everybody. If it is good for one group it has to be good for all of us.

"But, Richard, we could never get everybody to accept all of the changes that are required for what needs to be done in this country. Take Healthcare for example. Everybody has a different viewpoint on what the government should do in order to insure that every American had good Healthcare. How could we get everybody to agree on that one? The President and Congress will have to make that decision for us." Maybe, that is the solution.

Think for a minute about what you would do if it was all up to you. Wouldn't you look for a solution that involved you? Of course you would. Why do we have to keep repeating all of the mistakes of the past years?

Do we really think that the government can do a better job of helping us than what we could do for ourselves? How many people in this country think that the Government is doing a good job providing Welfare? What will cause the Government to be any more successful with Healthcare than what they did with Welfare?

Where will the **self-interest** come from on a National Healthcare program? Let me see. The people who will use the benefits of the program will not pay the majority of the cost of the healthcare benefits. If you don't believe that then tell me why they don't pay for them now? No, one of the major goals of Government Healthcare is to provide Healthcare Benefits for people who do not pay for them now. Those are the people who want the Government to create a new Government benefit.

When do we figure out that we can't act like children and pass everything that we are afraid of or might taste bad off to Mikey? When will we want to be part of the solution? Why do we have to look to **Rich** people to pass the cost to like we used to use Mikey to see if it tasted bad? Maybe, we need to think back to each of us helping people ourselves?

One of the things that has always bothered me has been the way that I react when I meet people on the street that are asking for my money. Has it ever happened to you? You are going downtown to that favorite Restaurant of yours. In my case it is the **Rendezvous** and they have the best barbecue ribs in Memphis.

The trouble is that the **Rendezvous** is downtown in an alley and you have to walk from your car and past a gauntlet of street people all asking for money. They all look just like some of the same people that asked me for money, when I was on R&R in the Philippines and trying to walk past all of the little kids in Poe City. Those memories come back about trying to help somebody only to end up with a part of your body missing when you reached for your wallet.

Every time I go downtown to the **Rendezvous** at night it ends up the same way. When I encounter the street people those memories come back and I walk as fast as I can past them into the Restaurant or my car. I have missed another opportunity to follow what Jesus said about helping our fellowman. I have sinned. I have fallen short again.

That is right I am human. I have my own set of memories and experiences and I factor all of these into how I relate with people in my world. Has there ever been anybody who was perfect? Yes, there was one person who was perfect. Let's see what did my Newspaper say on Christmas day?

There is no other character in history like that of Jesus.

As a preacher, as a doer of things, and as a philosopher, no man ever had the sweep and the vision of Jesus. A human analysis of the human actions of Jesus brings to view a rule of life that is amazing in its perfect detail.

The system of ethics Jesus taught during His Earthly sojourn 2,000 years ago was true then, has been true in every century since and will be true forever. Plato was a great thinker and learned in his age, but his teachings did not stand the test of time.

In big things and in little things time and human experience have shown that he erred. Marcus Aurelius touched the reflective mind of the world, but he was as cold and austere as brown marble. Thomas A. Kempis's Imitation of Christ is a thing of rare beauty

and sympathy, but it is, as its name indicates, only an imitation.Sir Thomas More's Utopia is yet a dream that cannot be realized.

Lord Bacon writing on chemistry and medicine under the glasses of the man working in a 20th Century laboratory is puerile.The world's most learned doctors until 150 years ago gave dragon's blood and ground tails of lizards and shells of eggs for certain ailments. The great surgeons a hundred years ago bled a man if he were wounded. Napoleon had the world at his feet for four years, and when he died the world was going on its way as if he had never lived.

Jesus taught little as to property because He knew there were things of more importance than property. He measured property and life, the body and soul, at their exact relative value. He taught much more as to character, because character is of more importance than dollars.

Other men taught us to develop systems of government. Jesus taught so as to perfect the minds of men. Jesus looked to the soul, while other men dwelled on material things. After the experience of 2,000 years no man can find a flaw in the governmental system outlined by Jesus. Czar and Kaiser, president and Socialist, give to its complete merit their admiration. No man today, no matter whether he follows the doctrine of Mills, Marx or George as to property can find a false principle in Jesus' theory of property.

In the duty of a man to his fellow no sociologist has ever approximated the perfection of the doctrine laid down by Jesus in His Sermon on the Mount.

Not all the investigations of chemists, not all the discoveries of explorers, not all the experiences of rulers, not all the historical facts that go to make up the sum of human knowledge on this day in 1912 are in contradiction to one word uttered or one principle laid down by Jesus.

The human experiences of 2,000 years show that Jesus never made a mistake.

Jesus never uttered a doctrine that was true at that time and then became obsolete.

Jesus spoke the truth, and the truth is eternal. History has no record of any other man leading a perfect life or doing everything in logical order. Jesus is the only person whose every action and whose every utterance strike a true note in the heart and mind of every man born of woman. He never said a foolish thing, never did a foolish act and never dissembled.

No poet, no dreamer, no philosopher loved humanity with all the love that Jesus bore toward all men. WHO THEN was Jesus?

He could not have been merely a man, for there never was a man who had two consecutive thoughts absolute in truthful perfection. Jesus must have been what Christendom proclaims Him to be---A divine being---or He could not have been what He was. No mind but an infinite mind could have left behind those things which Jesus gave the *world as a heritage.*

(From the Commercial Appeal December 25, 1993 reprinted from Commercial Appeal 1912 by C.P.J. Mooney. Editor.)

Thank you **Commercial Appeal**. That was a great Christmas present that you gave me when you ran that article. It helped me deal with the problem that I have always had with walking by the people on the street. I am not perfect and I need Jesus' help each and every day. Our government is in the same boat. As hard as it tries our Government is not perfect. The perfect world is not possible unless we turn toward God and away from man and government. Let's go back to my problem for just a minute.

You see those people on the street are looking for some money for their needs--not my idea of what their needs are but their needs. I can never understand why they are there and why they are asking for money.

I would not act like them if I needed the money. If I were down on my luck, the last place I would go and look for money would be in downtown Memphis. Have you been there recently? There is not a lot of people living and working there.

They have all moved out East to Germantown or Bartlett or maybe Tunica, Mississippi. No, I would pick a different place to ask for help.

But that is the major point. They are not me. I don't know why they are there. If I tried for my whole life, I could never understand why they are there. I also cannot understand why they are on a cold and lonely street corner instead of at the Salvation Army or some shelter set up by a church.

They are different from me and they always will be. If I try to help them from my own view of what they need I would not really give them what they wanted. They may just want some of my money to buy some drugs or some wine. I will never know. I also will never know why they don't go down to the local charity.

You see, our Government has tried to help people without realizing that they were only trying to help them according to what the people in the Government believed was their problems. It could have been help that was centered around a Liberal Belief or it could have been a Conservative point of view. In either case it would have been wrong.

People need help for **Their Own Reasons**--not yours or mine but theirs. That also causes the problem. In order to deal with your own problems, you have to want to solve the problems yourself.

"Wait a minute Richard you have made more than a couple of mistakes. First you are really confusing a bunch of people. How can you talk about God and talk about some things in such a, how would you put it--a less than Respectful manner? You need to treat some of those things in a more dignified manner."

Well, Mikey, you probably don't think that The Lord has a sense of humor do you? Tell me then why did he let all of us in Memphis think that we were going to get a National Football League Franchise then? No, I think God likes a person to have a sense of humor. What's your other problem?

"How come you talked about what happened to a car salesman and a college educated person like yourself? The real people don't relate to either of those kinds of workers. You guys had it made. You were in Management. What about what's happening to everybody else in the work place? What about the people who have to work for a living?"

Gee, that's an interesting question coming from you, Mikey. But I have decided to be nice to you as we are wrapping up this little old talk and I will tell you about somebody else. Do you remember my friend, Billie? Billie was the son of a U. S. Steel company worker and grew up in a true blue collar home in Chicago. You remember those union people that you are so careful not to make mad. Yes, Billie's dad was a laborer and his mother worked at home while Billie's dad worked at the plant.

Well, Billie worked his way through college the hard way. Working in a dirty factory making barbed wire while going to college. Billie was finally rewarded for all of his effort and had become an Accountant. Billie continued to work hard and finally thought that he had it made as the head of Finance and Accounting for a small Real Estate Company in Houston, Texas. Unfortunately for Billie, things were starting to change at the Real Estate Company. You see, Real Estate was in bad shape in Houston, Texas and Billie lost his job.

"Now Richard, don't you know that with all of the oversupply of Real Estate in Houston, Texas during that time, that a company had to reduce expenses in order to survive?"

Well, how did Billie's boss decide on what expenses to cut? He took his payroll register home and decided to fire the people that he was spending the most money on each month. In this case the losing numbers were Billie and the Sales Manager. Why was that such a dumb move for the company?

It was very dumb, when you consider that the Sales Manager was paid on commission only. He did not get paid a cent unless he made money for the company. Billie's main responsibility was to get the financing for all of the Real Estate Deals and the company was still doing some deals that were bringing in money. Firing both of these people was dumb. They both were generating more money than they cost. It was a numbers game though. Pick their number first before the other person's number came up.

Now, Mikey, I hope you see why we need to change the way the government deals with jobs and unemployment in this country. Regardless of your logic or Pat's, it is not happening like you think. People are being fired not for the Future good of the company. They are being fired so somebody else can have it good.

Sure, I know that this used to be okay when it was factory workers and we tried to support their Firings with **"a lack of production"**, but it still helped us and hurt them. Don't you see that has to change?

"What would you do about the Welfare women who continued to have more and more children? You know like some of those women that left those small children in that apartment in Chicago. You remember all of those kids that were fighting dogs for their food? How would we handle them?"

I didn't forget that. I was hoping that you would figure that out on your own. We have to look for a solution that answers a lot of questions. First question is, are you prepared to take those kids and raise them as your sons or daughters? Are you willing to take them away from a mother that you think is not treating them as she should?

Does it give you a tremendous problem, seeing several thousand dollars of taxpayer money go into that apartment and little go to feeding and providing for the welfare of those kids? Have you seen this before with all of our well intentioned welfare programs? Money goes to welfare mothers for children but instead goes to other things. It may go for drugs. It may go to a lot of other places. It doesn't go to help the children. It sounds a lot like my problem of giving money to street people. How can you really help the kids?

If you are not ready to have those kids come live with you, what are you prepared to do? Are you prepared to take those kids away from their mothers to be raised by the state that will become their mothers and fathers and have the government continue to raise those kids and the additional taxes that would be required. Are you prepared to throw more and more tax dollars at that problem? Are you ready to maybe try something else that would help both the mothers and kids?

Remember the Future Solution For abortion? Yes, letting women sell their babies to couples that couldn't have kids of their own. What about letting welfare mothers sell the children that they couldn't provide for to a Fair Corporation? This would totally get the government out of trying to meet the needs of women that couldn't support those kids. It would also stop sending money to them for the benefit of the kids. If there are problems in getting the kids that help, let's get those kids some real help.

"Wait a minute, Richard this would break up poor families. This would separate children from their mothers."

You wait a minute. Didn't you see those pictures on Television showing all of those starving kids in that cold apartment in Chicago? The apartment that several thousand dollars of welfare was going into and still the kids had to fight with dogs for food. When will we understand that just throwing money at the problem is not the solution?

Again, who wants to hold up their hands to be those kid's fathers and mothers. Regardless of any other factors that has to be addressed first. Those poor kids do not have parents that can care for them as they should. All of the money in the world will not change that fact. May I repeat myself those kids don't need our dollars, they need daddies and mommies. Let's appeal to the mothers and fathers of those neglected children.

Let's make them an offer that may appeal to their own self-interest. Let's offer them say $5,000 for every child that they agree to place up for adoption by a Fair Corporation. Let's give that child a chance to grow up and have a Future. Let's offer that mother and father a chance to start over. Maybe without the pressures of trying to support those kids they might make it.

"But Richard, are you suggesting that we go back to how it was in the 19th century when we had all of those horrible orphanages. You know like in the movie, *Annie*. Wouldn't that be horrible on the kids?"

As horrible as little kids fighting with a dog for a piece of meat while sitting in human waste? As horrible as all of the welfare money and food stamps going to support a Drug habit? What do you think that we have now for all of the money that we have thrown at the problem? We have that and more.

If you really care about all of those starving kids, you have two choices. You can either volunteer to adopt those kids yourself or you can create a **Fair Corporation** that is staffed and funded by people who want to give those kids a chance. Continuing to throw money down the endless pit of welfare will not work because government will never be able to truly supervise the parents that have brought those kids into that situation. What do you want to do?

Before we have to say good-bye, I want to thank you, Mikey for not trying to hit me over the head with any talk about my not being more respectful of my mother. I guess some of you Liberals do care about people's feelings.

Well, I knew that you always were a good person, but that just proves one of my points. Don't you see that if my mother and I can't even agree on what is **Fair**, how can you expect the millions of us in this country to agree? This gets to be a real big problem, when you are trying to get one group of people to pay the majority of the taxes for benefits to other groups. Don't you remember our first rule?

Everyone Acts in their own best self-interest.

I also remember, after I had come back from Vietnam and I was trying come up with a way to go to Law School. I had some pretty big dreams in those days. I even thought about going to some real good law schools like Stanford or Vanderbilt. The only problem was that even with the GI Bill and the fooling around money that I was able to scratch up, it was not going to be enough. Do you know what I did?

Why, I asked a **Rich** relative for his help. You see, I had an Uncle who was a retired Methodist Minister and a pretty successful businessman too. I asked mother to ask him for some help so I could afford to go to a good law school. Sure enough, Uncle Chester called and said that he would be happy to help me. He was going to come over that night and he had a way that I could achieve my dreams.

Uncle Chester came over just as he said. Do you know what his help was going to be? Uncle Chester wanted me to be one of his *AMWAY* sellers. Uncle Chester was an *AMWAY* distributor and would set me up to sell **AMWAY**. I could make a lot of money selling **AMWAY**. I also could make some money for him.

Now, do I think that Uncle Chester was an uncaring evil capitalist that was just trying to make some money off of my labors? I may have thought that at the time, but I see things differently now. He was just trying to give me some help from his own point of view.

To him, this was a way of sharing in the opportunity that he already had in selling **AMWAY**.

From his point of view, he was giving me what I had asked for when mother made that call for help. Uncle Chester also helped a whole lot more people get some real help than I will ever be able to do. He was a good Christian and was one of the Lord's hardest workers. Mother also told me a story about my grandmother and how your perception can be a lot different than reality.

Mother told me about how Grandmother always was struggling to have enough money to pay for the bare necessities. One time mother just knew that Grandmother was going to run short and wouldn't have enough money to buy an Easter Hat for the special Easter Sunday service. When she went over to Grandmother's apartment (Grandmother moved into her own place when my brother and I were a little more grown.), Grandmother showed her a new hat that she had bought.

he was real happy and looking forward to wearing it to church Sunday. Mother told me that's when she realized that Grandmother knew how to scratch and save so that she had a little messing around money for herself.

That's why we have to be careful about our opinions of how others should act and trying to come up with rules and laws that force people to act like we think that they should. We also have to be real careful about what we think is the truth. Sometimes things are a lot more complicated than we think.

We need to be a lot more open minded about those kinds of things. Rather than trying to force somebody to change to what we think, we need to be more accepting of them.
"Wait a minute, Richard, I appreciate those kind words that you had for

me, but I still have my job to do and I need to point something out to you. Have you ever thought that maybe you just were jinxed with having a bunch of bad relatives? You know the examples that you are using really involve your relatives. Maybe you are using what the analytical people call "A Biased Sample".

Maybe we haven't really stopped caring about people. You know this is just a temporary thing that we are going through now. There is no reason to make all of these changes."

Well, it looks like you still don't buy the concept of everybody acting in their own best **self-interest**. You probably also still think that the Government has this secret source of money and the **Rich** people have not earned that money but have stolen it from the Government.

Okay, here goes one more time and this time it's not some of my relatives. Do you remember when we were talking about the Job situation in this country? Do you remember me telling you about my experience working in the Oil business and how I lost my job? Do you remember how most of the people that I worked with were so relieved to see the job cuts stop with me and not them? Do you remember that story?

Well, there is another part to that story. It didn't end with just me and the rest of the useless bums that had it coming. It continued to grab more and more jobs. In fact most of the people who went to lunch with me on my last day with that company lost their jobs too. Losing their jobs were a real sock to them. They though that it would stop with me. They were wrong.

"But Richard, you are still living in the Past. That was what happened in the Oil Business in the Eighties. We are in the Nineties now and a long way from what happened in the Oil Glut. You are mixing apples with oranges. What is happening now is a lot different than reducing your expenses when nobody is drilling for oil.
 Get real."

You still don't get it do you? Do you want another example? Okay, let's take Healthcare for a minute.

Now, let's assume that you have a real good job in a Healthcare company and somebody that you know calls you and asks you for some help in getting a job with this fine company. What do you do? Do you really try to help them or do you just go through the motions and come up with a lot of excuses for not wasting your time. How has this changed from our past?

Well, as they say back in the good old days, people helped other people because they knew that it was the right thing to do. Most people really enjoyed helping somebody. There didn't have to be something in it for them. Everybody understood that when they helped somebody else that they could be that somebody asking for help. You just did all that you could to help somebody. No big deal. You were helping yourself in a roundabout way.

"Enough of this general talk. Specifics and Details. Who, What, Where. Inquiring minds want to know. Give us some more details. Are you making this up or did this really happen?"

Yes, Mikey, I will give you some more details and this is a real story. The story involves somebody that I know joining a large Hospital here in Memphis, Tennessee. Well, good old JR had landed a real big job. How big? Probably the biggest job that she ever had. Running a major department at this Hospital. How did I come to know this story?

That's simple. You see the person who asked that JR person for some help was me. Yes, I asked that good old JR to help me get a job with that major Hospital. Did she help? No, for whatever reason she wasn't able to give a lot of help. There was a lot of talk about how the Hospital had to watch expenses and more and more excuses.

"That's a real poor example, Richard. I tried to tell you that companies were going through major cost cutting plans.
What did you expect?"

The help or lack of help was what I expected. What happened next really surprised good old JR.? Yes, that person who had it made in the biggest job that she ever had. You guessed it. She became a part of the clean clinical term. She became a part of the Hospital's Cost Cutting Plan. It now became her turn to find out about cutting out unnecessary expenses. The fat that companies were cutting out of their overhead.

It had become her turn to go on a crash diet. Do we still believe that it will stop with them and not reach us? Do we still think that they deserved to lose their jobs? Do we think that it will all turn out to be a bad dream and wake up in our lover's arms in our own shower? Or do we wait and see it stop just at the water's edge?

At somebody else's door. No, not our door their door. Is it their own fault? If you still think that all of the problems that we have been talking about are somebody else's fault and that you are not part of the problem and solution, take this simple little test.

Have high school chemistry, physic or other science teacher give you a little test. This test would be a True and False test concerning laws in these sciences. My money says that you don't pass the test. You see a lot of those laws and principles that we learned in high school have changed. Man has developed new laws of science according to his current understanding of that specific science.

That is one of our biggest challenges that we all face in trying to have that future. We have to be prepared to change our minds about what we think is the truth. We have to grow as human beings. There is one Truth that we can start with and develop all of our growth. There is a God. He has given us the opportunity to learn and grow. We cannot just sit still and wait. We must change.

"But Richard didn't the last election that kicked out all of the bad liberal Democrats and brought in the smart conservative Republicans change that? Didn't they make a contract with all of us to shrink the government and get it out of our lives? They are going to end all of those horrible Liberal social programs that drained all our money out of the economy and rewarded people who weren't pulling their part of the wagon. Isn't that what you were getting at when you talked about the **Fair corporations**?"

Yes, Jim Bob that is a start to having our Future Solution, but there is another part. You see the problem was twofold.

It was never wrong to try to help people who needed our help. It was wrong to try to make the government do a job that each of us should want to do.

We should want to help all people who need our help. We should want to do that with joy in our heart.

"Wait a minute Richard; now that we finally got the Liberals thrown out of office, are you changing your stripes just to be different. Maybe Bubba was right about you being so illogical? Don't you know that was what the Liberals were trying to force down our throats when they were in power?"

No, Jim Bob you have overlooked a major point. There are still needs to help people that are in disparate conditions. For all of the changes that we have talked about there will still be people who need our help. There will still be poor people. There still will be people who have lost their husbands, wives, sons, daughters, fathers and mothers. There will still be people who don't have jobs. People who don't have roofs to cover their heads. People who are hungry.

People who need Healthcare. People who need help. They will still be with us. If we just stop with changing the government we will be making a big mistake. Those people still need our help.

"What can we do about helping them, Richard? Don't you understand that people are tired of throwing good money at those kinds of problems? That's what the election was all about. Don't you understand how people really feel?"

Yes, I think that I do understand Jim Bob. Do you remember us talking in the beginning about the elections that they have down in South America where they have revolutions and change the whole government? Do you remember that they still end up with the same bad leaders that they were trying to eliminate with their revolutions?

That's what we will end up with if we stop with just the government and don't ask ourselves what we are going to do to help the people that need our help. We will be only doing half of the job.

We will have changed our idea of the government being our **God** and looking to it for the solutions to our problems. We still will be forgetting **God** and what he told us to do. He told us to love our fellow man as we love him and ourselves.

We have to be prepared to start loving our fellowman again and being there to help him. Loving our fellowman again as much as we love ourselves is the key. We also have to forget the labels of Liberal and Conservative.

Just because the Conservatives won the Congress is not the answer. Even if the Republicans win the White House will we see true change?

They are all people struggling with a difficult job. Giving us what they think we want and trying not to make anybody mad. We are the only ones that can truly change our lives for the better. The change has to start with each of us first.

We have to make that last change in ourselves when we change our government. We have to be prepared to be the good shepherd that the **Lord** asked us to be when he left us here in charge. We have to want to try to help others who need our help. We have to change too .The key to unlocking the **Future Solution** is to finally realize that the solution to all of our problems has to start with **Ourselves**.

We have to be the ones who are willing to change first. The change has to start with us and not them. We are the ones who have to change. That's the answer to why our government has been letting all of us down.

We are the Government.

We are the ones who have allowed ourselves to become the criminals, the uneducated, the unemployed, the unloved and the uncaring. We have to change and it has to start with each of us. We have to be prepared to change our directions.

We have to start on a new direction. We can't just keep putting it off and hoping that somebody else will change first. It has to start now with each of us.

No, I don't believe in just continuing to go down the same one way street. I believe in looking for **Solutions**. I also believe in trying to do something about our problems and not just looking for somebody else to blame.

This year, I am going to remember a good line from the movie *The Untouchables*. Do you remember what the Sean Connery character would tell Elliot Ness, every time Elliot felt that he had encountered a major problem that would not go away? He said, "What are you going to do about it?"

"Richard, that's the movies, don't you know that doesn't happen in real life. What about what the doctors told you on your left eye? What are you going to do on that? Come on this is real life and what are you going to do about that? Are you just going to talk it away? Don't you see that you are in one of the same boats that people find themselves when something goes wrong in their lives? What are you going to do now?"

I guess, Jim Bob, that all of us get to this point in our life sooner or later. At some point in your life, this will hit you right in the face. You get some bad news and there is nothing else that anybody can do to help you. You are alone. You are back in your own room. What are you going to do? How do you live the rest of your life? What do you do? There may not be anything else that you or anybody else can do? So, what do you do then?

You still live your life as best as you can. That is what you and all of us can do. That will cause us to look to the present and the future. We cannot live in the past. It may not be our own fault. It may be somebody else's fault. It may not be anybody's fault. That doesn't matter.

All that matters is that we try and live our lives as best as we can. And we hope and keep our hearts, minds and eyes toward **The Future**. **A Future** where all things are possible. **That Future** may be the next day, the day after or it may be a long time away, but **That Future** is coming. **A Future** where all of our hopes and dreams are answered. **A Future** where we are all young again and we run without falling and play.

Today is now and not in **That Future**, so I will dream and pray. I will look toward **That Future**. I will also keep trying in this time. I will still ask myself what I can do about my problems. I will also remember that I am not alone. Others are struggling with their problems too. Well, when problems come at me this year and I hope for the rest of my life, I am going to not try to blame somebody else for my troubles and I am going to ask myself,

"What are you going to do about it?" I am also going to try to remember a story that I first heard from Zig Ziglar. Zig used to end some of his presentations by telling a story about a father who had a son who was born with very weak and almost useless muscles. Zig would talk about how when the father found out what his son's health problems were, he would not accept what everybody was telling him that his son would be in that condition for the rest of his life.

According to Zig, the father went to scores of doctors who told him the same thing over and over. There was nothing that could be done for his son. That was all he could expect for his son. The father would not give up and he kept looking for some doctor who could help his son. Finally, he found a Doctor who told him there was one solution to his son's condition but it would be very difficult.

He was going to have to work with his son to overcome his physical problems and most importantly he was going to have to keep his son away from other people who had problems like his. The doctor never wanted the man's son to see another patient who had his condition and think that it was hopeless. There was going to be a lot of hard work in working with a physical trainer to train the muscles and body of the man's son.

The man would have to want to see **The Solution** and be a part of **The Solution**. Well, they were successful and the boy went on to overcome the physical problems that he had been born with. He even went on to become a successful athlete in Canada. At this point Zig would always stop and think to himself about what the boy would have been able to accomplish if he had not been born with such a difficult physical condition?

Then he would turn to the audience with that smile and have the look that only Zig was capable of having and would talk about how that maybe having those problems may have given the boy the desire to achieve a lot that he wouldn't have had the desire to achieve if he had been born without those problems.

No, I think I will remember that when I start feeling sorry for myself. I also will ask myself, "What am I going to do about it?" I will also remember that I have to look for ways that I can help other people.

I have to be prepared to be that good shepherd that the **Lord** asked me to be.

I cannot run away from his words if I truly believe that he is who he said that he was. We may have gotten the Government out of our lives and acting as our god, but we still have to remember that **God** asked all of us to love our fellowman. I have to change too.

The meeting is over and we can all go home. Back to our yard work and our other chores. Good-bye Mikey. Good-bye Pat. Good-bye Jim Bob. Have a good life. Work hard and enjoy.

Just remember to ask yourself the important questions about your life. So, what's wrong with you? What are you prepared to do?

"What are You going to do about

It?"

1. The First Black American was Re-elected President.
2. The Second Black American was Re-elected President
3. The Democrats won and lost the House.
4. The Republicans won and lost the Senate.
5. A President tried to define the meaning of the word IS.
6. A President tried to define the meaning of the end of a Sentence, period.
7. The Press Spell checked every word of The President.
8. The Press Used a Thesaurus to explain every word of The President.
9. We lost over 3,000 Americans in an act of War.
10. We tried to make Peace with a country that wants to Exterminate the Jews and US.
11. The Wicked Leader of the Iraq is dead
12. The Wicked Leader of the attack and Murder of Over 3,000 Americans is dead.
13. Another Paul was elected Senator.
14. Another Movie Actor was elected California Governor.
15. Another ex-Demarcate Californian Governor was Re-elected Governor.
16. A recession has turned into something else.
17. We are trying to look like some other country.
18. Memphis, Tennessee didn't get a NFL team. We got the NBA when we already had the University of Memphis Tigers.(Not Memphis State)
19. The St. Louis Cardinals Won and Lost The World Series.
20. The Boston Red Socks Won and Won The World Series.
21. Mickey Mantle will run with the Lions again.
22. Stan the Man will fly with the Cardinals forever.
23. Bubba Retired.
24. My Best Friends Bill and Billy went to be with the Lord.
25. Zig led both of them.
26. I am really trying to be like Zig's Canadian Body Builder.
27. We have forgotten who really gave us this Country.
28. He has not forgotten US.

The Man Who Counts

It is not the critic who counts, not the man who points out how the strong men tumbled, or when the doer of deeds could have done better. The credit belongs to the man who is actually in the Arena; whose face is marred by dust, sweat and blood: who Strives valiantly; who errs and comes short again; who Knows the Great enthusiasms, the great devotions and spends Himself in a Worthy cause; who at the best knows in the end the Triumph of High achievement and who at the worst, if he fails, at Least fails While daring greatly, so that his place shall never be with those Cold and timid souls who know neither victory or Defeat.

Theodore Roosevelt

ABOUT THE AUTHOR

Author Biography

Richard Wayne Hatley, Retired Certified Public Accountant with MBA from Memphis State University is a writer and a Business Consultant with over Thirty years of experience in the financial affairs of corporate Business. He was the Chief Financial Officer for a Healthcare Corporation, Public Governmental Agency, Financial Institution and Retail Corporations. He currently is a financial consultant in private practice and lives with his family in Melissa, TX.

Richard is a graduate of Memphis State University in Memphis, Tennessee and holds both a B.B.A. in Accounting and a Master of Business in Finance. He was a member of the American Institute of Certified Public Accountants and Tennessee Society of Certified Public Accountants. He also has taught several college courses in Business Accounting and Income Taxes.

Richard has a wide range of experience in such industries as manufacturing, retail, automotive, financial services, energy, healthcare and hospitality. He also has had the opportunity to think about his most important area. **The Future**. This Book was originally started in 1993. It has been updated to reflex some of the recent events in trying to solve our problems. The Solutions are the same and will always be:

The Future Solution.

Richard Wayne Hatley
2013